Where Have All the Robots Gone?

Worker Dissatisfaction in the '70s

HAROLD L. SHEPPARD and NEAL Q. HERRICK
THE W. E. UPJOHN INSTITUTE FOR EMPLOYMENT RESEARCH
WASHINGTON, D.C.

 The Free Press, New York
Collier–Macmillan Limited, London

We see a potential problem of vast significance to all industrial companies. . . . This involves the slowly rising feeling of frustration, irritation and alienation of the blue collar worker, the "hard hats," if you will, but not just the activists in big cities. It involves a gut feeling on their part that industrial society has left them with the dull, hard, dirty jobs—and doesn't care.

—Walter Dance,
Senior Vice President of
General Electric, before
a meeting of GE stockholders

The Free Press
A Division of The Macmillan Company
866 Third Avenue, New York, New York 10022
Collier–Macmillan Canada Ltd., Toronto, Ontario
Library of Congress Catalog Card Number: 72–77285
printing number 1 2 3 4 5 6 7 8 9 10

Contents

Foreword

HARVEY SWADOS

Suddenly, in the seventies, we are becoming curious once again about vast numbers of our fellow citizens whose lives have been a matter of indifference to us for many years. In the 1950s, that unlovely decade, most of us were concerned with little beyond our immediate personal and family horizons; staying out of trouble and getting ahead were both the most approved and the most general of aspirations; social scientists were seriously arguing that the great problems of industrial society had indeed been resolved. In the series of seismic explosions of the 1960s, blacks and students forced the rest of the nation to confront their life problems. Now, as these two groups appear to be entering a new period of reconsideration and regrouping, we find ourselves shaken by the re-emergence of a force—the labor force—that had been, in comparison with civil rights activists and militant students, virtually quiescent since the 1930s.

In Lordstown, Ohio, close to 8,000 youthful auto workers in a bright new factory producing compact cars defied General Motors, the giant of the automotive industry. They walked out on strike—not for higher wages or increased retirement benefits, but for a voice in the management of the fastest moving assembly line in the world. Charged with acts of irresponsibility and sabotage, they responded with pleas for dignity and respect. It is more than possible that the rebellious behavior of these young workers, with their fondness for long hair, pot, mod clothes, and other tastes usually associated with the youth culture of the more privileged, may well be only the early warning signal of a whole series of new convulsions.

In Washington, D.C., David Brinkley has this in mind. From time to time, he brings to millions of seven o'clock news watchers vignettes of the lives of discontented young workers—Americans who have never before been in the limelight, and whom one might partially define as being more accustomed to viewing than to being viewed. What do they want, people are beginning to ask uneasily, what do they want?

The New York Times is running anxious front-page articles bearing such headlines as, WORKING YOUTH: THE 17 MILLION "INVISIBLE"

VOTERS. The underlying tone of anxiety may well derive from the fact that, throughout the country, in an election year, "there are an awful lot of Americans," as Anthony Lewis has written, "who feel like losers."

And now, you have a volume which probes that feeling, and which destroys some of that "invisibility"—along with certain of the myths that often tend to accumulate about those whose needs have been insufficiently considered and who have been taken all too much for granted for far too long. Part One, The Myth of the Happy Worker, includes a chapter by each of the authors on "Pockets of Discontent" and on "Who Are The Discontented Blue-Collar Workers?"

Fifteen years have passed since my essay, also titled "The Myth of the Happy Worker," appeared. At the time, I wrote:

> With the personnel man and the union leader, both of whom presumably see the worker from day to day, growing so far away from him, it is hardly to be wondered at that the middle class in general, and articulate middle class intellectuals in particular, see the worker vaguely, as through a cloud. One gets the impression that when they do consider him, they operate from one of two unspoken assumptions: (1) The worker has died out, like the passenger pigeon, or is dying out, or becoming accultured, like the Navajo. (2) If he *is* still around, he is just like the rest of us—fat, satisfied, smug, a little restless, but hardly distinguishable from his fellow TV-viewers of the middle class.

My distress had been occasioned, in part, by the reception accorded *On The Line*, in which I had attempted to fictionally convey the quality of life on an automotive assembly line, and to demonstrate its effects upon a mixed group of workers. Few readers during the 1950s wished to learn of these people and their problems. For most, the book no doubt smacked too much of the thirties, with that era's passionate (if often sentimental) concern for the downtrodden. Yet others were of the opinion that this fictional report from the factory was the product of an overheated imagination and was an untrustworthy projection onto others—primarily onto dull and contented clods—of a middle-class intellectual's sense of shock and dismay at the drab ugliness of factory life endured by those who were producing what the rest of us were consuming. They bridled when they read, in my subsequent essay, the statement that the men with whom I had worked on the assembly line "felt like trapped animals. Depending on their age and personal circumstances, they were either resigned to their fate, furiously angry at *themselves* for what they were doing, or desperately hunting other work that would pay as well and in addition offer some variety, some prospect of change and betterment."

This did not concur with what readers were being told in the popular sociological works of the period, and so they assumed that my impressionistic observations were basically unworthy of serious consideration. Only among those who retained vivid personal memories of the toll exacted by assembly line work was there aroused a certain shock of recognition that helped to keep my work from utter oblivion.

Therefore, it is with a certain sense of vindication that I observe the re-emergence into the public arena of the young worker (white and black, male and female), and particularly of the "Middle American" unionist who, in recent years, has once again been written off—this time as a simpleton or a willing dupe of reactionary demagogues. The investigation of his life-style by the mass media, and of his discontents by the social scientists, is long overdue.

I hasten to add that it is not simply with melancholy satisfaction that I greet the appearance of these researches of Dr. Sheppard and Mr. Herrick into the sources of worker discontent and its relation to our national situation; or that I learn from them that, "Our own evidence suggests that . . . the gap between the emerging class of workers . . . and [Erich Fromm-type] intellectuals has been *narrowing*—that an increasing proportion of workers themselves *are* repelled by jobs involving low tasks."

To the contrary: the reader of the pages that follow will not merely have his hunches or his suspicions statistically verified; he will feel the kind of exhilaration that must always attend the discovery of significant facts that he did not know before, and that he needs to know, about the attitudes of a large body of laboring Americans toward their work, their youthful aspirations, their political leaders. The results of the Sheppard-Herrick study should and will be studied, particularly in an election year, by factory managers and union officers, public officials and candidates for office, and by those who powerfully feel the need to change the course of American society.

Several aspects of the study are particularly worthy of note for readers who may tend to regard surveys of job satisfaction with a certain reserve (a reserve no doubt paralleling that with which social scientists contemplate imprecise, impressionistic sketches in their area of competence). For one thing, in the pages that follow there is no hint—as there has often been in other studies—that the research has been undertaken with an eye to smoothing out rough spots in labor-management relations and, so, increase productivity, maximize profits, and make stockholders more contented than the workers whose grievances have been "adjusted" and whose jobs have been "enriched." The news about dissatisfaction not simply with the way the work is supposed to be done but with the task itself, the genuine depth of worker discontent, may not be welcome to managerial and personnel people, but they can hardly question its objective quality, and they will have to contend with its profound implications.

Similarly, the authors spell out their chariness about the role of top union officials, not simply as labor's representatives at collective bargaining tables, but as interpreters of the underlying attitudes of workers toward their jobs. As Sheppard and Herrick point out, the officers of trade unions (despite the fact that they may have been elected democratically) are far more remote from the workplace than are such direct representatives as shop stewards, and that they suffer from a "trained incapacity (or occupational disease)" which "leads to an almost exclusive preoccupation with wage levels and/or job security."

With this mixture, then, of shrewdness and objectivity, of carefully structured questionnaires, and venturesome interpretations of findings that, upon occasion, they admit were "completely unexpected," the authors proceed to delineate for us a pattern of social and political confusions that will inevitably be of vital concern in the immediate future.

Consider the following pregnant lines about the youngest workers queried in the authors' urban area surveys in Pennsylvania and Michigan. Speaking of the 1968 election, they tell us that, "if they voted at all, *fewer* of them—compared to the oldest—voted for Humphrey, *fewer* voted for Nixon—but a much larger proportion chose George Wallace. . . . By a ratio of nearly 6 to 1 (23 vs. 4 percent), the young voters in our sample of white male union workers, compared to the oldest ones, chose the candidate who for them apparently expressed a challenge to that 'Establishment,' and who gave vent to whatever resentments and frustrations such men harbor." In a cool footnote, they conclude: "there is some reason to believe that last-minute frantic efforts of the labor movement to reduce the pro-Wallace sentiments among its members succeeded primarily among the oldest workers."

Why? An important reason, we are told, is "the change in the social character of the young workers of the new era."

And what, precisely, are the elements of that change? Not least among them is a concern with two problems more associated with young students than with older workers: "On the two issues of war and environmental quality, we cannot dismiss as cavalier talk the belief that a generation gap exists—at least among the kinds of white male union members we interviewed." And, again like many students, "the young worker—compared to the others—is not convinced that the major parties are concerned about him."

One gets the impression, however, that if young workers are separated from their elders along lines similar to those marking off students from their teachers and parents, the workers are, in addition, distinguished from others in the general community by the extent of their dissatisfaction with what they do for a living. The "blues," that deep-going discontent which all of us experience upon occasion, afflict these young people for very specific reasons. They are more oppressed than others by a lack of variety in the job, by a lack of autonomy in the job and by a lack of responsibility in the job. And for them, the task level is more important than the wage level.

In contrast to middle-class wage earners, we learn, their discontent does not decline as family income rises (by having more than one wage earner in the family). Quite the contrary: the "blues" are to be found most often among double-income families. The authors speculate that one cause for this may be a decline in self-respect among young men brought up to believe that males function at the highest level when they are the sole breadwinner, taking care of woman and household; but whatever the root causes, there would appear to be little question as to the reality of the phenomenon.

The discontented worker is also very often a man who feels a great discrepancy between his aspiration and his achievement. And this study further indicates that his discontent is not directly tied to family income. We might have expected to find that he has less schooling and more unemployment than others—but not that he is no more prejudiced (perhaps even less so) than the general sample. We might have expected to learn that he voted less in 1968— but not that he chose George Wallace disproportionately, in preference to the Democratic candidate.

Perhaps most striking, however, is the fact that these workers are far more alienated than others, and that alienation is "unquestionably related to the workers' choice of President in the 1968 election. The probability that this relationship is due to chance is only 1 out of a thousand."

A pattern begins to emerge. The man who voted for George Wallace in the 1968 Presidential election is more likely to be alienated. He is more likely to be discontented. He is more likely to be young—his median age is eight years younger than that of the Humphrey or Nixon voter. His median schooling (unlike that of the dissatisfied worker in general) is the highest—"a much larger proportion of them had at least one year of college." With a higher educational level and a lower age, he enters adulthood with greater expectations— and shortly discovers that his life offers fewer gratifications. His political mood, compared to that of other voters, is more independent; he is more likely to live in a smaller urban area; and nearly half of his number, as compared with one fifth of the Humphrey and Nixon voters, "have thought frequently about making a real effort to enter a new and different type of occupation."

This man, the authors assert, "is truly the worker with the 'blues' . . . He is not only alienated in the social sense (little faith in others, and pessimistic about the 'lot' of the average man), but also in the political sense."

What has to impress the reader is, first, the observation that this "minority" of Americans may very well be a growing, rather than a shrinking one, and, second, the perception that these men are no more static in their personalities than in their numbers. They are sorely troubled human beings whose troubles may overwhelm us all, and understanding is not to be found in condemnation. For me, a key word in the Sheppard-Herrick interpretation is "interplay"—the interplay, as they see it, "between the nature of the job a man performs and his moods, outlook, and behavior . . ."

It follows that, not only in this particular election year, but increasingly as populism reenters the American vocabulary, political figures committed to bringing about progressive change are going to have to face the life problems of the discontented factory worker—not his racial attitudes alone, nor even his passionate concern for the care and education of his children alone, but the totality of his discontent and the depths of its roots. And it cannot be left to the singular charismatic politician: society at large must come to grips, once and for all, with the terrifyingly complex nature of the interplay between the dismal tasks that we ask millions of people to perform in our industrial system, the vistas of other, better ways of living free, dangled tantalizingly before them by our schools and our entertainment media, and the absence of opportunity to effect genuine change in their working lives in any orderly way.

Implicit in this, then, we may read an indictment of politicians who have lost touch with those they would lead, union leaders who have lost touch with those they would represent, bosses whose interest in keeping in touch is limited to buying off a discontent whose depths they cannot plumb. The explosive potential of this discontent has the capacity to destroy the fragile facade of the American democracy.

But the conclusions, as well as the programmatic possibilities issuing from them, are for the rest of us to arrive at; the authors have provided us with suggestive data demanding further investigation—and positive action too, if anything is to be salvaged of the original American dream which dies a little every day in the dismal workplaces darkening the landscape from sea to shining sea.

Preface

Blessed be he who has found
his work; let him ask no
other blessedness.
—Thomas Carlyle

In today's highly regimented, increasingly automated, and deeply impersonal industrial society, the human being who has found fulfilling work is indeed among the blessed.

But more and more workers—and every day this is more apparent—are becoming disenchanted with the boring, repetitive tasks set by a merciless assembly line or by bureaucracy. They feel they have been herded into economic and social cul-de-sacs.

This is a book about American workers. Don't search in these pages for statistics on their incomes, unemployment rates, occupational accidents or disability compensation plans. But if you want to know how American workers think and feel about their jobs—and how these thoughts and feelings spill over into their non-work lives—you will find this book of interest.

We give a great deal of emphasis to two specific groups of workers. We speak at length and in detail about the so-called "Middle American," the white male blue-collar worker who belongs to a union, the "suddenly remembered American" or whatever term the reader uses to conjure up in his mind that large group of workers in our factories and offices whose feelings, desires, frustrations, and vested interests affect the directions in which our country will move during the 1970s and beyond. We don't mean that this is the only group that will affect those directions. We do mean, to quote Peter Binzen in his *Whitetown USA*, that "We neglect the American worker at our peril."

Second, we give more than casual attention to the young American worker: white or black, blue-collar or white-collar, male or female, and so on. We do this partly because of the sheer number (over 22 million) of workers under age 30. The numbers of young workers, furthermore, are increasing and will continue to increase during the early 1970s. But above all, these young workers are more dissatisfied, more oriented toward change, and have higher expectations of work than their older counterparts.

IS THE AMERICAN WORKER UNIQUE?

Are we sure that all the words and pictures about American white workers, concerning such issues as politics, their jobs, and the world in general are strictly American? Based on some recent trips to a few European countries (mostly on this side of the Iron Curtain), we came away with the feeling that many of the main themes expressed in the complaints (and the touted feats) of European managers, union leaders, and journalists were not too different from what we have been subjected to here in America over the past few years; the indifference and/or rebellion of young workers, the resistance of workers to factory discipline, the declining "quality of work," high absenteeism and turn-over, and so on.

Even on the other side of that Iron Curtain, we find some doubt that modern-day workers living in socialist regimes are so different from their British, French, German, or American counterparts. Jan Szczepanski, the eminent Polish sociologist, in his book, *Polish Society*, has detailed the lack of consistency between a worker being an "owner" of his factory (along with hundreds or thousands of other similar owners) and being an employee on an assembly line. "The socialist revolution does not change their relationship to the machine, nor does it change their position within the technological struc-ture of the factory."

THE JOB ITSELF

In the spring of 1970, an Assistant Secretary of Labor, Jerome Rosow, au-thored a report for the President on *The Problems of the Blue-Collar Worker*. In the election campaign of that same year, a spotlight of rhetoric was beamed on this group of workers by politicians anxious to garner their loyalties. This was at a time of widespread reports on blue-collar workers' growing feelings of neglect. They felt left out, it was said, by attention given the protests of the Nation's more overtly disadvantaged groups—Blacks, Chicanos, Puerto Ricans, and Indians. Part of the "re-discovery" of the "Middle American" worker on the part of both parties and the press stems also from the inroads that George Wallace made among enclaves of white workers in the urban cen-ters of the country in his bid for the Presidency in 1968 and 1972. This book should yield some further understanding of these problems. Indeed, much of the research on which the book is based was stimulated by such concerns.

In the following year, President Nixon made at least three speeches ex-tolling the traditional values of the work ethic, and deploring its decline. In April 1971, he told the Republican Governors' Conference at Williamsburg about his thoughts on the rewards of honest toil. "Scrubbing floors and emp-tying bedpans," he claimed, have "just as much dignity as there is in any work to be done in this country—including my own." In September of the same year, before a joint session of Congress (and three days after a Labor Day statement containing the same theme), he again declared that, "No work is demeaning or beneath a person's dignity if it provides food for his table and clothes and shelter for his children."

While it was little remarked upon at the time, the President's Labor Day address recognized our radically changing work values and staked out a major new area for societal concern: the *quality* of work. President Nixon said that new needs of the American worker are now taking their place alongside the old economic needs. He identified some of these new needs as self-respect, individual dignity, and the necessity for avoiding the dehumanization of work by technology.

"In our quest for a better environment," Nixon said, "we must always remember that the most important part of the quality of life is the quality of work. And the new need for job satisfaction is the key to the quality of work."

We also believe that America—along with many other developed countries—is no longer dominated by the work ethic of the past, which stressed work for its own sake. According to this ethic, the rewards from work were the satisfactions derived from serving God: "To select a calling and follow it with all one's conscience is a religious duty."[1] It was this specific type of ideology, originally formulated and diffused by Calvin and his followers, that provided the social-psychological basis for the factory discipline necessary to carry out the extreme division of labor of the industrial age. But today we are entering upon a post-industrial society and, as the President said on September 6, 1971, the American worker has "new needs." Could it be that the search for the restoration of a *relevant* work ethic will have to consider the evaluations that workers place today on their job tasks?

Work itself—the job itself—is thus a major focus of this book. Our observations and conclusions about contemporary work attitudes are based on three separate empirical surveys, the results of which lead us to believe that we can no longer rely on the traditional moralistic appeals to achieve "good work." Many of our observations also have a bearing on the general discontent and the gropings for new political loyalties that seem to characterize the workers interviewed.

One of our overall generalizations (backed up by factual survey findings) is that the "new" worker—compared to his predecessors, or the younger worker of the past—is much more anti-authoritarian,[2] and thus rebels at the lack of variety, autonomy, and challenge to his potential that characterize so many jobs today.

Therefore, one of our themes is that technology, whether it has changed or remained the same insofar as these features are concerned, is not always the same when it comes to the worker's *reaction* to the machine. The machine and man *interact* with one another. To be more specific, different men react to a given technology (or to the tasks "determined" by that technology) in different ways.

We also maintain that, (1) technology is not the unmovable, unchangeable God that many of us (non-Marxists as well as Marxists) were taught to believe, and (2) for those machines or workplaces that might be invulnerable to "humanistic" redesign, there is no law that says a specific individual must remain tied to them for his total working life. Some of our chapters refer to the few efforts made to date to apply these two principles.

But our major emphasis is on the notion that certain kinds of jobs are undesirable—not only for the individual worker employed at them, but equally important, for the general society. For example, the statistical analysis of some of our findings leads to the conclusion (at least, for us) that for *non*-authoritarian workers, jobs with little variety, autonomy, and responsibility can lead to socially and politically undesirable attitudes and behavior. Our emphasis is on the proposition that the goal of reducing or eliminating such jobs is not only in the interest of the individual worker or the individual employer, who frequently pays the cost of such jobs in the form of absenteeism, turnover, poor quality products and low productivity, but also in the interest of the consumer who suffers from the low quality of goods produced under these conditions. It is also in the interest of labor unions, which have made great progress in eliminating many of the grosser forms of poor working conditions, job insecurity, and wage inadequacy, and which may have now reached the point at which new needs, desires, and gripes are beginning to emerge precisely among those very members who have reaped the benefits of that progress. We even believe that government can no longer remain aloof and neutral in this area. Having played a major role in legislating and enforcing fair labor standards (including minimum wages and occupational health and safety), is it possible that government will increasingly find itself forced to cope with the less tangible facets of worklife that affect the legitimate concerns of the state?

1. There are findings in our analysis of one project, consisting of interviews with nearly 400 white male blue-collar union members (in two northern states), that should make all these and other groups in America sit up and take notice that the mainstream of American workers contains a significant number of men who are unhappy with their jobs. Their discontent has many roots, but one of those is intimately tied to the very nature of their jobs. Employment experience, level of wages, and other working conditions naturally are critical elements. However, emphasis here goes beyond job security and income adequacy, and deals with *work itself*.

2. The findings from the interviews with a larger, national sample of 1,533 employed workers (conducted for the Department of Labor in 1969 by the University of Michigan) tell us that the nature of work itself is foremost among the causes of discontent. A large portion of workers said that the nature of their jobs was more important to them than security or pay. Further, analyses of the interviews suggested that they were telling the truth, since elements of autonomy, opportunity for personal growth, interesting work, and so

on, were more highly correlated with overall job satisfaction than were good pay or security.

Thus, we are asserting that much of the discontent can be traced to what men do in order to earn their daily bread. We must begin to examine how their daily tasks can be altered, or how the world of work in general can be rearranged so that no one individual has to be tied down to undesirable tasks for an interminable number of years. We are asserting that in the new epoch, workers will not accept monotonous and dead-end tasks as readily as we believe workers in past decades did.

There are many solutions. We make no special plea for any single approach. This book is not a "pitch" for one technique, gimmick, or work philosophy over another. Instead, it is a presentation of some facts about the lives of American workers and the extent to which the content of those lives cries out for greater, and concerted, action.

SIGNIFICANCE OF THE BLUE-COLLAR SURVEY

The examination of specific groups such as our white male, blue-collar union members is rare in writings of this sort. We usually find only feature stories based on intensive interviews with a dozen or so individuals, and these stories then frequently become the basis for careless generalizations about whatever broad social class, group, or race they happen to belong to. Or else we get carefully designed reports of how the "average" American feels, or behaves, regarding this or that feature or issue in American politics, social relations, economic crises, and so on. But neither approach brings us close enough to the specific issue under discussion. It is not enough to know how "Joe," the construction worker, approached in his local bar (or in his living room) reacts to some social issue. Neither is it enough to know what overall percentage of all American voters or workers say about the same topic. What we need are both nationwide surveys to establish norms, and surveys of specific subgroups to compare and contrast with these norms. This book attempts to fill this need— at least partially.

But more information than is provided by overall comparisons and contrasts is necessary to complete the portrait. The "more" requires that we look into the *relationships* between one set of conditions and another (in other words, between certain types of work and certain kinds of worker responses). This book is also an attempt to provide that "more." But no one ever provides "all."

While we are not entirely innocent of the crime ourselves, one of the pitfalls we tried to avoid in the pages that follow is the sin of "generalized slogans." Such expressions, according to Richard Titmuss, of the London School of Economics, "rarely induce concentration of thought; more often they prevent us from asking significant questions about reality."[3] In other words, we have tried, in this study, to avoid talking about such broad categories as "Americans," or "blacks," or "whites" (this list of social categories is endless), or how this or that group feels or acts. We have also sought to avoid another shortcoming that consists merely of reporting how *individuals* feel or act. "Americans," or "blacks," or "whites," (you add the other infinite rubrics) have other characteristics. They are also: (a) "big city" dwellers, suburbanites, small towners, or rural area residents; (b) old, middle-aged, or young; (c) with a lot or a little of education; (d) members or non-members of unions; *ad infinitum*. It even might make a difference in attitudes and behavior whether or not a "big city" dweller, for example, was born in that urban area, or in another urban area, or in a rural environment.

ON HUMANIZING WORK

Michael Maccoby, the author of the Introduction, is a prominent behavioral scientist and a practicing psychoanalyst (he studied under Erich Fromm).[4] His contribution to this volume consists of an overall perspective on the changing character of workers, and how this affects the major issues dealt with in our general report.[5] Technology, education, and the mass media— along with a rise in the general level of affluence—have made a difference in the types of human beings socialized in our economy and civilization. In particular, their *diminished* authoritarianism affects their reactions to the nature and quality of work tasks.

Maccoby's discussion deals, in part, with the relationship of worker personality and adaptation to varying types and styles of work. His preface is also important because of its attention to the phenomenon of "alienation" and the self. Is alienation from society, as we define it, something to bemoan, or might it suggest a lack of alienation from oneself? As Maccoby defines it, alienation from oneself is a pathological symptom of a dehumanized society. "The growing dissatisfaction of the workers may signify a change in the American character in the direction of stronger demands for a productive and stimulating life." But what if these demands are not accompanied by increased opportunities for such a life? What are the political implications, for example?

THE MYTH OF THE HAPPY WORKER

Studies of specific subgroups in the labor force, such as our young workers, or white male blue-collar workers of all ages, are difficult to interpret without some knowledge of the expectations and situations of the total work force. In order to get this general feel for overall values and expectations, our first chapter gives an overview of the workforce as a whole. This overview identifies the "pockets of discontent" in the total labor force—that is, workers in certain socio-economic groups who are more likely to express discontent with their work than are members of other groups. (For example, young black workers are more than five times as likely to be dissatisfied with their jobs than black workers age 45 and older.) We identify these subgroups not only by personal characteristics such as race and sex, but also by occupational differences as well.

The second part of this chapter points out the job characteristics which are most important to the work force as a whole, and the job requirements which are most highly associated with work satisfaction.

Chapter 2 jumps directly into the question of who are the discontented workers among the white males we surveyed in the summers of 1970 and 1971.[6] Our definition of "discontent," and identification of the characteristics of workers with such discontent should raise some new (and revive some old) questions about the nature of our society and its values, and about the impact of job tasks today. This chapter, along with others in the volume, delves into some of the political implications of the malaise, discontent, or alienation that prevails among many of the workers reached by our interviewers.[7]

BLUE COLLARS ON BORROWED TIME

Chapter 3, on the nature of the workers' job tasks, is basic to the entire volume. It investigates the possible effects on workers of differences in the amount of variety, autonomy, and responsibility in jobs today, and the relationships of such differences to factors of age and education, place of birth, and so on.

More specifically, this chapter seeks some answers to questions such as the following:

> Does the nature of work tasks have a relationship to a worker's attitudes about his job and to management?
>
> And, perhaps more important, does every worker reporting that his job has little variety, for example, feel the same as far as his *disturbance* over the lack of variety is concerned?
>
> If not, how do differences in how much he is bothered by this affect other facets of his work and non-work life?

While we have stressed the point that we are not advocates of any one set of solutions to the problems associated with the nature of job tasks, nevertheless, we have gone into the responses of workers themselves to help formulate several proposals for change or improvement, such as the notion of job rotation, and programs for education or training for better jobs. Our interest in this type of question is not so much what percentage of all our workers would be for or against such ideas, but rather which *types* of workers are the most or the least in favor of them. Is age a critical factor, for example? Or is it more than that? Might, for instance, their interest in job rotation or upgrading training opportunities be affected by social-psychological considerations?

Throughout this study, we call attention to the critical part played by worker's *expectations* about their jobs and about their lives in general. To put it more accurately, we have emphasized the critical role played by the *discrepancy* between such expectations and real achievements, as perceived by the workers themselves. The nature of the job tasks performed by the worker cannot be separated from this issue, which in turn, overlaps into some political and social ramifications. What price do we pay for the deep concern among young workers about their lack of mobility in the jobs they have now? Can we afford to neglect the fact that half of the young workers in jobs with little variety, responsibility, and autonomy, would leave the world of work entirely (that is, retire right away), if they had the chance? Regardless of this issue among the young workers, what is the effect of the opinion among workers in such low-level tasks that employers place too little emphasis on the *quality* of their work?

These and other questions are dealt with in Chapter 3. Some of the other questions include discussions about the adequacy of take-home pay and total family income. To what extent is it true, as suggested (but not demonstrated) in the much publicized Department of Labor report on problems of the blue-collar worker (by former Assistant Secretary of Labor Jerome Rosow), that the "economic squeeze" is felt most among middle-aged workers?

And just how confident are workers about finding a new job if they become unemployed? Who are the most optimistic? The least optimistic? Such questions revive the familiar issue of the relative importance of job security and income adequacy—compared to the *intrinsic* job task satisfaction—at a time when unemployment rates have risen. When problems of economic insecurity are, in general, resolved, does this mean that all's well in the world and that no *new* goals will emerge on the horizon of the workers' job environment? We think that our findings shed some provocative light on this and related issues.

We mentioned earlier that workers in poor jobs (in terms of task level) have negative evaluations of their employers' interest in the quality of their work. The same is true when it comes to evaluations of their unions. Workers in poor tasks are more likely to give a low rating on how helpful their union is to its members.

In this respect, then, unions and employers should have a common interest in coming to grips with the central thrust of our inquiry. However, at a conference in Williamsburg, Virginia, held in April 1971, with union leaders, company officials, and others interested in worker alienation, there was little acceptance of what we believe should be a common concern. That conference revealed to us how far we really have to go in convincing the leaders of major institutions that a crisis exists and that action far beyond what we have seen is imperative.

Much of the thought behind the analysis of our research with the white male, blue-collar workers was stimulated by certain ideas of Erich Fromm, especially his ideas concerning the effects of the nature of a worker's job on his "political personality" or social character.[8] The causes and effects of authoritarianism have long been a major preoccupation of Fromm. Our empirical findings tend to support his fears that bad jobs make workers more susceptible to political demagogy. But, surprisingly enough, the workers in our sample most alienated by dehumanized jobs and most ready to be actively destructive (that is, by voting for George Wallace) were *not* those with authoritarian personalities. Quite the contrary! The discussion of our concrete statistical analyses and their bearing on Fromm's formulations is a major focus in several of the chapters (especially Chapters 3, 4, and 5). Suffice it to say at this point that authoritarianism is intimately related to the world of work and to a worker's alienation, but not precisely in the manner we had expected from our reading of Fromm's works.

The effects of a man's job task, and degree of authoritarianism, on his alienation and political orientation are the main concern of Chapter 4. It is in that chapter that we move more directly into the world of politics. We have tried, as simply as possible, to unravel the complex path from a worker's job and his personality to his estimate of how effective he is in the decisions of government, and to his choice of candidates for the Presidency in 1968. We think our findings should be of more than passing relevance to the elections of 1972 —and those to follow.

So far, this Introduction may have led the reader to believe that we have been blind to the "real" world of economics—specifically, of unemployment and of wages—of its relationship to the allegedly less important, less real phenomena of workers' feelings and attitudes about their jobs. But we have not been blind to this issue. Chapter 5 on "Economic Factors and the Impact of Meaningless Work," deliberately addresses itself to this issue. Job security and anxiety about it are, of course, of tremendous and top-priority importance. In this section of our volume, we have been able to test some of the notions underlying the cynicism of many public leaders and academic authorities about the importance of "work itself." If alienation or job satisfaction, for example, *is* unimportant among workers who have gained a high degree of economic security (as measured by past unemployment experience and level of wage), we should expect to find that differences in job tasks make no difference in worker alienation or job satisfaction. But is that what we really find? We leave it to the reader to determine the answer for himself, after examining the analyses presented and discussed in this chapter.

Union leaders will be interested in how their members with economic security rate their unions' helpfulness, depending on the kind of job tasks they perform. Democrats and Republicans also will be interested in these same workers' party preferences. Our dissection of the interview results suggests another look at the conventional beliefs concerning the relationship of unemployment experience to party choice. Our evidence points to a breaking with tradition among workers of today: Low wages and unemployment experience combined are no longer the guarantee for pro-Democratic loyalties.

THE YOUNG WORKER

The next two chapters deal with the favorite topic of many social commentators: the youth scene. Chapter 6 is aimed at drawing a portrait of a national sample of all employed workers under 30 (more than 22 million of them, of all races and sexes), and is derived from the Department of Labor study carried out by the University of Michigan.[9] Chapter 7 returns to the under-30 workers in our special sample of white male union members. Both chapters, we think, answer some of the vital questions in the minds of many Americans, for example:

> Are young workers unique in their work attitudes, including their feelings about doing something worthwhile in their job roles?

> How do race, sex, and education affect young workers' attitudes toward their jobs?

> Are they really as irresponsible about work as so many adults say they are? Or do they feel that the kinds of jobs they are in allow for little feeling of responsibility and usefulness?

> How does this relate to the possibility that the "Now" generation has far higher expectations of life?

> Taking just the young white male union members, what do they think of their employers, their unions, and the current political atmosphere?

> Are they any different from the older workers in what they want to hear from political candidates?

One of our major conclusions is that, if any one thing sets apart the young workers in contemporary America and goes a long way in explaining much of their other behavior (in the work and political spheres), it is their *anti-authoritarianism*. This, to us, suggests an emerging new "social character"—to use a concept developed by Fromm. If our hunch is correct, as such young workers grow older, their anti-authoritarianism will not diminish. The implications for the future of work in America may be revolutionary in scope. They suggest that our institutions will have to bend—indeed to change—in order to make greater, more fruitful use of this new social character, since this character is much more difficult, if not impossible, to modify. And what of the future generations of young workers—those individuals now in their early teens or younger?

The political ramifications of this change are also discussed in Chapter 7, and they shed a great deal of light on the question of where political candidates such as George Wallace get their support.

OPPORTUNITY: A SECOND KNOCK

But the young cannot claim all our attention. Older workers, too, have their expectations and needs. For a certain portion of them, there is an unmet need for change, particularly in terms of occupations. While the subject of "mid-career" malaise and radical job shifts among the upper classes (professional and highly technical personnel, for example) has become a popular theme in our mass media, little attention has been paid to the possibility that for older (over-40) blue-collar workers as well, there is a similar desire. This is the theme of Chapter 9.

What proportion of the 40-and-older white male union workers fall into such a category? And how do they differ from the men of their same age group who rarely, if ever, think about moving into a completely different kind of job and who would *not* take advantage of a program sponsored by government, companies, or unions to educate them for a really better job? Our data point up the reasons why such programs might be necessary—not only for the individual worker himself, but for the welfare of society and the economy in general.

Chapter 10, on "Second Careers," by Alan Entine, spells out the successful results of a project at Columbia University designed to move professionals into second careers that are very different from their previous occupations. His chapter is included here because it shows that such an idea is not utopian, that it can be done, even for blue-collar workers.

POSSIBILITIES FOR CHANGE

A critical question, of course, is who is doing what now about changing the nature of work and its organizational setting? Chapter 11, by Harvard Professor Fred Foulkes is one attempt to answer that question. As he properly points out, the problem of work today is not limited to blue-collar workers: "a mounting wave of unrest . . . is sweeping the ranks of middle management." We may be dealing with a cultural phenomenon affecting all social classes (which is part of Michael Maccoby's viewpoint). Foulkes, who has written an important study on *Creating More Meaningful Work* (American Management Association, 1969), presents a brief but telling summary of recent attempts to cope with the work-related problems of today's workers. If he is correct in his estimate of how many companies are carrying out new and innovative ideas to meet such problems, we have barely begun to scratch the surface. The impression he actually leaves is a confirmation of the survey of employer points of view and policies, presented in Chapter 12.

Chapter 12 goes beyond the usual approach to the issue of work satisfaction (based only on interviews with *workers*), and gets at the degree of recognition and acceptance by corporation presidents, middle management, union presidents, and shop stewards—and workers themselves—that the nature of job tasks *is* a critical factor in the life of individuals, organizations, and society. The data are based on a third survey, conducted among such groups or organizational representatives, and it includes the relative priority placed on this issue by each of such groups. We know that little will be done on the issue as long as unions, companies, and government agencies fail to "get the message" from workers, as expressed in their verbal attitudes and overt behavior (ranging from low production and poor quality of output to outright sabotage), that the restructuring of work tasks and organizational climate is long overdue. Accordingly, we felt it indispensable to learn just how such organizations feel about, and what they are doing about, the problems involved.

The Williamsburg Conference was one way of sounding out some selected representatives of unions, companies, and government. On a more systematic basis, we canvassed the views of management and union leaders on such questions as their willingness to sponsor experiments in job content improvement; their opinions on the relative importance of improving opportunities to do interesting and satisfying work (as compared to the need to improve, for example, wage levels, health and safety practices, etc.); and whether or not they felt that the Federal government, unions, and companies should concern themselves with job-content problems.

The discrepancies between the responses of employers, foremen, union officials, and union stewards, *and* those of workers themselves go to the heart of the survey and analysis. Some of the findings confirm Michel Crozier's observation that people in positions to make decisions in large organizations are frequently not in a position to know about the actual situation and individuals being affected, and people in the situation are likely to experience and know about the problems being tackled, but are not in a position to make decisions on those problems.[10]

In other words, workers' preferences on many of the items covered were far apart from those of employers—and even those of union officials. Union stewards, who are closer to the everyday worklife of union members, do not always rate job-related issues in the same way as do union *officials*. For example, by a 2 to 1 ratio, stewards—compared to union officials, as well as employers and foremen—believe that workers are less satisfied now than in the past with pay, fringe benefits and working conditions.

—Harold L. Sheppard

and

Neal Q. Herrick

This book is a product of a pleasant division of labor between the two authors during 1970–71, when Neal Herrick was on leave from the Department of Labor as a Federal Executive Fellow at the Upjohn Insitute for Employment Research, of which the second author, Harold Sheppard, has been a staff member since 1963. Each chapter is the sole responsibility of its author. Chapters 1, 6, and 12 were written by Herrick; Chapters 2 through 5, and 7 through 9, by Sheppard. Chapter 10 (on an experiment in second careers at Columbia University) was written by Alan Entine, of the Stony Brook campus of the State University of New York; and Chapter 11 (on current efforts to cope with workers' job dissatisfaction) was authored by Fred Foulkes, of the Harvard Graduate School of Business.

NOTES:

1. Adriano Tilgher, "Work Through the Ages," reprinted in Sigmund Nosow and William H. Form, eds., *Man, Work, and Society* (New York: Basic Books, 1962), p. 19.
2. See Chapter 4, page 80 for a detailed definition of "authoritarianism," as used in this book. Briefly, it refers to a tendency on the part of individuals to defer to superiors, or to be strict with subordinates, to be resistant to change, and to be anti-democratic.
3. Richard M. Titmuss, *Commitment to Welfare* (New York: Pantheon Books, 1968), p. 124.
4. The two have also recently co-authored *Social Character in a Mexican Village* (Englewood Cliffs, N.J.: Prentice-Hall, 1970).

    Maccoby is currently the director of a study on technology, work, and character sponsored by Harvard's Program on Technology and Society—as well as a Fellow of the Institute for Policy Studies in Washington, D.C.
5. Based on his remarks at a Williamsburg meeting in April 1971, which convened labor and company officials along with government representatives to discuss some of the issues presented in this volume. A report on this conference, by Charlton Price, is now available: *New Directions in the World of Work* (Kalamazoo: W. E. Upjohn Institute for Employment Research, 1972). The conference was sponsored by the Institute, as part of a grant from the Ford Foundation.
6. They were randomly selected from membership lists of the AFL-CIO in the following urban areas: Pittsburgh, Philadelphia, Allentown–Bethlehem, York–Lancaster—all in Pennsylvania; and from lists of the United Steelworkers and the United Auto Workers in Kalamazoo, Michigan. The cooperation of the officers and staff of the unions involved, especially Michael Johnson, of Pennsylvania's AFL-CIO along with Fred Hoehler, Director of the new AFL-CIO Labor Study

Center in Washington (and formerly at Michigan State University) is gratefully acknowledged; also that of Professor Subhash Sonnad, of Western Michigan University (Kalamazoo) who supervised the survey in that urban area. A major part of the research in this sample of workers—as well as the Williamsburg Conference—was financed by a grant from The Ford Foundation.

Chapters 2–5 and 7–9 in this book are based on these interviews.

7. The interview schedule used with the Pennsylvania and Kalamazoo blue-collar workers is reproduced in Appendix B.

8. For an early summary of his views, see his "Freedom in the Work Situation," in Michael Harrington and Paul Jacobs, Editors, *Labor in a Free Society* (Berkeley: University of California, 1959), pp. 1–16.

9. The general report on this study is *Survey of Working Conditions* (Washington: U.S. Department of Labor, Employment Standards Administration, 1971).

10. Michel Crozier, *The Bureaucratic Phenomenon* (Chicago: University of Chicago Press, 1964).

Introduction

MICHAEL MACCOBY

During the past generation, social and cultural changes in the United States have led to rising expectations and demands about life and work. Modes of work and life styles that were acceptable in the past are increasingly felt as oppressive by young workers in factories, offices, and development labs. It is no longer considered sufficient to have a "decent" job that pays enough to provide adequate food and shelter. The goal of comfort and security is still central for the majority of production workers, employees, and service workers. However, as the analyses by Sheppard and Herrick show, for many workers the quality of the job is as important and after reaching a certain level of income and safety even more important than increases in wages. Herrick's investigations begin to suggest that management, and even union officials, tend to over-estimate the workers' satisfaction with work conditions and to underestimate a growing consciousness that the quality of work needs to be improved.

What is meant by improving the quality of work? Most workers have never been stimulated to evaluate their work in broad human terms, and less to consider alternative ways of designing tasks. In those few companies where workers have been encouraged to critically analyze their jobs, a general consensus emerges of negative and positive work attributes. In general, workers want to avoid jobs that are monotonous, repetitive, over-controlled, and isolated from interaction with others. In contrast, they seek jobs that require activeness—planning and judgment—autonomy on the job, variety, and that are demanding enough to stimulate learning. Beyond these psychological factors, workers are also concerned with the dignity associated with the job and with opportunities for career development. They are also increasingly concerned that the work be "meaningful," that it involve clearly useful tasks and require sufficient skill to be worthy of respect.

Taken together, these requirements move in the direction of humanizing work. In contrast, dehumanized work is a job which makes the worker into a machine part, totally controlled, fully predictable, and easily replaceable. For quite a while, there has been evidence that, when work is less dehumanized, most workers are more satisfied and there is less absenteeism and turnover. In the recent past, however, Americans appeared more willing to adapt themselves to mechanized work. Many appeared to have been satisfied by such jobs, as long as they paid a decent wage. There are a number of reasons for this.

1. Some industrial workers, such as the ones described by Frederick Winslow Taylor, were immigrants, for whom the pay and standard of living were superior to what they had known before. Indeed, before the wave of immigration in the 1880s, there was a growing movement to democratize the workplace. The immigrants generally came from traditional cultures where one accepted his place in society. Furthermore, the worker might gain satisfaction from his role in the subculture rather than in the factory. At home, he might have headed a patriarchal family. There, he was respected by his wife and children, and he could feel compensated for the dreary work.

2. Other factory workers, including early union organizers, considered the first priority for workers to be decent wages, health and unemployment benefits, and the establishment of collective bargaining principles. In return for security and benefits, management retained control of design and organization of work. Many people accepted the notion that work had to be organized so that human considerations would be sacrificed for maximal efficiency. It was generally taken for granted that the requirements of advanced technology should determine the work, and that maximum specialization and repetitiveness, combined with minimal training, was the most profitable approach. Even many humanists accepted this idea and aimed for a shorter work week as the main relief from dehumanization, ignoring the probability that to be creative in leisure while mindless and passive in work demands a schizoid attitude.

Today, these attitudes of workers are changing, and industrial experiments indicate possibilities for modifying technology and the organization of work. As Sheppard's studies indicate, younger workers are more democratic and less authoritarian. Members of the new generation are more self-affirmative and expect to be treated with respect by their employers. They seek work that allows them to be more active and autonomous. Judson Gooding's interviews with workers, as reported in his *Fortune* articles during 1970–71, supports these findings. Gooding also suggests that many are resentful and rebellious, and he cites incidents of industrial sabotage as protests against dehumanized work.

What are the forces that have led to this new character and ideal of workers which is so different from the old stereotypes? It is probable that changes in technology, education, and the organization of work, have all played a role.

Technological developments have led to increased productivity and consumption of goods. The average American industrial worker now enjoys a standard of living that seems fabulous to most of the world. Once a certain level of affluence is taken for granted, this tends to undermine the attitudes based on the principle of scarcity, that one must sacrifice individual expression and growth in order to survive. Furthermore, Americans are less willing to passively accept their fate; the fatalistic ethic of traditional societies has been replaced by the values of the American technological society which Tocqueville described in the early 19th century. This ideology, reinforced by the achievements of science and industry, suggests to Americans, rightly or wrongly, that there are no limits to possibilities for improving society. Therefore, the American worker is especially likely to feel that change for the better is possible.

Technology has also been responsible for the development of mass communications networks which have spread the values of autonomy and technological progress into every home. Neither "ethnic" families from eastern and southern Europe nor farmers from middle America can hold the cultural line against the onslaught of radio, television, and juke boxes. Furthermore, the consumer goods themselves, on display in stores, worn by working-class people, and driven by them on highways, are themselves a media message, suggesting that everyone can participate in the affluent society.

The traditional authoritarian submissiveness is also undermined by the movements of rock music, civil rights, and war protest. The media have reported and also stimulated the challenge to traditional values that has dominated the twentieth century. Children no longer blindly accept the authority of parents; the paterfamilias can no longer demand respect, but must earn it. Students question the knowledge of teachers, and are no longer bedazzled by degrees and titles. Black Americans have rejected the servile role and the racist image. Women are challenging inequality and lack of opportunity structured by the male-dominated bureaucratic-industrial society. These challenges to authority are often harsh and bitter; sometimes they express resentment and revenge. But they also reaffirm humanistic and democratic principles of the American Revolution submerged during the period of rapid industrial growth and immigration, including the right to pursue happiness and to have a voice in decisions which determine one's life. As the concepts of community control and decentralization have gained new life, so too the goal of industrial democracy.

Education has also made a difference. Some of the radical critics of schooling, myself included, have denounced the factory-like organization of the schools, the conventionality and abstractification of what is learned, and the boring, non-productive atmosphere. These criticisms make sense when the actual is contrasted to the possible. Schools are not sufficiently oriented to the development of individual potentialities. The content and structure of pedagogy can be significantly improved. However, the attacks on schooling gain support mainly from the upper-middle class on the one hand and the ghettos on the other. In the former case, this is because parents want the public schools to feature the latest innovations, to prepare children to make it in the competitive world of professions and corporations. In the case of the ghettoes, the schools have simply been unequal to the task and have often used force because they are unable to teach.

However, this is not the case for the whole country. A recent census study reported that the percentage of Americans with a high school diploma has almost doubled from 38 percent in 1940 to 75 percent in 1970. (The percent with college degrees has gone from 6 to 16 percent; the proportion of those with one or more years of college has gone from 13 to 31 percent in the same 30 year period.) For many young Americans, particularly those who are to become blue-collar workers, the atmosphere of local schools is both more stimulating and democratic than either the home or work place. At school, these young people are expected to learn, to develop competence, and to play with their peers in democratic groups, which stress fairness and competence, rather than seniority and submissiveness. In contrast to many factories, their school work allows variety and some initiative, and achievements are recognized. Students are sometimes pushed around by their teachers (and teachers are sometimes pushed around by students), but students are generally not exploited. Thus, one finds in Sheppard's studies that for white male blue-collar workers, years of schooling is positively correlated with democratic attitudes, while workers with less schooling tend to be more authoritarian. This finding explains why the auto companies have discovered that young workers with high school diplomas are more likely than the older generation to find assembly work oppressive and to rebel against it. The young people compare this mechanized organization of work with their other experiences and against their values; the contrast increases frustration and anger.

American workers may also be influenced by new models of organization in the workplace, particularly on the managerial level. The requirements of advanced technology have led to an increase in projects and teamwork. The old-style bureaucratic structures no longer serve for industries which are oriented to innovation, nor to those which emphasize service. Some corporations have adopted new programs or organizational development (sometimes including sensitivity groups) in order to develop team work and smoother interpersonal relationships. Furthermore, managers have been taught new ideologies of human relations, stressing the importance of autonomy, and the quality of the work itself. These models may also have some effect on stimulating new attitudes and hopes on the part of both white-collar, and blue-collar workers.

It should be added that dissatisfaction with mechanized work is not limited to factory workers. Engineers in highly technological organizations also bridle at being highly controlled parts of a megamachine in companies that develop large electronic or aerospace projects. (See, for example, R. Richard

Ritti, *The Engineer in the Industrial Corporation*, Columbia University Press, 1971). These highly schooled individuals feel deep dissatisfaction in jobs which do not demand a fuller use of their skills. In large part, this is because they are thus unable to show their abilities, and have no chance to make the first team. A significant number, however, seek work which allows initiative and growth.

Indeed, the growing dissatisfaction on the part of workers to being over-controlled is experienced in all parts of the society, even on the part of many symphony orchestra members. These young musicians contrast the model of the chamber group or the rock combo, organizations combining cooperation with individual expression, with the orchestra which demands submission to the absolute authority of the conductor. There are, of course, differences in orchestra conductors. Some are martinets, who require musicians to fit into a hierarchy at the cost of their dignity and sense of self, and others are more humane teachers and coaches. However, the structure of the orchestra tends to make the individual into part of a machine, while that of the chamber group tends to develop a sense of relatedness and mutuality.

The spirit of the times and the prevailing ideology is anti-bureaucratic and suspicious of all hierarchy. Such is the extreme expression of this spirit that some young people reject all forms of structure and interdependence and glorify an ideal of individualistic egoism. However, the importance of this strident anti-social childishness tends to be exaggerated by those who favor pyramidal structures and rigid control. In contrast, the goals of workers who want to improve the quality of work are not narcissistic; to the contrary, they seek personal development and a less schizoid relation to their work.

Indeed, the question may be asked as to which workers today are satisfied with being a part of a megamachine. What does it mean to be adapted to mechanized work which requires little or no autonomy and activeness? Sheppard's data demonstrate that the most authoritarian workers are the ones who complain least about dehumanizing work. These are individuals who assent to the statements that:

"The most important thing to teach children is absolute obedience to their parents."

"Any good leader should be strict with people under him in order to gain their respect."

"A few strong leaders could do more for this country than all the laws and talk."

The authoritarian character has been described by Erich Fromm as that of a person whose sense of strength and identity is based on a symbiotic sub-ordination to authorities, and, at the same time, a symbiotic domination of those submitting to *his* authority. That is to say, the authoritarian character feels himself strong when he can submit and be part of an authority which (to some extent backed by reality) is inflated, and when, at the same time, he can inflate himself by incorporating those subject to his authority. This is a state of sado-masochistic symbiosis, which gives him a sense of strength and identity. By being part of the powerful organization—the megamachine—the authoritarian feels big; if he were alone, by himself, he would shrink to nothing.

Since the authoritarian men are the ones most satisfied with routinized, repetitive work, this implies that adaptation to mechanized work has important social implications. These individuals tend to be the most anti-democratic in their roles as husbands, fathers, and citizens as well as in the factory and in trade unions. They are the men who try to crush independence in their children and who treat their wives as chattels. They are likely to support the oppressive elements in schooling, and whatever political positions are taken by "strong leaders" who are contemptuous of citizens' rights.

It is of course true that human beings are capable of adapting to dehumanizing conditions. However, such adaptation tends to be extremely costly, individually and socially. The authoritarian personality is one form of adaptation to the megamachine. Another form is the passive compliant personality, resigned and without hope. A third form is the depressed, schizoid individual who goes through the motions, whose deadened attitude freezes an unbearable feeling of rage; such workers tend to escape from factories into a world of canned dreams. As Harold Wilensky has shown through interview studies, they spend their "free time" watching TV, tortured by feelings of guilt and waste.

The relationship between adaptation to work and the personality of workers is one which merits particular attention. There is evidence suggesting that the mode of work is a key element among the character forming elements in a culture or subculture. For example, in a traditional farming society of small land owners, workers tend to develop the productive-hoarding character traits that fit them for their work. The traits of compulsive saving, independence, cautious conservativism, patience, and suspiciousness of strangers are all highly adaptive for the small farmer's mode of production.[1] In contrast, the peons who were landless and under the control of semi-feudal masters on haciendas in Mexico and other countries tended to develop traits of submissiveness, passiveness, and dependence which were rooted in the receptive character. These character traits are still adaptive for landless agricultural workers in traditional societies. The character traits most adaptive to a society's mode of production become the attitudes which determine cultural and political attitudes. The independent-hoarding small farmer is conservative in his politics, although he may become rebellious and militant in defense of his traditional rights, and particularly when his property is taken from him. The passive-receptive laborer is unlikely to concern himself with his rights, and tends to follow strong leaders who offer him something for nothing.

Since each type of work organization tends to produce a character type most adapted to it, one cost of structuring work in a particular way must be measured in terms of the kind of person molded by it. It should be kept in mind that the relationship between work and the individual's character is an indirect as well as direct one, since the traits needed in work tend to be the ones developed in the family and also by the schools. Parents tend to emphasize traits that are adaptive to work as they know it, and they may lobby for school programs they believe will effectively develop a "successful" child. Our society is, of course, much more complex than any traditional culture. Here, these are different social classes and, within each, there are different kinds of work which allow the development of many types of character. However, the way work is organized in factories and industries which employ hundreds of thousands may have a decisive role in the formation of our national character.

Today, as we have suggested, the character traits required by mechanized work and the traits stimulated by schooling and popular culture do not always coincide. Increasingly, children from blue-collar families are being raised according to the values of autonomy, democracy, and meritocracy. The values of the megamachine, compulsive order and obedience, no longer take root in children who are encouraged to be both more democratic and self-indulgent. At best, they are also stimulated to be more daring and unconventional in their approach to learning and to develop their own intellectual interests. One may expect, if the upper-middle class critics succeed in further reforming schooling to stimulate active learning in the "open classroom" and through teaching by dialogue, the effect will be to create an even greater tension between the mechanized workplace and the character of the workers.[2]

The results of Sheppard's studies suggest that workers who experience most intensely the conflict between their needs for self-realization and the monotony of the mechanized workplace will be the ones who are most alienated from the society. Can one expect it to be different?

To consider the problem one of "alienation" may muddy the water, unless the meaning of the concept is clearly understood. Indeed, the term has at least two basic definitions which are not only different, but in certain contexts have opposite meanings. In the sense that Sheppard uses the term, alienation implies deep dissatisfaction with the society, often to the degree that the individual seeks radical change in the status quo. A second meaning taken from traditional psychiatry refers to the separation of mind from emotions. In terms of this definition, the alienated individual feels "depersonalized" and cannot experience the full reality of himself. For example, the alienated person in this sense may be the one who adapts himself to mechanized work by cutting himself off from his feelings of anger, becoming emotionally deadened and passive. Alienation from self, which characterizes many "normal" people, is *the* human problem of industrial society. The movement to humanize work can be summarized as man's struggle to create conditions which do not alienate him from himself.

In terms of the self, who will be the more alienated, the worker who is adapted to mechanized work or the one who resists it? Will the individual who is most alienated from dehumanizing social conditions be more alienated from self than the one who accepts these conditions without protest?[3] It seems unlikely, even more so if we consider the opposite of each type of alienation. The opposite of alienation from society turns out to be the national problem most discussed by intellectuals 15 years ago, namely conformity. In that sense of the term, alienation is a potential for progress, depending on whether or not the alienation becomes a stimulus for constructive change. The growing dissatisfaction of the workers may signify a change in the American character in the direction of stronger demands for a productive and stimulating life. Or, if no change is possible, such alienation may only increase the worker's sense of powerlessness and his feeling that he is a "loser" in the meritocratic game of life. As a result, such an individual may be attracted to violence or to movements like that of George Wallace, based on resentment, which shape a particular consciousness of powerlessness and make it the basis of a political ideology.

The opposite of alienation from self is more difficult to define. It is perhaps best formulated in terms of mature individuation. The psychologically unalienated person is productive in work and love; he is in touch with himself, others, and society. Such an individual has perfected his capacity to understand and create, in areas of human relationships as well as art, science, athletics, and industry. In this context, the organization of work can be measured in terms of whether it increases human alienation or whether it moves toward improving possibilities for fuller human development. In this sense, the "problem" of alienation will not be solved unless the quality of work is improved, so that the worker need not sacrifice his dignity and potential in order to earn a living.

How will these changes take place? The humanization of work is not a problem to be solved simply or mechanistically. It requires systemic changes in people, organizations, and perhaps even in the larger society. We can begin to learn from studying the experiments in job improvement that have taken place over the past decade in some forty American corporations.[4] These programs have been of two main types, either changing specifications of jobs within existing structures, or developing new, generally more automated factories, such as the one created by Lyman Ketchum of General Foods, where from the start, work is organized to be freer and more interesting.

We do not yet have sufficient data from these experiments to arrive at definitive conclusions about what works best. On the basis of preliminary reports, the new factory model appears a particularly promising way to improve work. However, there is considerable evidence concerning resistances to changing the nature of work within existing structures. In one company, it was discovered that a program including on-the-job education with job enlargement, while extremely satisfying to those workers involved, was not readily accepted by the rest of the organization. Workers left out of the program felt a natural resentment. And some managers were threatened by the program and its effect on the workers. One manager who favored the program cautioned that, "Before we continue the education of people, we must understand that the result of education is a freer man and not a more controllable man."

One finds managerial coolness or active opposition to job enrichment programs, even where there is evidence that these programs are profitable for the company in terms of more efficient work, drops in absenteeism, and less turnover. The reason is that humanizing work gives more initiative and autonomy to the worker. He or she becomes less controlled by the manager. Once the worker is given responsibility for an area of work, he is no longer a simple part in the machine, easily replaceable on the manager's whims. In the new situation, there is less need for managers, since workers take over many managerial functions. Those managers or foremen who are needed must win the respect and confidence of the workers; they can no longer manage on the basis of autocratic authority. Thus, while programs to improve work appeal to democratic workers and productive managers, they are resisted by individuals who are authoritarian, threatened by freedom and spontaneity. As one manager of an auto company asked during a discussion of humanizing work, "Where will it all lead?" Once the worker is encouraged to question and think, one can no longer predict what he will think about. For example, as he gains more responsibility, the worker may become more concerned about the products he makes. He may object to making products that are shoddy or destructive. Some people have faith that greater freedom will in the long run humanize our society; for others it conjures up only fears.

Given the resistances and costs of humanizing work, few industries will move in this direction solely in terms of their own initiative, although some particularly creative managers have dedicated themselves to improving the nature of work. Generally, these innovators must explain their efforts to the company in terms of profits in order to "rationalize" their creative vision so that it is acceptable within the corporate world view.[5] In some areas of industry, the movement to humanize work may also gain support from increased international competition, forcing steps to increase efficiency. However, the movement depends also on the role taken by labor unions. As Herrick points out, high union officials are now far less concerned with the humanization of work than they are with the bread and butter issues of pay and benefits. Probably, some union leaders would have resistances similar to those of the managers who are threatened by autonomous workers. The free worker is more likely to question the organization and decisions of the union as well as those of the industrial organization. As Marcus Raskin argues, the unions have bargained away the quality of work for security and benefits, and have become a powerful force to keep the workers "in line."[6]

In conclusion, it should be emphasized that the major reason to humanize work is to create an America in which resources are organized optimally to allow each individual to develop himself to the fullest, and in which projects are carried out by free people, none used as an object by another. Progress toward this goal will require that individuals become more self-directed, less competitive, and more responsible. The process of humanizing work will enrich the lives of many people, and at the same time, move towards a society which *needs* free and active citizens.

NOTES:

1. See Erich Fromm and Michael Maccoby, *Social Character in a Mexican Village* (Englewood Cliffs, N.J., Prentice-Hall, 1970).
2. This problem of course also exists for those middle class students who, in the past, graduated to work at low-level bureaucratic jobs. In the future, such jobs are the ones which are most likely to be replaced by computer systems, which will eliminate paper work and paper workers.
3. A meaning of alienation related to this is the use of the term by Hegel and Marx, based on the distinction between existence and essence, in the sense that alienated man is not what he could become. An alienated man may be one who has surrendered himself in order to serve the machine. As Erich Fromm points out, this concept of alienation is close to the prophetic view of idolatry in the Old Testament. See his *Marx's Concept of Man*, (New York, Ungar, 1961).
4. According to Fred K. Foulkes. See his book, *Creating More Meaningful Work* (New York, American Management Association, 1969), and his Chapter 11 of this volume, which describe some of these experiments.
5. At the Williamsburg conference on the quality of work—sponsored by the Upjohn Institute in April, 1971—one manager presented his vision and another corporate-governmental official insisted that the manager's "real goal" must be making money. This official could not conceive that an industrial manager might have the same creative goal as an artist, who, of course, also wants to sell his product. In other words, the concept of an unalienated industrial manager clashes with a world view that is rooted in a materialistic social character. There is a strong tendency for people to rationalize their own attitudes in terms of an ideology which attributes them to "the nature of man." Thus, those who are concerned solely with making money argue that this is human nature. Such people are the ones who most challenge the idea that blue-collar workers may want autonomy and interesting work as much or more than pay increases.
6. *Being and Doing* (New York: Random House, 1971).

Part One

The Myth of the Happy Worker

Chapter One

Pockets of Discontent

In simple bewilderment we watch the spread of violence through what once were peaceful streets. We note in anguish the rise of crime unprecedented in America; and we blame it on our racial problems while ignoring its rise in lands where race is no factor; or we blame it on poverty, forgetting that in the 1930's when poverty was a common possession, crime was endurable. Earnestly we grope for clues to explain the revolt of the young, the persuasion of alcoholism, hallucinatory drugs, pornography. Explanations become dust even as we touch them. The hungry psyche has replaced the hungry belly.
—*Robert Ardrey*[1]

Until recently, "tough-minded" men of affairs ridiculed any concern over workers' feelings, saying that workers cared about only one thing: pay. The worker exchanged his time, they said, for an agreed upon sum of money with which he then purchased his pleasures.

This appears to be changing now—and for very good reason. Not because McGregor conceived the theory that workers have a natural inclination to be productive.[2] Not because Maslow conceptualized an industrial world where—once worker's security needs were met—their self-fulfillment needs would be intensified.[3] Not even because of the influential writings of Erich Fromm and other philosophers. Worker dissatisfaction metamorphosed from a hobby horse of the "tender-minded" to a fire-breathing dragon because workers began to translate their feelings of dissatisfaction into alienated behavior! Turnover rates are climbing. Absenteeism has increased as much as 100 percent in the past 10 years in the automobile industry.[4] Workers talk back to their bosses. They no longer accept the authoritarian way of doing

3

things. In short, workers themselves are beginning to tell us the same things about their feelings and needs that McGregor, Maslow, and Fromm told us in the past. They are telling us in capital letters and those letters spell out a need for action.[5]

Corporate managers are becoming interested in such previously academic questions as, "Who is dissatisfied?" and "Why are they dissatisfied?" and "What are the implications of this dissatisfaction?" This chapter comments on these questions, drawing on the data from a national survey of workers conducted in November and December of 1969 by the Survey Research Center at the University of Michigan.[6] Since it is based largely on one-time survey data, it cannot answer questions regarding trends (for instance, "Are young workers becoming more dissatisfied than in the past?") The first table in Appendix A indicates the percentages with negative attitudes toward work and life, by a number of socio-economic groupings. A re-survey is planned for early in 1973, however, and it should help us find answers to many such questions. For the time being, we must confine ourselves to describing the subgroups that were most dissatisfied, and commenting on the work features which seem to go hand in glove with dissatisfaction. There will also be some discussion of dissatisfaction with life in general, particularly as it relates to dissatisfaction with the workplace.

Black workers under age 30 were much more dissatisfied with their jobs than any other group. Thirty-seven percent expressed negative attitudes toward their jobs. The group with the second highest proportion of dissatisfied workers was made up of workers aged 29 and under with some college education. Females aged 29 and under were the third most dissatisfied group. It is striking that, of the ten most dissatisfied groups, all were made up of workers age 29 and under, except one. The exception was composed of individuals with some college experience who made less than $5,000 per year.

From the preponderance of young groups among the most dissatisfied, we might speculate that the groups expressing the least job dissatisfaction would be made up of oldsters. Indeed, this seemed to be the case. Among the least dissatisfied group, only 6 percent expressed negative attitudes toward their jobs. This group was made up of workers age 45 and over making $5,000 or more per year. As expected, older males were consistently among the most satisfied workers. Also highly satisfied were workers having an income of $10,000 or more, and, in addition, falling into any one of the following categories: having a white skin, being over 44 years of age, not having been to college, or being married.

PATTERNS OF DISCONTENT

The older a worker is, the more likely he is to be satisfied with his job—regardless of income. The higher his income, the more likely he is to be satisfied—

unless he is under age 30. In this age bracket, chances for satisfaction do not improve until the $10,000-per-year mark is passed.

This chapter discusses the associations of various factors such as age, income, race, sex, etc., to job satisfaction. In addition, a few comments on life satisfaction are thrown in for good measure. Table 1 in Appendix A shows the percentage of workers in these socio-economic groups who expressed negative attitudes toward work[7] and life.[8]

INDUSTRY AND OCCUPATION

If you want your sons and daughters to have the very best chances for work satisfaction, advise them either to prepare for a career in the construction industry or to go into business for themselves. In construction work and among the self-employed chances of dissatisfaction with work were only 1 in about 20. They might also aspire to technical, professional, and managerial occupations, where their chances of dissatisfaction with work would still be low: only about 1 in 10.[9] They should avoid, however, service occupations and the wholesale-retail industry. In either category, chances for dissatisfaction were nearly 1 in 4. Prospects in the manufacturing industry were not much brighter.

INCOME

This may come as a shock to your sons and daughters, but the old saying, "I've been rich and I've been poor and believe me rich is better," was still valid in November and December 1969. About one of every five workers making less than $5,000 a year was dissatisfied with his job. Moving to the $5,000–$10,000 income range, the percentage of workers dissatisfied with their jobs dropped almost in half. For workers making $10,000 or more, only a hard core 8 percent were dissatisfied.[10]

AGE

"Say what thou wilt, the young are happy never.
Give me bless'd age, beyond the fire and fever."

Sir William Watson might have been talking about the American worker. The older the worker, the less likely he was to be dissatisfied with his job. One of every four workers under age 30 felt dissatisfied. Only 13 percent of workers aged 30 to 44 expressed negative feelings toward their jobs. The percentage dropped to 11 for workers between 45 to 54 and to 6 percent for workers aged 55 and over. Perhaps younger workers are more dissatisfied because they are a "new breed" with higher expectations than their elders and no sobering contact with the 1930s to influence their values. The opposing view is that young workers—as did their elders before them—will become more satisfied as they grow older and accommodate themselves to the realities of the industrial world. While the truth no doubt lies somewhere in between, its "new breed" aspect is fraught with significance for the future.

Somewhat apart from the subject of work satisfaction—but nonetheless having wide-ranging applications for employment policy—is the finding that only 10 percent of employed persons age 55 and over reported dissatisfaction with their lives. This was as low a percentage as for any age group and takes on real significance when contrasted with findings in 1965 and 1968 that between 27 and 30 percent of retired persons were unhappy with their lives in general.[11] These data would suggest that the trend toward early retirement plans is in precisely the wrong direction, at least from the point of view of satisfaction with life. Perhaps some innovation such as a major public service program for older workers should be considered. If pure volunteerism does not provide sufficient rationalization for people to become active, it may be that some economic incentives, such as nominal compensation, travel expenses, etc., could be used.

RACE

Blacks were about twice as likely as whites to be dissatisfied with their jobs (and with their lives). The ratio of two dissatisfied blacks for every one dissatisfied white held until age 44. At that point, the percentage of dissatisfied blacks dropped to 7 as compared to 9 percent for whites aged 44 and over.

The first significant drop in dissatisfaction for both blacks and whites occurred after age 30. For both races, the 30 to 44 age group included only about half as many dissatisfied workers as the under-thirties. The fact that young blacks were the most dissatisfied segment of the labor force and that older black workers were among the most satisfied suggests that, while the generation gap may not be a racial phenomenon, it is far more intense among blacks than among whites. It is interesting to note that, while the dissatisfaction of blacks with both their jobs and their lives decreased sharply after age 44, there was a noticeable increase in their tendency to be depressed.[12] One last comment on the black generation gap: Twice as many blacks over age 44 were dissatisfied with their lives as were dissatisfied with their jobs. Older whites were just about as likely to be dissatisfied with one as with the other. This seems to give further support to the idea of a unique generation gap among blacks. Perhaps older blacks feel that being employed is reason enough to be satisfied with their work lives. Problems of housing and social discrimination may account for their greater tendency toward dissatisfaction with life in general.

The black worker appeared quite indifferent to the benefits of being in the $5,000–$10,000 personal income category as compared to the under

$5,000 bracket. The percentage of black workers with negative attutudes toward their jobs was the same regardless of income: 22 percent. Even black workers making $10,000 and over maintained that same percentage of "dissatisfieds," but there were so few of them (only 13) that the figures have no statistical reliability. No other group of people (with the single exception of workers under 30) were just as dissatisfied in the $5,000–$10,000 salary bracket as in the under $5,000 group. Even the dissatisfaction of young workers seemed to dissipate when they earned over $10,000 per year. Further, the decline in dissatisfaction was not a sporadic thing. With all other groups, dissatisfaction with work decreased steadily as income increased.

Also, the same disinterest in money appeared in the life dissatisfaction data. The percentage of blacks dissatisfied with life remained the same until the $10,000 per annum mark was reached. This latter characteristic, however, was shared by blacks with certain other groups (female workers and people with some college education).

BLUE-COLLAR VS. WHITE-COLLAR

Many jobs which were blue-collar in the old mechanized society are now, with the automation of work, shifting to white-collar status. Our sample reflects this change. It contains 709 blue-collar workers as compared to 753 who were classified in the white-collar category. Even disregarding technological changes, many white-collar jobs (secretaries, clerks, etc.) involve the same routinized types of work as blue-collar workers—but under cleaner conditions.

Despite the fact that white-collar workers, on the whole, earn more than blue-collar workers, the percentage who expressed negative attitudes toward work was not significantly smaller.[13] That is, 17 percent of blue-collar workers expressed negative attitudes toward work as compared to 13 percent of their white-collar brothers.

Young workers are color blind—at least with regard to the color of their collars. Identical percentages (24 percent) of blue-collar and white-collar workers under age 30 expressed negative attitudes toward their jobs. However, in the 30–44 group, the percentage of dissatisfied white-collar workers shrank to a low of 9 while the percentage of dissatisfied blue-collar people diminished only slightly to 18. At 45 and above, the two groups maintained similar percentages of dissatisfied workers.

The big sensitivity to collar-color seems to occur in the "middle years." At this stage of their lives, nearly twice as many blue-collar as white-collar workers were dissatisfied with their jobs. One reason for this overall dissatisfaction with work may be that blue-collar workers may experience an "economic squeeze" during their middle years—as suggested by Jerome M. Rosow.[14] Blue-collar workers usually achieve their top earnings earlier in life.

White-collar workers, however, do not "plateau" early but begin to reap the rewards of their greater education in their thirties.

Now let us see how groups of blue-collar and white-collar workers in the same income brackets view their jobs. As expected, in both groups, as income went up, dissatisfaction went down. More important, among blue-collar and white-collar workers who make the same amounts of money, differences in dissatisfaction tended to diminish. Holding income constant, blue-collar workers were somewhat more dissatisfied. But the two groups are never separated by more than a few percentage points, with the largest differences between them occurring in the upper income brackets: Eleven percent of the blue-collar workers making $10,000 and more were dissatisfied with their jobs as compared to 7 percent of the white-collar workers[15] in that income group.

EDUCATION

Surprisingly enough, almost identical percentage of workers among the following three groups expressed dissatisfaction with their jobs: those with an elementary school education or less, those with a seventh to twelfth grade education, and those who had progressed beyond high school.[16]

In the various age brackets, when workers who had no college were compared to those who had gone beyond high school, a significant difference did appear—but only with regard to *life* satisfaction, not *job* satisfaction. In the "middle years" (30–44), 19 percent of the workers with a high school diploma or less were dissatisfied with life as compared to only 8 percent of those with advanced education. On the other hand, there was a tendency among educated young workers to be less satisfied with life than their contemporaries who had no college experience. In the 45 and older group, the percentage of "dissatisfieds" was the same for the two groups. These findings seem to relate to the fact that, during the "middle years," workers are very sensitive to disadvantages of education, occupation, and so on, but that they adapt to these disadvantages as they grow older.

Among workers with comparable incomes, college experience was a real handicap to attaining job satisfaction. Those who had progressed beyond high school and were making less than $5,000 per year tended to be more dissatisfied than workers in the same income bracket who had not been to college. The same held true for workers in the $5,000–$10,000 bracket. Only when an individual with education beyond high school began earning $10,000 a year was he as satisfied with work as his less educated brother.[17]

SEX

Women have by far the worst of it in the American work force. They are more likely to express negative attitudes toward both their work and their lives.

One is reminded of Freud's desperate question, "What do they want? What in God's name do they want?"

The answer, however, does not seem unclear. They want more money! They want comparable jobs and equal pay![18] Among men and women in the same income ranges, differences in work dissatisfaction tended to disappear. So much for the job dissatisfaction problem among women! The theoretical solution is simple: equal employment opportunity!

Women's higher level of dissatisfaction with work does not appear to be related to age. As with men, fewer women in the higher age groups reported job dissatisfaction and the difference between women and men remained about the same all along the age spectrum.

Female dissatisfaction with life does not appear to begin until about age 30.[19] Until then, the proportion of dissatisfied women is about the same as the proportion of dissatisfied men. In the middle and older years, about twice as many women as men were dissatisfied with their lives.

But how about the differences in negative attitudes toward life? Do they also disappear when income is held constant? The answer is yes and no. In the low income brackets, women were somewhat less likely than men to express dissatisfaction with life. Above the $5,000 level, they were significantly more likely to be dissatisfied. No ready explanations suggest themselves.

MARITAL STATUS

To marry would seem to substantially increase one's chances of being satisfied with both one's job and one's life.[20] When only 9 percent of married people report negative attitudes toward life as compared to 26 percent of "unwed workers," this must say something important about marriage.

It is best, however, not to jump to conclusions when dealing with gross percentages. For example, when the data are grouped by age, the difference in job satisfaction almost disappears. Unmarried people are, after all, concentrated in the under 30 age group, and young workers, as we have seen, tend to be highly dissatisfied.

However, marriage itself—rather than some associated characteristic— seems to be tied to life satisfaction. Unmarried young people were twice as likely to be dissatisfied with their lives as their married counterparts. Unwed workers in their middle years were three times as likely to experience this general unhappiness. At age 45 and over, the ratio of the unmarrieds to marrieds expressing life dissatisfaction jumped to almost 5 to 1.

Arranging the "marrieds" and "unmarrieds" by income category also supports the notion that something other than marriage *per se* is responsible for the differences in job satisfaction. Since unmarried people—being generally younger—were likely to earn less than the marrieds, they were naturally less satisfied with their jobs. However, unmarrieds making less than $5,000 were no more dissatisfied than marrieds in that income range. Neither were unmarrieds making $10,000 or more more dissatisfied. Some difference still remains, however, at the $5,000–$10,000 level, in that 20 percent of the unmarrieds were dissatisfied with their jobs as compared to 12 percent of the marrieds.

Income can cure a lot of things but it doesn't seem to make the unwed condition any more tolerable. Among workers making less than $5,000 a year, unmarrieds are twice as likely to be dissatisfied with their lives as marrieds. But unwed workers earning more than $5,000 are almost three times as likely to be dissatisfied with their lives as their married counterparts.

WORK FEATURES ASSOCIATED WITH DISSATISFACTION

A major source of disagreement among union officials, government people, employers and academics when they get together to discuss the problem of worker discontent is the question: "What's bugging them anyhow?" In general, the union and government people seem to believe that it is a matter of dollars and cents, while employers and academics feel that workers are angry because they expect—but do not get—fulfillment from their work.

Of course, when we talk of the "worker" we are talking about a non-existent person. No doubt, some workers are motivated solely by money and look at the world of work as a market place where they can exchange their time for money. There are other workers, however, who wish to be active in their jobs and express themselves through the medium of work. This chapter proposes only to speculate on the preponderant or average causes of discontent.

What's Bugging the Labor Force in General

We can speculate that young people might be dissatisfied for different reasons than those in their middle years or older people, that blacks might have different causes of dissatisfaction than whites, and that women might have different grievances than men. Later chapters will discuss the youth question. Differences between the races and sexes must await other analyses. At this point, let's look at what is bugging the average worker, the labor force as a whole.

Importance of Work Aspects

The University of Michigan's national sample of 1,533 workers were asked how important they considered the various aspects of work. The information on the percentages of workers who considered each of 25 aspects of work to be very important may be surprising to those who believe workers are interested mainly in pay.

Of the 5 top-ranked work features, only one had to do with tangible or economic benefits. And that one (good pay) was ranked number 5. Interesting work, enough help and equipment to get the job done, enough information to get the job done, and enough authority to do their jobs—all were very important to more workers than was good pay.

The work aspects rated sixth, seventh, and eighth in importance were: opportunity to develop special abilities, job security, and seeing the results of work done. Of the top eight possibilities, six had to do with the content of the worker's job.

As contended by some, workers might overstate their concern with the non-economic aspects of their jobs in order to put themselves in a more favorable light. I would suggest, however, that we take the worker at his word and seriously question our traditional notions regarding his needs and priorities.

Between Expectation and Reality

In addition to being asked how important they considered these work aspects, workers were also asked to what extent each aspect was present in their jobs. This provided a rough indication of the aspects of work which the most workers felt to be in need of improvement. That is, where more workers felt an aspect of work to be very important than believed it to be characteristic of their jobs, it was a sure sign that some workers were expecting more of their jobs (with regard to that aspect) than they were receiving.

This was true for 10 items, of which 3 were economic and 7 concerned job content. Appendix A, Table 3, shows the "satisfaction gap" (or lack of one) for all 25 aspects of work.

The item with the largest satisfaction gap was "good pay," with 64 percent ranking it very important and only 40 percent stating that it was very true of their jobs.[21] Second was the "opportunity to develop one's special abilities," an intrinsic feature; and third was the "adequacy of fringe benefits." "Interesting work" was fourth, and "enough help and equipment to get the job done" was fifth. While these figures indicate that more workers feel their jobs fall short with regard to pay than on any other aspect of work, let's be sure we are clear on the fact that this is only an indication of the number of workers who feel a discrepancy between their desire for good pay and the fulfillment of this desire. It does not measure the seriousness of this discrepancy to the people affected.

Correlations of Work Features with Job Satisfaction

Now, let us take an indirect approach to the question: "What's bugging the worker?" Instead of relying on direct answers to direct questions, we will relate the extent to which the worker says certain features are present in his job to other statements he makes about job satisfaction.[22]

The right-hand column of Appendix A, Table 3 shows the correlations of the 25 aspects of work with job satisfaction. It is significant that the two work features which have the most to do with job satisfaction are part of the job content; the work itself: being given a chance to do the things one does best, and whether or not the work is interesting.

The folklore favorite, "good pay" is tied for third place with "I have an opportunity to develop my special abilities." In fifth place is the opportunity to see the results of one's work.

By all available measures—direct and indirect—it appears that the chance to do meaningful work and to achieve and grow on the job is of great importance to the average American worker—perhaps even overshadowing financial considerations. It also appears that this chance is sadly lacking in the average job. While Jerome Rosow's "economic squeeze" is certainly a major problem, what may be bugging the worker even more—especially the worker who is not feeling the economic squeeze as acutely—is the scarcity of meaningful and satisfying work.

NOTES ON POLICY IMPLICATIONS

The most general and pervasive conclusion is similar to one stated by President Nixon in his September 6, 1971 Labor Day Address: ". . . we must always remember that the most important part of the quality of life is the quality of work, and the new need for job satisfaction is the key to the quality of work."

We believe that this need for job satisfaction can best be met through the humanization of work: through restructuring the work situation so that jobs provide autonomy, interesting work, and the opportunity to be active, to grow, and to achieve. This is the thread that runs through all the chapters of our book—supported by empirical data from three separate pieces of research.

Industry Differences

The widely varying rates of dissatisfaction in the various industries suggest a targeting of efforts to improve the quality of work. Just as society gives particular attention to industries which have exceptionally high accident rates, perhaps special assistance might be tendered by the government—and special concern shown by employers and unions—in industries which have particularly high dissatisfaction rates. We understand that work is being done by the U.S. Department of Labor in cooperation with the Census Bureau to annually measure dissatisfaction rates among 38 or 39 industry and occupational classifications.

Small Business

Work dissatisfaction (and life dissatisfaction) were practically nonexistent among the self-employed. This supports the theory that a condition of satisfaction is independence of action. It also points out the possibility of improving the structure of work by encouraging—through taxation or other incentives and aids—economic possibilities for the very small businessman. A detailed examination of the occupations of the 205 self-employed workers in our sample would be a logical first step.

The Senior Citizen

Major programs to employ the aged are needed. When only 5 percent of the sample of employed persons aged 55 and older are dissatisfied with their lives, and when previous studies have shown that between 27 and 30 percent of retired persons express negative attitudes toward life, it is time to develop programs allowing older people an alternative to dropping out of life. As Erich Fromm points out, the human being is by nature active and, when inactive, he begins to die.

Black Workers

This study tells us nothing new. It has long been apparent that the healthy dissatisfaction of black people cannot be removed solely by equal employment opportunity. There must also be "equal consumer opportunity": The minority group dollar must buy the same amounts and kinds of housing, education, and consumer goods. Having said this, however, it is still clear that proportionate representation of minorities—not only in the labor force as a whole but at all income levels—is necessary before there is even the chance of "equal consumer opportunity."[23] An excellent first step in this direction would be a results-oriented approach to administering the President's Executive Order on discrimination in Federal contracts. Basically, this would mean making an initial presumption, without any on-site investigation, that establishments progressing satisfactorily toward employment parity[24] are eligible bidders for government contracts and—only where targets and goals are not met—would the question of procedures (such as advertising as an equal opportunity employer, giving acceptable employment tests, and so on) be at issue.

Women Workers

Is it possible that women workers' greater dissatisfaction with their lives may be significantly related to their long-standing second class citizenship in the workplace? It is true that women have problems other than their disadvantages at work, but it would seem that—as with blacks—the basic dignity of satisfying and meaningful employment is a prerequisite to general feelings of worth and satisfaction with life.

Blue Collars on Borrowed Time

In a sense, the young blue-collar worker is living on borrowed time. The young white-collar worker can usually look forward to doing more interesting work at higher pay as he moves into his middle years. The blue-collar worker has no such great expectations, or, if he has them, he is most sadly disappointed. As he passes his thirtieth and thirty-fifth birthdays, he becomes increasingly aware that there is no place for him to go (grow) at work. His income has leveled off and his work becomes fixed. He apparently resigns himself to a personally unrewarding work life and perhaps denies the importance of continued personal growth. In 1970, Congressman Henry S. Reuss of Wisconsin proposed a sabbatical plan for workers who were unable to finish high school or to complete college. It might be more practical and less expensive to adopt an innovation of the General Foods Corporation as a standard labor practice.[25] General Foods (in at least one of its plants) pays workers on the basis of the number of different jobs which they can do, rather than on the basis of the particular work they are doing at any one time. A General Foods worker in his thirties is unlikely to have learned every job in the plant. He still has something to gain and somewhere to grow as he becomes older. Another possible approach could be the establishment of a worker "loan bank" for education and training. The users would repay the loans from increased earnings.

We should be very careful, however, not to view worker dissatisfaction as only a blue-collar problem. It is a workplace problem and should be approached with general remedies as well as with solutions aimed at particular groups, such as the blue-collar worker in his middle years.

NOTES:

1. Robert Ardrey, *The Social Contract* (New York: Atheneum, 1970), p. 93.
2. Douglas McGregor, *The Human Side of Enterprise* (New York: McGraw-Hill, 1960).
3. Abraham H. Maslow, *Eupsychian Management* (Homewood, Illinois: The Dorsey Press, 1965).
4. Judson Gooding, "Blue Collar Blues on the Assembly Line," *Fortune* July 1970, p. 70.
5. In Gallup Polls since 1963, the percentage of white Americans expressing satisfaction with their work has been steadily declining—from 90 percent in 1963 to 83 percent in 1971. See Gallup press release, September 26, 1971.
6. This survey was commissioned by the U.S. Department of Labor and was directed first by Robert L. Kahn and later by Stanley E. Seashore of the Survey Research Center.
7. These data show the percentages of respondents who answered, "Not at all satisfied" or "Not too satisfied" (rather than "Somewhat satisfied" or "Very satisfied") to the question: "All in all, how satisfied would you say you are with your job?"

8. These data show the percentages of respondents who answered, "Not very satisfying" (rather than "Completely satisfying" or "Pretty satisfying") to the question: "In general, how satisfying do you find the way you are spending your life these days?"

9. Structural work occupations, the construction industry, and self-employment were also conducive to satisfaction with life in general. Workers in these categories were less than one-half as likely as most other workers to report dissatisfaction with their lives.

10. The data for life satisfaction closely parallels these ratios and percentages.

11. These findings are reported in Robinson and Shaver, *Measures of Psychological Attitudes*, University of Michigan, 1969. They resulted from the work of Bradburn, Caplovitz, and Noll.

12. That is, blacks age 45 and over are somewhat more depressed than young blacks (according to a University of Michigan depression scale based on a series of questions completed without the assistance of the interviewer). This suggests that their failure to express dissatisfaction with objectively dissatisfying conditions may be debilitating in other ways.

13. Significant differences were found by the computer when it compared indices derived from a battery of job satisfaction question, but as measured by responses to the single question: "All in all, how satisfied would you say you are with your job?" The differences were not significant even to the .05 level of probability.

14. Jerome M. Rosow, "The Working Man Does Need Help: Another View," *The Washington Post*, August 23, 1970, p. B 3.

15. Blue-collar workers making over $10,000 per annum, however, had the lowest percentage of any group (4 percent) who were dissatisfied with life. Is it possible that pay without freedom and opportunity for growth can buy off-the-job complacency, but not on-the-job satisfaction?

16. Mean job satisfaction scores were also computed on the basis of whether the respondent felt it was "very true," "somewhat true," or "not at all true"; that in his job, "the work is interesting," "the pay is good"; and 23 other work features. While a significant correlation was found, it should be kept in mind that a worker's appraisal of his job is not necessarily the same thing as his satisfaction with it.

17. The low-income college man, however, is less dissatisfied with his life than others in his income bracket. And in the $10,000+ group, only 4 percent of college people are dissatisfied with their lives as compared to 8 percent of those who never went further than high school. It is only in the $5,000–$9,999 range that education appears to breed dissatisfaction with life in general.

18. In his unpublished paper, "Sex Differences in Compensation," Malcolm S. Cohen of the University of Michigan finds a $2,500 per annum difference in personal income between male and female non-professional workers age 22–64 with a steady job and working the same number of hours.
19. See Chapter 6, "The Now Generation of Workers."
20. Due to the small number of unmarried people in the sample, it was not possible to separate the different effects of marriage (if any) on males and females.
21. The major "satisfaction gap" for workers under 30 years of age was between their desire to develop their abilities and the lack of an opportunity to do so. See Chapter 6.
22. This was accomplished by running product-moment correlations measuring the extent to which components such as "good hours," "time to get the job done," and so on, were associated with satisfaction.
23. Life satisfaction, however, cannot be achieved merely by radical improvements in the economic sphere. As Aiken, Ferman, and Sheppard found in their *Economic Failure, Alienation and Extremism* (Ann Arbor: University of Michigan Press, 1968), p. 156:

   The *social* fact of being a Negro in American society . . . does carry with it more connotations than can be gleaned through . . . measures of economic insecurity and deprivation, even through degree of education. It is not completely accurate, therefore, to say that if Negroes had the same economic, occupational and educational status as white—at this point in history, at least—all of their outlooks on life and society would be no different from those held by whites.

24. Minority group representation—within each of the standard job levels—which is comparable to minority group representation in the labor market area.
25. See a brief description of the "socio-technical" approach at General Foods by Charlton Price, in his *New Directions in the World of Work: A Conference Report* (Kalamazoo, Mich., and Washington, D.C.: Upjohn Institute for Employment Research, 1972).

Chapter Two

Who Are the Discontented Blue-Collar Workers?

> *What accounts for this malaise? One possible answer*
> *has to do with workers' perceptions; they may think*
> *they're much worse off than they really are.*
> *—Elliot Carlson*

The 1970s began with a new kind of national soul-searching about the worker with the "blues," the "suddenly remembered Americans," the "hard hats," and those disenchanted with the work place and the world around them. This soul-searching is directed at the broad, hard-to-define group of middle-income white workers, and especially blue-collar men, who feel alienated and at dead ends. The movie, "Joe," a caricature of this "social type," heightened the mass culture interest and curiosity (but not necessarily the knowledge) about this group. To be sure, concern with this segment of the working population is not a new one. Few need to be reminded of the many studies and journalistic accounts of the 1940s and 1950s that flooded the bookstores and newsstands of those years.

Actually, it has occupied the attention of social scientists and other observers of the work and non-work worlds for many decades. Karl Marx's sensitivity to the issue of worker alienation permeated much of his writings. He even constructed a "job satisfaction" questionnaire for use among European factory workers (but without observing the best of standards regarding objective wording of the questions). Interest in and concern with alienation in the work world has been a major preoccupation of thoughtful observers of society, the economy, and politics.

Much of Erich Fromm's writings imply that the job itself—especially the dreary, repetitive type—is the critical variable in the development of "traits of violence, anger, sadism, slight depression and indifference." More is involved in the creation of such traits than just the nature of the job performed by the worker, to be sure. A worker's reaction to his job may also be affected by factors such as his family status. For example, such things as marriage, number of dependents, and how many other members of a family are also in the labor force affect job attitudes. Other factors that cannot be ignored include, above all, a worker's aspirations in life—and the extent to which his job destiny and achievements have lived up to his expectations. His total family income, his own individual earnings, and education, might also be related to whether or not he has the "blues." We will return, however, to the notion that "the job itself" is a critical variable—a theme that permeates much of this total report.

The purpose of this chapter is to take one group of workers (in the sample of white male blue-collar union workers) with certain selected characteristics that may be some reflection of the "blues," and to compare them with other workers *without* such characteristics. There is some basis for believing that the groups of workers interviewed come close to representing the so-called "middle American white worker," the phrase that conjures in our minds that part of the American labor force which is now moving into the spotlights of journalists, philosophers, politicians, and social scientists.

Two sets of questions were used to isolate those workers we define here as "discontented" or having the "blues." They are somewhat different from the definition implied in the previous chapter.

The first set consists of three questions designed to determine the degree to which workers' aspirations have been met, regarding (a) how their current job measures up to what they wanted when they first took it: "How well would you say your job measures up to the kind you wanted when you first took it? Is it very much like the kind of job you wanted? Somewhat like the job you wanted? Or, not very much like the kind you wanted?" and (b) their own judgments as to their current achievements since leaving school: "Compared with what you had hoped for when you finished school, are you better off than you hoped for at that time? Not as well off? Or, just about as well off as you had hoped for?" and (c) their judgments as to where they are now, as compared to ten years ago, in the things they've wanted out of life: "Compared with where you were 10 years ago, are you further ahead in the things you've wanted out of life? Behind? Or, just about the same as where you were 10 years ago?" Using different "weights" for the three different possible responses to each of these three questions, an Aspiration-Achievement Discrepancy Index was devised.

The second dimension in which the workers were categorized relates to their perception of promotion or mobility chances on their current job: "Different jobs and types of work vary in how much opportunity they provide a person to *advance* himself, to get ahead in that line of work, or to be promoted. How is it on your job?" (Worker presented card with following choices):

a. "On my job there is no real chance to get ahead."
b. "There is some chance to get ahead on my job, but very little."
c. "The chances of getting ahead are above average."
d. "On my job there are excellent chances of getting ahead, in comparison with other lines of work."

The discontented workers—the ones with the "blues"—are those who scored high on the Aspiration-Achievement Discrepancy Index and who also replied that they have no real, or very little, chance of getting ahead on their jobs. Nearly 30 percent of these white male blue-collar workers (103 in number) qualified for membership in the discontented or "blues" club. The purpose of this chapter is to present and discuss the differences between these discontented workers and the others who were not discontented.

We are not making any claims here, however, about what precise percentage of all workers who are white male union members have the blues. Instead, the focus of this chapter is to ascertain the degree to which these 103 workers are unique with respect to *other* selected characteristics reported by them in the survey. The characteristics to be compared include the following items obtained through the personal interview schedule used in the survey: age and education, hourly wages and family income, number of earners in the family, dependents, adequacy of take-home pay, nature of job tasks, political efficacy, alienation, choice of 1968 presidential candidate, and race attitudes.

Evaluation of Current Job. Before presenting these comparisons, however, a more concrete portrait of the workers with the "blues" may be useful. Taking each of the four separate questions used to identify them, how do the discontented workers compare with the other workers in our sample?

The fact that a worker is in the "discontented" category does not mean that he is negative in all three of the dimensions involved in the Aspiration-Achievement Discrepancy Index. It would, therefore, be interesting to see how, for example, what proportion of the Pennsylvania[1] workers with and without the blues stated that their current job is not very much like the kind they wanted when they first took it. Their answers to this question reveal the extent to which the process of occupational choice, vocational counseling, and advice plays a role in the life chances of the kind of men working in the jobs and industries covered by our survey. The workers' judgments as to how well their jobs "stack up" with their original hopes are one of our best indicators of discontent.[2] Fifty-three percent of the workers with the "blues" and five percent of the others stated that their current job is not very much like the kind they wanted.

This finding (and many others reported elsewhere in our total report) throws into question the proposition put forward in the mid-1950s by Robert Dubin and other industrial social scientists that the job was no longer the source of workers' "central life interests."[3] Dubin was not referring to the possible impact of the work environment and of job tasks on the psychology of workers, although many industrial sociologists have tended to minimize (or to neglect altogether) such impact. Dubin was referring to the job mostly as a source of interpersonal, "social" relations. But this should not be taken to mean that a man's reaction to working in a foundry will be no different from his reaction to working in a florist shop. Our own survey suggests further that different epochs may yield differences in the "saliency" of the job in the lives of workers. In a section below, we shall have more to say about the workers' ratings of their jobs regarding such matters as the degree of variety, autonomy, and responsibility that their jobs allow or make possible. In other chapters, we will consider the possibility of the emergence of a new type of worker—especially among the young—who *does* care about, or is affected by, the nature of the tasks he performs to earn a living.

Achievements since Leaving School. Seven out of every ten Pennsylvania workers with the "blues"—but only one out of every seven in the remaining group—complained that, compared with what they had hoped for when they finished school, they do not feel that they have progressed very far toward their goals.[4] This contrast between 70 and 14 percent warrants some consideration of the possible role of education in the development of worker malaise or discontent, and it will be discussed in a later section of this chapter. Of the three items used to measure the discrepancy between aspirations and achievement, this particular one about hopes upon finishing school (or upon entering the labor market, to express it differently) yielded the highest percentage of "disappointment" (31 percent) among all the workers as a whole.

Personal Progress over the Past Decade. No simple measure of change over the past ten years—for example, in median earnings—can, by itself, assure us that white skilled and semi-skilled workers will feel that they are further ahead or behind in the things they have wanted out of life, in comparison with where they were 10 years earlier. Recent Census data comparing 1960 with 1970 reveal that for *married* white skilled and semi-skilled workers (craftsmen and operatives) living in metropolitan areas of the North and the West, median earnings have increased, in real dollars, by 29 percent. Such averages, however, tell us nothing about the possibility of "skidding." More important, demographic and income data are imperfect substitutes for data concerning group *perceptions*. And group perceptions are "hard facts" no less than reported average incomes. They influence behavior and other attitudes just as much as do income, age, and education. In our sample, 11 percent say they are *behind* where they were 10 years ago. And for just those in the "blues" category, the proportion rises to 29 percent. Only 4 percent of the "non-blues" workers feel the same way. To express this relationship differently, among those Pennsylvania workers saying they are behind compared with 10 years ago, 77 percent are in the "blues" group, in contrast to only 23 percent of the remainder.[5]

The comparisons presented so far merely fill out the details of the two contrasting types of workers and as implied earlier. By definition, the discontented worker will be sharply different from the others in the answers to the questions used to distinguish the discontented from the others.

The first three items used to define the workers with the "blues" all have an aspirational "success" or "achievement" content. In a society such as ours, with its traditional stress on these goals or values (as well as its stress on equalitarianism, or at least equal opportunities to succeed), attention must be paid to how members of that society *perceive* their progress. Measures of such perception should be an integral part of any effort to construct "social indicators."

Mobility Chances on Current Job. The fourth item directly inquires about this facet by asking the worker how much he believes his current job provides any chance of promotion or opportunity to "get ahead." By definition, all of the workers in the "blues" category see very little or no chance. But such an answer is not sufficient for designating a worker as being discontented. Even among those not in our discontented group, more than half (54 percent) say that they see very little or no chance for advancement in their current jobs.[6]

Such responses, however, refer to how the worker views his promotion chances. They do not tell us how workers *react* to such an outlook. The fact that a job contains no chance for advancement is not by itself a perfect or absolute measure of discontent. The president of a giant corporation, for example, may not be able to get any further ahead, but we can presume that this fact (which he very likely acknowledges) doesn't bother him much of the time, if at all. We cannot assume, in other words, that all persons in "dead-end" jobs are deeply upset about their lot. Because of this, if a worker in our interviews perceived little or no chance for getting ahead on his job, he was also asked, "How frequently does it bother you that there is very little or no chance to get ahead on your job? Nearly all the time? Very often? Sometimes? Rarely or never?"

We have, therefore, information about both types of workers (with and without the "blues") who say they are in dead-end jobs. This information tells us whether there are differences in how much being in such jobs is salient to them and how serious it is to them.

If the basis for our classifying workers with and without the "blues" were purely arbitrary and capricious, there should be *no* difference between the responses of the two types of workers to the follow-through question quoted above. But they *are* different. Among discontented workers, 27 percent replied that they are troubled nearly all the time or very often because of slim chances for getting ahead. Among only those workers not discontented who also said there was little or no chance for getting ahead, the percentage bothered by this nagging feeling was only 10 percent. In other words, discontented workers are more likely than "contented" workers to be disturbed by their lack of mobility opportunities on the job. This finding is not an artifact or tautology. That is, the differences in the saliency of poor promotion chances are not a result of the method we used to define discontented workers.

DEMOGRAPHIC AND ECONOMIC DIFFERENCES

The preceding section was largely devoted to explaining what is meant here by worker discontent, and to showing the kinds of replies that were used to identify such white male union members. These questions have a heavy success-theme component and demonstrate the degree to which a worker's achievements have kept up with his aspirations. The data so far pertain to the workers' own perception of their achievements and failures, their own estimations of the chance to get ahead in their current jobs. To resurrect an old sociological aphorism, "If men *define* situations as real, they are real in their consequences." The "reality" of their situation may, of course, affect how men view that situation. But we cannot evade the hard fact that the definition—the way people see and evaluate events, experiences and conditions—affects behavior and critical perspectives that influence their lives. We will see this, for example, when we report on their voting choice in the 1968 Presidential election.

But what really is their situation? For example, are age and education related to whether or not the workers in our study have the "blues"? What about earnings and family income?

Age. Workers with the "blues" tend to be slightly older than the others, but apparently not to any great extent, as suggested by the following table:

	Workers with the "Blues"	Others
under 40	28%	36%
40–49	32	26
50 and older	40	38
	100%	100%

But age by itself is a poor "predictor" variable on many crucial issues in the field of worker behavior and attitude research. As we shall see later, the *joint* effect of age and education may indeed be highly influential in the generation of "worker malaise."

Education. Here, too, amount of schooling, by itself, does not help us much to understand the two different groups under our social analysis microscope. Education, like age, can only be used in this type of analysis (especially within a given social class, in this case, blue-collar workers of one sex and race) along with other factors. Because of this, we have combined these two variables, amount of schooling and age, in order to determine their joint relationship to amount of "worker blues." By doing this, we might be on to something that warrants a larger, more systematic study. The evidence suggests that more educated, older workers run the greatest risk of developing the "blues." Let's rank the four age-education groups according to their percentage with the "blues":

Age and Education	Percent with the "Blues"
50 or older, high school degree	37%
50 or older, no degree	33
under 50, no degree	31
under 50, high school degree	28

Older, better-educated workers are more likely to have the "blues," but *younger* better-educated ones have the lowest proportion. For anyone with a one-track mind without any sensitivity to the dynamics of human behavior and attitudes—especially as these change during a person's life career—this may indeed seem a paradox. Students of the labor movement, labor economists, demographers, and others are generally unaware of what might be called adult socialization; that is, what happens to men and women after they cease to be children and adolescents, and the impact of adult experiences on other aspects of their lives, behavior, and outlook.

Census reports are not an adequate source for such knowledge. As Herman Miller of the Bureau of the Census has himself stated, ". . . census statistics are very limited for an analysis of the thesis that blue-collar workers are alienated, troubled or forgotten."[7] On the other hand, few specialists in the area of adult socialization research have attempted to apply their knowledge to what labor economists, demographers, and others have been trying to explain (to themselves as well as to others) for many years.

The emphasis here is that either the amount of education a person attains tends to affect his career aspirations as he enters the world of work, or persons with high aspirations tend to be the ones obtaining more education than those with lower aspirations. This is not the place to indulge in any scholarly polemics about which is cause and which is effect (except to express my opinion that each factor can be *both* cause and effect).

The more critical point is, to quote Orville Brim in his survey of adult socialization research (in John Clausen's *Socialization and Society*[8]), that "many American males must adjust their career aspirations of *earlier* years to the probable realities of the levels of achievement to be reached in their lifetimes." (Italics mine.) Brim cites studies indicating that in time, high-career-aspiration graduates from high school achieve less than their aspirations. The greater a person's education achievements, as measured by years of schooling, the greater are his life and job aspirations, but it may turn out that higher aspirations mean a greater risk of non-achievement of those hopes and dreams. "The White Male Worker and the American Dream" is an apt description of what this chapter is all about.

The implication is that many of the workers (aged 50 or older) in the Pennsylvania sample who, 30 years ago or more acquired a full high school education, started out with great expectations, and that during the intervening three decades or more, many of them endured socio-economic "environmental insults" that (1) lowered their actual achievements, and (2) thus gave them the "blues" and made them discontent, as defined in this chapter. Older workers with less education may have had the same adult experiences but their disappointment was less.

In the relatively lower discontent among the young higher-educated workers of 1970, can we see some portent of a change in how much they will become "blue" in 10 or 20 years? Young white males will not change into blacks. They will not change into women. But all of them will change into *older* white males—death being the only alternative. The challenge to our society is not to lower the opportunities for education, but rather to create opportunities after that experience commensurate with the aspirations derived from the educational experience. There is no certainty that we are preparing to meet that challenge.

Hourly Wages and Family Income. As might be expected, the workers with the "blues" have a higher proportion of low wage-earners (in our group of union members, below $3.50 an hour). Very few worked at jobs paying less than $2.50 per hour. Half of those with the "blues," as opposed to only 38 percent of the other workers, earned below $3.50. The contrast between the two groups is even stronger when we look at the proportions earning more than $4.00 per hour. Among the discontented workers, less than one-fifth (19 percent) earned as much, while among all others the proportion was more than two-fifths (44 percent).

The data on family income and discontent are consistent with those above. Among the discontented group, 37 percent reported family incomes of less than $8,000—compared with 30 percent of those without the "blues."

Adequacy of Take-Home Pay. Actual wages are not by themselves a complete explanation of the discontent that may develop among male blue-collar workers. Their own judgments as to whether or not such wages (take-home pay) are good enough to take care of their families' wants and needs may also contribute significantly. Obviously, the higher the hourly wages, the smaller the proportion of workers who are discontented. But *within* each wage category, the rate of discontent is different depending on how adequate the worker *feels* his take-home pay is.

Many factors, such as size of family, influence such feelings, but we will not get into those details here. Taking all the workers in the Pennsylvania sample, 23 percent of those workers who say their pay is adequate are discontented. This is exactly half the proportion of the group feeling that their take-home pay is not good enough to cover their families expenses—45 percent. In other words, the workers stating their take-home pay is not adequate are twice as likely to be discontented as workers satisfied with their level of take-home pay.

The workers' own judgments about sufficiency of take-home pay is a far better "predictor" of discontent than actual wages. I mean that, 35 percent of the workers earning $3.50 an hour or less have the "blues," but this is not much greater than the 27 percent reporting discontent among those earning above that rate. The contrast is nowhere near as great as the 45 vs. 23 percent when the workers' own judgments on wage adequacy are considered as an influence on discontent.

What is equally provocative is that as long as the worker views his take-home pay to be not good enough to take care of his family, his actual wage level matters precious little! Among workers who earn under $3,50 per hour and who feel this way, 44 percent are discontented; among workers feeling the same way but earning over that wage rate, the rate is 45 percent. Even among the workers saying their take-home pay is adequate, wage levels do not make too much difference, although the ones in the higher wage bracket are slightly less discontented than workers in the lower bracket (21 vs. 26 percent).

The group with the highest proportion of discontent are the older workers (50 and over) who say their pay envelopes are not fat enough: 52 percent in this group are discontented. And the group with the second highest proportion of discontent are the younger workers also reporting inadequate take-home pay—42 percent.

Education and Wages. Since education plays an important role in the development of people's expectations, is higher discontent also to be found among those workers with high education but employed in low wage jobs? We found the education-wage variable to be relevant to discontent only among the under-50 workers in our sample. Among those under the age of 50 in the Pennsylvania sample, workers with a full high school education but working for less than $3.50 per hour had the highest rate of discontent—38 percent, compared to only 20 percent for all others under-50.[9]

Number of Family Earners. It is part of current conventional wisdom and practice to report findings which show, as reported earlier, that the higher the hourly wage or salary, the higher the total family income, the more content people will be, and let it go at that. The finding certainly confirms our assumptions—which are, to be sure, rooted in a great deal of reality.

It is also part of this conventional wisdom to point to the growing number of married women joining the labor force, and then to conclude that such a phenomenon is good, since it obviously adds to total family resources to enjoy the fruits of American society. "Money buys happiness," the saying goes. Certainly, as already reported, the higher the wages, or the higher the family income, the lower the proportion of men with the "blues." And anything that contributes to more income (such as a working wife) must be good.

But part of the function of good social science is to re-examine conventional wisdoms, to take a careful look at unexamined assumptions or popular beliefs (and even of time-worn assumptions in the world of researchers, not to mention critical decision-makers in the private and public sectors of society).

To just what extent does the participation of a male worker's relative (his wife and/or child) reduce the odds that he will have the "blues," as defined in this report? Or, indeed, does such participation increase those odds? The latter question is the issue posed by the results of our analysis. The analysis, in fact, suggests that this participation tends to increase malaise.

Workers with the "blues" have a far greater proportion with one or more additional family members working than do the workers without the "blues." The following table presents the findings for the group of Pennsylvania workers:

Percent of Pennsylvania Workers with One or More Additional Family Members in the Labor Force

	Workers with the "Blues"	Others
All Ages	45%	32%
under 50	48%	35%
50 and older	41%	26%

The table also indicates clearly that the pattern holds even when age is considered: regardless of age, workers with the "blues" have higher proportions of discontent when other family members also work. Furthermore, the data suggest that younger workers (with and without the "blues") have a higher proportion when other members in the family work. Among a younger group in our sample—those under 40 but not shown in the table—the proportion with additional earners is even higher, but only among the younger workers with the "blues." Fifty-five percent of these under-40 discontented workers have one or more additional family members in the workforce, in contrast to only 33 percent of the under-40 group who are not discontented.

All this leads to the thought that the phenomenon of two or more earners in the working class family is not the unmixed blessing it is assumed to be. To put the above facts in a different form, only one-fourth of the single-earner Pennsylvania workers have the "blues." But among workers with additional earners in the family, discontent goes up to nearly two-fifths, 38 percent.[10]

The risks of discontent are greater for workers with other family members also working, but the lower the earnings or family income, the greater this difference in degree of discontent between workers with one earner and those with two or more earners in the family. The basic finding, is a critical one. And it goes far beyond pure sociology—perhaps to the heart of some current social policy issues affecting work and the family.

The findings that (1) age and education combined, and (2) number of family earners affect workers' discontent lead to the question: What is the joint influence of age, education, and number of family earners on the odds for a worker developing the "blues?"

Among higher education men, 40 and older, with at least two earners in the family, 39 percent were discontented. On the other hand, younger men with the same schooling but with no additional family earners reflected an extremely low rate of discontent—only 14 percent.[11] As young blue-collar workers with a high school education or more become older and as their wives enter the labor force, especially if out of economic necessity, will we witness an increase in their discontent in future decades?

Between the 1960 Census and the Current Population Survey of March 1970, the proportion of white skilled and semi-skilled workers with wives in the labor force jumped from 32 to 44 percent. But this rise is no clear justification for drawing conclusions about "progress." In this connection, it may be of some relevance to note that for married men aged 45–54, in this occupational group of whites, the proportion with wives in the labor force was 35 percent as of 1960, but ten years later, the proportion with working wives changed very little, to 41 percent.

It is quite possible that more sophisticated analysis, using true cohort analysis over a ten year period (with the same individuals) would reveal that even in an objective sense, as measured by such things as percent of workers with working wives, little progress has been made. Is it only coincidental that in our survey, among the workers 55 and older, the proportion saying they were behind compared with ten years ago was greater than among younger workers? But more to the point, those with an additional wage-earner in the family had a much higher proportion saying they were behind in the things they've wanted out of life compared to ten years ago, than the oldest workers with only one wage-earner (25 percent vs. 11 percent).

These findings were completely unexpected. The specific inquiry concerning the possible relationship of discontent to number of family wage-earners was not originally planned: after all, we have all been taught to believe that the more earners in the family, the more money, and the more money, the lower the odds for being "blue." Any *post hoc* explanation must at best be on the level of plausibility. (This explanation was stimulated by some clues suggested to me by Eugene Litwak of the University of Michigan, who has been conducting unstructured interviews with Detroit lower-middle-class workers.) Getting ahead, striving, wanting a share of the "good goods" of affluent America, which keeps persuading us to want more, and to feel we deserve more—all these things characterize workers just as much as they do the other strata of American society. It may be that for the working class stratum, "machismo" is a factor—even among white males, although a much more extensive analysis to verify ethnic differences in this masculine pride is needed. It may be that such men don't feel that they've really succeeded if, *all by themselves,* they can't provide their families with the necessary income to pay for the level of living to which they aspire.

Perhaps the belief that satisfaction among male workers should increase as family income is improved through their wives' employment is a projection on the part of the people who write about such problems. These people are primarily professional, upper-middle-class individuals. Perhaps these professional males feel no threat to themselves if their wives work. Indeed, they may even feel proud and may gain satisfaction if their wives are so engaged outside the home. And the wives themselves may work, not so much for the purpose of adding needed income to the family fortune, but more for achieving certain "self-fulfillment" needs.

The working-class context may be sharply different from the professional class situation, and the professional-class individuals who write about worker discontent may, out of ignorance of this difference, be making some wrong assumptions when attempting to understand discontent in terms personally familiar to them.

Finally, to return to the possible influence of "machismo," it must be reported that the authoritarian men in our Pennsylvania sample had a smaller proportion of wives working than the non-authoritarians.

Number of Dependents. Workers with the "blues" have proportionately more dependents than the others. Very few of them (6 percent) have no dependents, in contrast to 14 percent of the workers without the "blues." At the other end of the scale, 26 percent of the "blues" workers have at least four dependents, in contrast to only 19 percent of those without the "blues." The contrasts are especially great among those workers earning less than $4.00 an hour. In that lower earnings group, discontent among those with many dependents (four or more) is much higher than those with three or fewer dependents. The influence of family size on discontent among low-income groups cannot be ignored.

THE "BLUES" AS AN INFLUENCE ON CRITICAL SOCIAL ATTITUDES

Up to this point, we have shown what we mean by worker discontent, and have identified the workers who are characterized by this presumed ailment in terms of age, education, income and earnings, number of family earners, and number of dependents. These variables may be among the possible conditions (I hesitate to say "causes") of worker discontent.

Now we want to deal with another question: To what extent does such discontent affect (or how is it related to) other aspects of the workers' behavior and attitudes? There may be some social-psychological factors that are associated with having the "blues," but which we cannot say with any certainty are dependent variables. In other words, they may be neither the result of a worker having the "blues," nor the cause. Along with discontent, these other variables may both be the result of something else. We just don't know, given the type of analysis used here. But in certain instances, we cannot ignore the possibility that some of the variables are among the causes, and that some may be effects.

Nature of Job Tasks. How workers feel about their jobs is a good example of this problem. We have assumed in this study that because of the definition of discontent used here, there should be some relationship of this type of discontent to the worker's perception of the nature of his job.

The workers were asked an intensive series of questions, spelled out in greater detail in subsequent chapters. Many of them were adapted from *Industrial Jobs and the Worker,* by Arthur N. Turner and Paul R. Lawrence of Harvard's School of Business.[12] In this study, Turner and Lawrence developed an index of workers' perceived task attributes.[13] For our own study, we used their questions designed to tap such job task dimensions as variety, autonomy, and responsibility. On the basis of the responses to the six questions asked to measure the workers' perceptions of these selected facets of their jobs, it was possible to devise a Total Task Index (the higher the score, the lower the variety, autonomy, and responsibility). The score distribution was divided into approximate quartiles, from the most positive to the most negative scores.

The following table shows a strong relationship between the two variables of worker discontent and a Negative Job Task Index. Seventy percent of the workers with the "blues" fall at the negative, bottom half of the Job Task Index, while only 41 percent of those without the "blues" are in this negative category. Forty percent of the discontented are in the "most negative" category. Within each of the two groups (those with and without the "blues") there is no Job Task Index difference between the young and old workers.

Distribution of Total Task Index
(Pennsylvania Only)[14]

Rank Position of Scores		Workers with the "Blues"	Others
Most Positive	1	11%	25%
	2	19	34
	3	30 ⎱ 70	24 ⎱ 41
Most Negative	4	40 ⎰	17 ⎰
		100%	100%

Let us look at the responses to the specific questions used to develop this index. When asked about the degree of variety they have on their jobs, nearly three-fifths (59 percent) of the discontented workers reported little or no variety in what they do on their jobs. On the other hand, the proportion of the workers without the "blues" reporting little or no variety in their jobs was less than half the proportion among the "blues" workers—only 27 percent. In other words, low job variety is associated with worker discontent.

When asked to describe their jobs in terms of the degree of freedom or autonomy they have to do their work as they want, more than two-fifths of the "blues" workers (43 percent), but less than one-fifth (18 percent) of the workers without the "blues" replied that they had little or no freedom to do their work as they wanted to.

Answers to a second question designed to tap the autonomy allowed by the job similarly showed that 44 percent of the discontented workers, but only 17 percent of the contented ones (an almost perfect match to the previous finding) felt almost none, or at most one-fourth, of their potential ideas, and skills are being used on their jobs.

These two questions concerning the workers' feelings of autonomy on their job were so critical in the overall Job Task Index that a separate Autonomy Index is worth reporting here. Using the two questions together to construct such an Index, we found the following proportions with feelings of low autonomy: workers with the "blues," 55 percent and others, 25 percent. Job Task Autonomy, therefore, must be seriously reckoned with in seeking to understand (and hopefully, to reduce) worker discontent.[15]

These two general measures of the worker's perception of the quality of his job—variety and autonomy—suggest, in my opinion, a widespread discontent that cannot be dismissed by cavalier talk about the great "progress" that white skilled and semi-skilled workers have made over the past ten years— again as measured merely by earnings, family income, labor force participation by their wives, and so on. It is more than suggested by the kind of statistical analysis presented here that there is a relationship between the odds for a worker being discontented and the lack of variety and autonomy his job provides him. Analysis of the questions concerning responsibility on the job (including the use of their potential ideas and skills) reveal a similar pattern.[16]

There are other aspects of the worker's job in relation to our measure of discontent that are found in the 1971 interviews with the 101 workers in Kalamazoo. First of all, the discontented workers report that they are frequently dissatisfied with the job to a far greater extent than the workers not discontented (33 percent as compared to only 5 percent). When asked how satisfied they are with their pay, fringe benefits, and working conditions, only 13 percent of the discontented workers, in contrast to 34 percent of the others, indicate they are very satisfied. Virtually the same results are found in response to the question asking how satisfied they are with their opportunities to do interesting and enjoyable work.

The Kalamazoo workers were also asked whether they are more satisfied or less satisfied than they were three years previously with opportunities to do interesting and enjoyable work. Only one-fourth of the discontented workers, but nearly half of the others, reported progress (more satisfied) on this facet of their work lives. At the other end of the scale, only 6 percent of the workers without discontent said they were less satisfied than three years ago, in contrast to 20 percent of the discontented workers, with opportunities to do interesting and enjoyable work.[17]

These workers were also asked what their choice would be if they were completely free to go into any type of job they wanted. Would they: (1) want the same type they now hold, (2) want to retire, or (3) prefer some other job to the kind they now have? Only 29 percent of the discontented workers, but 45 percent of the others replied that they would want the same type of job now held. Expressing this finding in another way, among all the Kalamazoo workers saying they would want the *same* type of job they hold now, only 17 percent are discontented. But among those preferring a different type of work, the proportion of discontented workers jumps to 38 percent—more than twice the proportion among the contented. On a similar question, only 10 percent of the Kalamazoo blue-collar workers indicating they don't want to change jobs even for more money, "because the one I have is a good one," expressed discontent. But among those saying they would quit their jobs if they had anything else to do, or would take almost any other job in which they could earn as much as they are earning now, the rate of discontent rises to 35 percent—more than three times the rate among those not wanting to change jobs.

We may not be able to change the nature of jobs in any given state of a society's technology, although this is being hotly debated by experts dealing, for example, with job redesign potentials. But what about those institutions or patterns that now operate under the assumption that individuals must remain in jobs providing little or nothing in the way of variety, freedom, and the use of potential ideas and skills? Why should any man, for example, be forced to work for 30 to 40 years on an assembly line or in a foundry? It may no longer be sufficient to consider "early retirement" as a "solution" to such a fate. Given the type of results revealed in the survey discussed in this chapter (as well as results of other studies), I cannot believe that we are dealing with an "academic" issue, or one that is merely a projection of how professional, upper-class intellectuals would feel if they were in similar jobs. This is a charge frequently made by critics of any notion that the nature of job tasks should be an object of concern by union leaders, managers, government officials, and other persons in important decision-making roles. Moreover, these feelings may "spill over" into other social and political dimensions of blue-collar worker's human life and behavior—as this entire report seeks to explore.

Political Effectiveness. Three well-known questions were asked to find out how much workers believe they are, or can be, personally effective in the political process, as a sort of Index of Political Effectiveness:

"There's little use in writing to public officials because often they aren't really interested in the problems of the average man."

"The way people vote is the main thing that decides how things are run in this country."

"People like me don't have any say about what the government does."

Workers who are not discontented register a slightly higher score on the Political Effectiveness Index than those with the "blues"—54 percent vs. 46 percent. The difference between the "blues" workers and those without the "blues" is especially strong among the older workers. In the 50-plus age group, less than two-fifths of the "blues" workers, but more than half of those without the "blues," scored high on this Index.

Suppose we combine both variables of discontent and job autonomy to see how they relate to political implications. Workers in Pennsylvania with the "blues" and with low job autonomy differ sharply from those who are content and who have high job autonomy when it comes to degree of political efficacy. Only 41 percent of the first group, in contrast to 56 percent of the workers with fewer complaints about life and the job, have a high score on political efficacy. We will return to other more overt political implications, when we report the actual 1968 voting choices of the discontented workers.

Alienation. A number of measures have been used by sociologists for more than two decades to ascertain what has variously been called alienation, anomie, estrangement from society, personal futility, and other related but not always clearly defined terms. In our own survey, three statements from a much longer possible list were used for this purpose. The worker was asked to what extent he agreed or disagreed with them:

"These days a person doesn't really know who he can count on."

"In spite of what some people say, the lot of the average man is getting better, not worse."

"It's hardly fair to bring children into the world with the way things look for the future."

On the basis of responses to these three statements, an Alienation Index was constructed, and the analysis of the relationship of this Index (with four categories from high to low alienation) to worker discontent reveals, once again, that our original definition of the "blues" is not a mere exercise in methodology. For example, among the workers with the "blues," only one-sixth were in the lowest alienation category, in sharp contrast to nearly one-third in the case of the workers not discontented. On the other hand, 17 percent of the non-"blues" workers, and 25 percent of the discontented were in the highest alienation category. Even when age is held constant, the relationship prevails. Discontented workers, regardless of age, are more alienated.

Distribution of Alienation Scores among White Male Workers (Pennsylvania Only)[18]

		Workers with the "Blues"		Others	
Lowest Alienation Scores	1	16%	} 49	31%	} 65
	2	33		34	
	3	25	} 50	18	} 35
Highest Alienation Scores	4	25		17	
		99%		100%	

One concrete example of the difference between the workers with the "blues" and their happier counterparts can be seen poignantly in the contrasting proportions disagreeing with the statement about the lot of the average man getting better, not worse. Among the discontented, 37 percent disagreed with this proposition, a proportion twice that for the workers without the "blues" (18 percent). The Kalamazoo interviews revealed almost identical findings: 38 percent of the discontented workers, but only 14 percent of the others, disagreed that the lot of the average man is getting better, not worse.[19]

Apart from the issue of the difference between the "blue" and non-"blue" workers, the findings on the first item may be considered alarming. Of the Pennsylvania workers interviewed, exactly three-fifths agreed with that statement. Even among those without the "blues," the proportion was high, 56 percent—although the proportion for the workers with the "blues" is still greater, 71 percent.

It should be clear by now that the two dimensions—(1) the discrepancy between aspirations and achievements (along with job mobility chances), and (2) feelings of alienation—are intimately related. A separate chapter deals in greater detail with the nature of the alienated workers in our sample.

We now know that the workers with the "blues" are alienated men in the social psychological sense. They are also the ones who feel they have little influence over the political decision-making process in our country. In other parts of this volume, greater attention is given to those workers who are characterized by the opposite characteristics—the men who are non-alienated and who feel politically effective.

As will be discussed in greater detail in Chapter 4, a critical problem in any democratic society like ours is the proportion of its citizens who not only feel politically effective but who are also non-alienated. At this point, we want only to combine the separate data on alienation and political efficacy and then to determine to what extent the discontented workers in our study are different, if at all, from the other workers—those with little discrepancy between their aspirations and achievements and who also are more likely to feel some chance for advancement on their jobs.

In other words, what proportion of the discontented are both alienated and feel politically ineffective? What proportion are the very opposite—non-alienated and with high political efficacy? On this very important question, we have the combined results of the Michigan and Pennsylvania interviews.

The discontented workers comprise a much higher proportion (32 vs. 18 percent) of men who have little trust in others, who are convinced the lot of the average man is getting worse, who are pessimistic about the future in general, and who also are not confident about any impact they might have in the political process, or in the degree to which government has any concern for them. In vivid contrast, more than two-fifths of the workers who are not discontented are non-alienated and feel politically effective—the very opposite characteristics. To repeat, they also have few men (only 18 percent) who reveal high alienation and little political effectiveness. The degree to which workers feel that their life and job expectations have been realized, and that their job-advancement chances are good, quite clearly is related to—perhaps even affects—their total alienation. The two measures of alienation and political effectiveness together might actually be treated as a more sensitive litmus test of general alienation—and it makes a difference whether a worker is characterized by this overall malaise. It is a malaise that should be of major concern to all of us concerned with creating and sustaining a viable, humane democratic society.

POLITICAL AND RACIAL IMPLICATIONS

To brand the discontented workers as part of the "Establishment" simply because they are white and are members of unions is a pitiful commentary on the Orwellian, Kafka-esque sickness of our times. (Indeed, our interviews with such men suggest that they feel left out of the "Establishment," which for many consists of unions as well as other institutions and organizations.) To prey on their political impotence and personal futility by directing their resentments against other groups in the society—as is done by persons in the public limelight (such as Spiro Agnew and George Wallace)—is perhaps worse. We don't know what all of this means in the 1970s, with some national leaders acting and speaking in ways that can lead to further polarization, but at least we do know the following on the basis of this one study:

The discontented workers—the ones who feel they have not succeeded in getting the things they've wanted out of life compared to 10 years ago; the ones who feel their job is not like the kind they wanted when they first took it; the ones who feel they are not as well off as they had hoped for when they left school and who complain about little chances for advancement in their jobs—disproportionately voted for George Wallace in 1968.[20] The following table, which combines both the Pennsylvania and the Kalamazoo data, indicates this vividly:

1968 Presidential Choices

	Discontented Workers	Contented Workers
Humphrey	48%	46%
Nixon	21	35
Wallace	18	8
Other or Refused to Answer	13	11
	100%	100%

The percentage of discontented white male blue-collar workers voting for George Wallace was more than twice the percentage of Wallace voters among those not discontented.[21] Our statistical analysis convinces us that it is not a "fluke" that the discontented workers in our sample had a very high percentage voting for a person like George Wallace.

To round out this portrait, the discontented workers, to a greater extent than the other workers in the sample, disagree that Negroes want to get ahead by using the same methods as other Americans have used to get ahead, and feel that unions and/or management are doing "too much" in providing good training or good jobs for minority groups like Negroes and Puerto Ricans.[22]

If responsible public leaders and organizations seek to reduce such high percentages, they must also look for the conditions that lead to such political choices among workers and members of other social classes. And those conditions include the discrepancy between human hopes and human achievements—much of which is rooted in the realities of the work situation itself.

SUMMARY

Our analysis, very briefly, suggests the following:

1. If thwarted in their striving to make real the "American Dream," higher-educated workers will be more likely to take on the symptoms of discontent, alienation, malaise, or the "blues" by the time they reach middle age.

2. The fact that relatively high family income has to be obtained by more than the individual wage-earner himself is not in itself any guarantee that such a worker will feel less alienated than workers earning such high income by themselves. In the current gropings to concoct "social indicators," we must

pay attention to the conditions under which workers achieve a "high" income and their judgments of those conditions.

3. The nature of the job itself (that is, how much a worker's tasks allow for variety, autonomy, and responsibility) cannot be separated from the off-the-job facets of a worker's well-being, attitudes, and behavior. But even if they turned out not to "spill over" into non-work life, the phenomena of low variety and of low autonomy on the job warrant some positive action by employers, unions, and government.

4. Especially when we consider jointly on-the-job and off-the-job dimensions, these factors and conditions may play a major role in such important matters as the worker's perception of his political effectiveness, his voting choices, his evaluation of minority group workers, and his degree of alienation.

We have presented here a portrait of white male union workers with the "blues," as defined by a series of questions bearing on the congruity or discrepancy between life and job aspirations, and by the worker's perception of his chances for mobility in his present job situation; of workers who feel they have little effect in the political process of our country; of men who say they have little variety, autonomy, or responsibility in the performance of their daily job tasks; and of men who express little confidence in their fellow men and in the fate of the "average man,"—feelings some social scientists have labeled as *alienation*.

The workers with such attributes, especially the ones with both a low level of political effectiveness and a high degree of alienation, are telling us something about their dissatisfaction with the responsiveness of the general community to their needs; something about their feelings of powerlessness to control the features of their job and life situations—a lack of (or a loss of) attachment to, or trust in, the major social institutions of the society—and a lack of faith in the trustworthiness of other persons in general.

While there is much that might be done to change the nature of his job situation (in terms of job redesign, job rotation, "enrichment," and/or upgrading opportunities), we also feel strongly that leadership in the many institutions impinging on the worker's life can and does play a role in directing and articulating his social and political responses to his total social condition. It is a striking and provocative fact that a variety of polls have indicated that many of the voters for Wallace (typically from the white working class) were previously attracted to a political figure like the late Senator Robert Kennedy. Their life and job situations had not changed: what changed was the "leadership environment." At the same time, factors outside that environment—such as those dealt with in this volume—are also relevant.

We haven't tried to settle here the academic and methodological disputations about the exact, precise, referent of such terms as the "blues," alienation, or anomie. It was more important to show that workers with the socio-economic characteristics chosen by us to get at something that is "bugging" them are different from other workers, and that it makes a difference whether workers have or do not have these characteristics, regardless of the label or labels used to classify them. The fact that it makes a difference is grounds for starting the careful search for effective solutions. And one part of this search must be directed at the content of their work lives.

NOTES:

1. A good part of this chapter will report only on the results of the Pennsylvania interviews conducted in the summer of 1970. The Michigan survey (in Kalamazoo, with 101 members of the auto workers union and the steelworkers union) was carried out one year later, and analysis of these interviews was not completely carried out to include all of the findings at the time this chapter was written for publication in this volume.

2. In our total sample of 371 workers, 22 percent voiced discontent with their jobs. The University of Michigan's *national*, across-the-board sample yielded only 13 percent, thus indicating less of a discrepancy than among these white male union member workers. At the other end of the scale, 63 percent of the nationwide survey said their jobs were very much like the kind they originally wanted. This large proportion must be compared to the 37 percent of our sample with similar feelings.

3. Robert Dubin, "Industrial Workers' Worlds: A Study of the 'Central Life Interests' of Industrial Workers," *Journal of Social Problems*, January, 1956.

4. In the Kalamazoo sample, *none* of the discontented workers felt that they were better off compared to what they had hoped when they finished school. Nearly three-fifths said they were not as well off as hoped for.

5. Among the Kalamazoo workers, *all* of the workers saying they are behind were discontented, in sharp contrast to only 19 percent of the remainder.

6. For the total Pennsylvania group, 68 percent say they see little or no chance for advancement in their current jobs. In Kalamazoo, the percentage was 58 percent.

7. "A Profile of the Blue-Collared American," published as a chapter in Sar A. Levitan, Ed., *Blue-Collar Blues: A Symposium on Middle America* (New York: McGraw-Hill, 1971).

8. John Clausen, *Socialization and Society* (Boston: Little Brown and Co., 1968), pp. 203–205.

9. In the Kalamazoo sample, which is by far a much younger group than the one in Pennsylvania (three-fourths were under 50), the education-wage level hypothesis was definitely confirmed. Those with a high school degree but earning less than $4.00 an hour had the highest rate of discontent—36 percent—in contrast to only 20 percent of the rest of the sample. The finding for this Michigan group is therefore almost identical to that for those in Pennsylvania. Nearly *all* of the high eeucation-low wage group were under 50.

10. Among the Kalamazoo workers, about one-fifth of the single-earner workers, but nearly one-third of the workers with additional earners, are discontented.

11. Unmarried young men in this group had a "blues" rate of only 10 percent. For the married, high school graduate with no additional earners, only 17 percent had the "blues."

12. Arthur N. Turner and Paul R. Lawrence, *Industrial Jobs and the Worker: An Investigation of Response to Task Attributes* (Boston: Harvard University Graduate School of Business Administration, 1965).

13. They also found a close relationship between such task ratings by the workers themselves and ratings obtained through "objective" measurements and observations.

14. The same general relationship between task levels and discontent was discovered among the Kalamazoo workers:

		Discontented	Not Discontented
Most Positive	1	5%	31%
	2	30	32
	3	43 ⎱ 65	21 ⎱ 37
Most Negative	4	22 ⎰	16 ⎰
		100%	100%

15. The severity of negative tasks (how frequently workers are bothered by being employed in them) is more dramatically related to the "blues." Among the discontented, 36 percent registered an extremely high degree of dislike for such tasks—but among the contented, the proportion drops to a mere 9 percent.

16. Analysis of the Kalamazoo interviews reveals the same thing. On each of the separate components of the task rating index, workers with the "blues" report the least variety, autonomy, and responsibility.

17. To repeat, these specific questions were asked only of the Kalamazoo sample, and are the subject of greater scrutiny in Neal Herrick's contribution to this volume.

18. The same results were found in the Kalamazoo sample: 50 percent of the discontented workers, but only 32 percent of the others, had high alienation.

19. In a forthcoming report on white workers and their political psychology and behavior, Thomas Pettigrew (Harvard) uses this same question (concerning the lot of the average man) as a measure of "relative deprivation." He found it to be a highly sensitive indicator.

20. Contrary to our expectations, non-voting was no greater among the workers with the "blues" than among the other workers.

21. Only 77 discontented, and 201 contented workers actually voted. The remainder were either too young to vote, or did not vote, despite their eligibility.

22. Based on the Pennsylvania data only. In addition, among the discontented workers, 42 percent expressed negative views of new workers and also disagreed that Negroes want to get ahead using the same methods as other Americans have used. But among the contented workers, the proportion is only 27 percent.

Part Two

Blue Collars on Borrowed Time

Chapter Three

Job Tasks and Workers' Lives

> *Without work all life goes rotten.*
> *But when work is soulless, life*
> *stifles and dies.*
> *—Albert Camus*

America, as it journeys to the moon and labors mightily for a cancer cure, is doing precious little to correct the humdrum, unchallenging nature of the workplace. We are beginning to move into the era of the "anachronistic factory" which, "based on misconceptions and unacceptable assumptions about people, deteriorates and drives away able men and women."[1] We intend in this chapter to draw attention to this doleful fact with concrete findings—and to provide ammunition for the argument that we need desperately to increase our concern about the very nature of work itself. We also want this chapter to stimulate effective discussions among leaders in industry, the labor movement, and government that will lead to greater action in solving job-related problems.

Since the chapter deals directly with the possible effects of the tasks that workers perform (specifically, in terms of task variety, autonomy, and responsibility), it should be considered basic to the total volume.

Much of the argument to date for paying greater attention to work-related problems (many of them, for example, stemming from the prolonged effects of work simplification or fragmentation in the past) has been addressed to employers—in such terms as the effects upon turnover or absenteeism rates, and hence productivity. Another argument could be addressed to labor leaders, by pointing out that workers with lower level skills (in other words, very little variety and autonomy called for in their jobs) are less enthusiastic about their unions. In such a way, employers and labor leaders might both be motivated to take a greater interest in the nature of job tasks.

43

There is no guarantee, of course, that exposure to empirical, factual research results can change organizational priorities.

There is an equal, if not more compelling type of appeal: Suppose we were to find (as often occurs) that, while the absenteeism records and the union attitudes of workers in the lower skills are no different from those of workers with higher skills, their degree of alienation or feelings of political impotence, is nevertheless different?

Suppose we find that workers in lower task jobs tend to be less trustful of the social order, have less credibility about their individual impact on governmental decision-making?

Suppose we find that—regardless of absenteeism, productivity, or union loyalty—they register a greater discrepancy between their life hopes and their actual life achievements?

It seems to me that responsible men and women—apart from their roles as employers or labor leaders—should be interested in the possible role of the workers' jobs in the development or reinforcement of such beliefs, even if job traits do not appear to affect productivity or union attachment. Government and voluntary associations should have an active interest in such phenomena, too.

There is also involved the general issue of the development of our nation's human resources—the dimensions of which must include the role of work in our lives and in the fruitful use of our natural resources. "Fruitful" here means development of the individual for his *own* sake, and not merely for the benefit of public and private organizational goal attainments.

A major focus of this chapter and the one that follows is on the way white male union members (in our four selected urban areas of Pennsylvania and one in Michigan) rate their job tasks and the degree to which such task ratings are related to a host of other factors—such as job satisfaction, alienation, race and political attitudes, voting choices, etc.

Human beings differ from one another in the kinds of jobs they have, and in how they view the nature of the tasks involved in those jobs. There is no such thing as *the* worker. Hollywood's "Joe" is a monolithic caricaturized stereotype which has caused nothing but harm to the cause of gaining greater and more accurate understanding of—not necessarily sympathy for—the workers of contemporary America.

Some people may believe that differences in task ratings by workers could turn out to be a matter of caprice, unrelated to anything else—including the job tasks when classified by outside, "objective" observers. But as the following pages indicate, caprice does not rule. There is enough here to demonstrate that real variations do exist among job tasks, that workers reflect these variations in their own task ratings, that these in turn are related to other critical features in the lives of the workers interviewed. And these relationships also warrant increased attention on policy and program levels.

DESCRIPTION OF WORKER'S JOB TASK RATINGS

There is an infinite number of dimensions surrounding an individual's job. We never are able to look simultaneously through all the windows upon the world. And the number of questions that could be used to tap every job aspect is similarly without end. In this study, we have consciously chosen to concentrate on three major dimensions as measured by six questions adapted from Arthur Turner and Paul Lawrence's *Industrial Jobs and the Worker: An Investigation of Response to Task Attributes.*[2] The basic framework of this report is organized around classifications of what may be called the intrinsic features of a job, those features not readily identified as part of the monetary compensations or physical environment (e.g., noise and safety hazards) of the workplace. The fact that our focus is on some selected intrinsic job features does not mean that economic or physical factors should be ignored, or that they are of less importance. We will have much more to say about economic security for the worker, in other sections of this book.

Before citing and discussing these questions about job tasks and their answers, it is, above all, important to make clear that in the Turner and Lawrence study that served as one of the models for our own research, the two researchers found that the job task ratings by the workers themselves were closely related to the researchers' own objective observation of these job tasks. Turner and Lawrence's own rating procedure illuminated "differences between jobs which workers themselves perceived and considered relevant." In other words, whenever a worker indicated to the interviewers that his job was of a certain nature, the odds were that the job *was* of that nature. In our own study, therefore, we omitted any attempt at direct, observational confirmations of the workers' job task ratings.[3]

We are confident, based on the Turner and Lawrence experience, as well as our own internal evidence, that the ratings of job tasks by the workers in our own study bear a high relationship to the reality to be found in their work situations. However, we have to add that the relationship is not one-to-one. As indicated later, it is possible that the same set of job tasks may be rated differently (in terms of its variety, for example) by workers who differ in personality structure, especially regarding their degree of authoritarianism.

The first intrinsic aspect of these job tasks concern the amount of variety the worker feels he has on his job, and we asked the following question to measure it: "Do you have variety on your job (can you do different things, change methods, location, speed of working, and so forth)?"

"I always do the same thing on my job; there is no variety."
"I mostly do the same things, but there is a little variety."
"I have to do quite a number of different things on my job."
"There is a fair amount of variety."

"I have to do a lot of different things on my job; there is a great deal of variety."

The answers to this question reveal a wide range of job task variety, as judged by the Pennsylvania workers themselves:

	Percent	
"I have a lot of different things on my job; there is a great deal of variety."	27%	
"There is a fair amount of variety."	18	} 45%
"I have to do quite a number of different things on my job."	19	
"I mostly do the same things, but there is a little variety."	20	} 36%
"I always do the same thing on my job; there is no variety."	16	
	100%	

More than two-fifths report a lot or a fair amount of task variety.[4] But as can be seen from the same table, more than one-third (36 percent) indicated little or no variety on the job.

This group was asked a further question, designed to ascertain just how serious to them, how salient, such lack of variety was: "How frequently does it bother you that there is only a little or no variety on your job?"

"Nearly all the time?"
"Very often?"
"Sometimes?"
"Rarely or never?"

Three-fifths said they were bothered by the lack of variety either sometimes, very often, or nearly all the time. In other words, about 22 percent of all the Pennsylvania workers said they had little or no variety on their jobs and were sometimes, very often, or nearly all the time, bothered by this fact. Almost identical percentages were found among the Kalamazoo workers.

The second dimension has to do with autonomy on the job as measured by two questions:

a. "Which statement best describes the kind of job you have?"

"I have no freedom at all to do my work as I want to."
"I have little freedom to do my work as I want to."
"I am fairly free to do my work as I want to."
"I am completely free to do my work as I want."

b. "Which one of the following items best describes how much of their potential ideas and skills are being used on the job by the people working on the same general kind of job as yours?"

"Almost none of what they can offer."
"About one-fourth of what they can offer."
"About half of what they can offer."
"About three-fourths of what they can offer."
"Almost all of what they can offer."

The answers to the first part of this inquiry were as follows:

	Percent
"I am completely free to do my work as I want."	19%
"I am fairly free to do my work as I want."	56
"I have little freedom to do my work as I want."	16 ⎫ 25%
"I have no freedom at all to do my work as I want to."	9 ⎭
	100%

Workers responding "little or no freedom" were, as in the previous question, asked how frequently it bothered them; 70 percent (18 percent of the total sample) said it bothered them sometimes, very often, or nearly all the time. Among the Kalamazoo workers claiming little or no freedom (17 percent), three-fourths were bothered to the same extent.

On the second part, asking about how much of workers' potential ideas and skills are used on the job, they answered as follows:

	Percent
"Almost all of what they can offer."	30%
"About three-fourths of what they can offer."	19
"About half of what they can offer."	26
"About one-fourth of what they can offer."	13 ⎫ 24%
"Almost none of what they can offer."	11 ⎭
	99%

Turner and Lawrence's measures of worker ratings of responsibility consisted of three questions:

a. "Some jobs provide a great deal of opportunity to learn more about the work and enable a person to increase his knowledge of the process and his skill; other jobs provide very few such opportunities to learn more. How is it on your job?"

"There are very great opportunities to learn more."
"There are fairly good opportunities to learn—above average."
"There is little opportunity to learn."
"There is almost no opportunity on my job to learn more about the process or to increase my skill."

b. "Is the quality of your work the most important thing to you, or is it less important than quantity, speed of working, or other things?"

"Quality is by far the most important thing on my job."
"Quality is the most important thing, but quantity or other things are important, too."
"Quality is emphasized but not as much as quantity or other things."
"Quality is given very little importance on my particular job."

c. "Which of the following statements fits your job?"

"Almost anyone could do my job."
"A good many people could do my job."
"Only a limited number of people could do my job."
"Very few people could do my job."
"Can't answer; hard to say."

On the first of these questions designed to measure degree of worker responsibility on the job (as perceived by the worker), the responses in the Pennsylvania group were as follows:

	Percent
"There are very great opportunities to learn more."	23%
"There are fairly good opportunities to learn—above average."	35
"There is little opportunity to learn."	25 ⎫
"There is almost no opportunity on my job to learn more about the process or to increase my skill."	17 ⎬ 42%
	100%

When asked how frequently it bothered them that they have little or no opportunity to learn more about their work, 60 percent of these workers reporting little or no such opportunity (25 percent of the total sample) said sometimes, very often, or nearly all the time.[5]

The second question, asking about importance of quality of work, yielded the following replies:

	Percent
"Quality is by far the most important thing."	44%
"Quality is the most important thing, but quantity or other things are important, too."	37
"Quality emphasized but not as much as quantity or other things."	13 ⎫
"Quality is given very little importance. . . ."	6 ⎬ 19%
	100%

The third item used to measure how much responsibility the worker feels his job contains resulted in the following responses:

"Very few people could do my job."	10%	
"Only a limited number of people could do my job."	37	
"A good many people could do my job."	34	} 52%
"Almost anyone could do my job."	18	
"Can't answer; hard to say."	1	
	100%	

More than half of the Pennsylvania workers said that almost anyone or a good many people could do their job. In Kalamazoo, the proportion was nearly the same (48 percent). Such findings can be used as a measure of the esteem of such jobs as seen by the workers themselves. The high proportion stating that almost anyone or a good many people could do their jobs indicates, in my opinion, a widespread feeling of low regard for the kinds of jobs many workers perform.

TOTAL TASK INDEX

While these six separate questions and their responses are interesting in and of themselves, it is more useful to combine the answers to all of the questions, with each answer being given a special weight.[6] In this way, we can (1) derive a more general, overall picture of how each worker views a number of aspects of his job, and then (2) determine to what extent this overall index relates to other selected features about the worker. Such features include:

1. The usual demographic items such as age, education, and place of birth;
2. Economic factors such as wages and employment experiences;
3. Two types of social-psychological variables: (a) those relating directly to the job but not included in the overall six-item index, and (b) those which may seem at first to have little connection with work;
4. Political behavior and related attitudes; and
5. How the worker would respond to some selected possibilities for dealing with his current job situation or aspirations (specifically, training for better jobs and job rotation).

For the Pennsylvania workers we classified the range of overall scores into four groups roughly equal in number, ranging from those workers with the most positive (high-level) job tasks to workers with the most negative (low-level) tasks. For the Pennsylvania group, in the most positive one, there were 56 cases; the next most positive group, 76. These two groups (51 percent of the 258 cases for which we have complete job index scores) constitute the workers described here as having positive (high-level) job tasks. The third group numbered 65; the fourth group, with the most negative task perception scores, contained 62 workers. These last two groups, totaling 127 (49 percent of the total for which we have complete task scores) are the workers referred to in this report as having negative (low-level) job tasks.[7]

Among the six separate questions used in our classification of workers according to the job tasks, no single item differentiates between the highest and the lowest groups as much as the one question asking about degree of variety. The second most important differentiator consists of the two questions used to determine the degree of autonomy the worker feels he has on his job.

RELATIONSHIP OF JOB TASK RATINGS TO OTHER JOB ATTRIBUTES

If these weightings or groupings have any basis in reality or any usefulness, they should be related to other measures of the way the workers feel about their jobs, measures not used in our definition or classifications of job tasks described by the workers. For example, nearly half (46 percent) of all the workers with positive ratings of their job tasks told us that if completely free to go into any type of job they wanted, they would still want the same type of job. In contrast, only 30 percent of the group with negative task ratings said the same thing. The job task ratings of these workers, in other words, are related to other job-related phenomena.[8] Job attachment is thus related to the intrinsic nature of the job in which these men work.

A second example, and perhaps a more striking demonstration of the insights revealed through use of the Total Task Index, is the clear-cut relationship of that Index to the kinds of choices the workers make when asked how they felt about changing their jobs.

As the following table indicates, the Pennsylvania workers with the most positive ratings are far less likely to want to change jobs than those with negative ratings.

Relationship of Job Attachment to Job-Task Levels

	Most Positive			Most Negative
	1	2	3	4
1. Highest Job Attachment: I do not want to change jobs even for more money because the one I have now is a good one.	40%	36%	17%	15%
2. Lowest Job Attachment: I would take almost any other job in which I could earn as much as I am earning now. I would quit my job right now if I had anything else to do.	0 2 } 2%	3 4 } 7%	9 8 } 17%	18 8 } 26%

The Kalamazoo data duplicate the Pennsylvania results. For example, the proportion in the two highest task levels who don't want to change jobs even for more money is double that among those in the two lower task-level jobs (38 vs. 19 percent). And only 4 percent of those in the high tasks, compared to 19 percent of the others, would take almost any job paying the same or would quit right now.

In another question, we asked how well the job measured up to initial expectations—a question used in our analysis of discontent, presented in the previous chapter. The proportions in the two lowest task levels telling us that their jobs are not very much like the kind they wanted are greater than the proportions indicating the opposite. Conversely, workers in the two highest levels who say their jobs are very much like the kind they originally sought outweigh by far those who evaluate their current jobs as not measuring up to the kind they wanted.[9]

Relationship of Job Expectations to Job-Task Levels

	Most Positive			Most Negative
	1	2	3	4
A. Percent saying job very much like kind originally wanted.	57%	43%	19%	19%
B. Percent saying their job not very much like the kind they originally wanted.	7	12	22	37
Ratio of A to B	*8.14*	*3.58*	*0.86*	*0.51*

Again, on a different question—one that has become a classic in job satisfaction literature—

> If you could retire with as much money as you need for a good pension, and not have to work anymore, would you do it right away, or would you wait a while? (If "Wait a while"): About how many years would you wait?[10]

Even when age is taken into consideration, the answers to this question are related to the workers' job tasks: in each age group, workers with positive scores are less likely to say they would retire right away or wait less one year, and more likely to wait at least ten years before retiring.

Half of even the under-40 workers in low-level tasks told us they would retire right away if they had a good enough pension. I suggest this is a reliable symptom of some form of "alienation from work." There are wide variations in worker attachment to their jobs within and between age groups, according to job-task level. It rises to 64 percent among the oldest workers (55 and older) in poor tasks, but is as low as 34 percent among the youngest in positive tasks.

The wide contrast among the oldest men in job attachment between those in high-task levels and those in low ones raises a question about retirement policy. If it is deemed wise and/or practical (the two words are not synonymous) to advocate early retirement, one might argue that it will be more difficult to deal with older workers in "good" jobs, as far as intrinsic task levels are concerned. But on the other hand, if it is deemed not so wise and/or practical to advocate an early retirement policy, the challenge lies among those older workers employed in the less attractive jobs. There is evidence that the longer a worker remains in an occupation with unattractive tasks, the greater the chance that he will desire early retirement—actually an escape from such jobs. But why should workers be allowed or required to remain for 20–30 years in such jobs?

This might also be the place to remark on the overall proportion of the total group of workers interviewed who would choose to retire right away. That proportion is exactly half of the group, ranging from about two-fifths of the youngest to three-fifths of the oldest workers.[11] What does this tell us about the basic attachment to work among today's workers in America, especially those below 55? Who are the young Pennsylvania workers (38 out of the 91 under the age of 40) who tell us that they would retire right away if they had a good enough retirement income? Does this tell us something about them, or their jobs, or both?

We do know that more than half of them are on jobs they describe as having little variety, little autonomy, and little responsibility. Could this be among the reasons that would impel them to answer that they would retire immediately if they had an adequate pension? The findings on other questions confirm this lower job attachment among young workers. On one question previously cited, only 13 percent of the under-40 workers said they didn't want to change jobs, even for more money, because they considered their current jobs good ones (compared to 26 percent among the 40–54 year olds, and 44 percent among the oldest workers, 55 and older). Thus, among the younger workers, nearly 90 percent find their present jobs so unattractive that they are ready for a change.

Management Interest in Quality Work

We have no certain way of knowing which is cause and which is effect (or whether we are dealing altogether with effects of something else not plumbed by our questions and analysis). But the answers to the next question, concerning management's emphasis or lack of emphasis on quality work,[12] are definitely related to the workers' rating of their job tasks. "Does management where you work put emphasis on your doing quality work, or do they emphasize other things such as quantity of output?"

"Management puts heavy emphasis on the quality of my work."

"Management emphasizes the quality of my work more than they emphasize other things such as quantity."

"Management emphasizes other things such as quantity more than they do the quality of my work."

"Management puts almost all the emphasis on things other than the quality of my work."

The majority (61 percent) of the workers with the most positive ratings of their job tasks reported that management in their companies puts a heavy emphasis on the quality of the work they perform, while the majority (54 percent) of the workers with the most negative tasks reported that their employers stressed quantity more than quality; the more positive the job task, the greater the proportion reporting management's stress on doing quality work. The bars in the graph represent the ratio of (1) workers citing heavy emphasis on quality work to (2) workers citing emphasis on other things such as quantity more than quality, or almost all emphasis on non-quality aspects. The

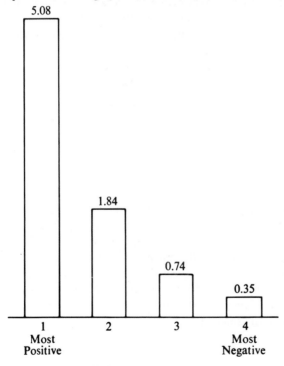

Pennsylvania Workers' Rating of Management's Emphasis on Doing Quality Work, by Job Task Rating

JOB TASK LEVEL

Kalamazoo data reveal the same relationships between task level and the worker's rating of management's emphasis on quality of work.

Furthermore, among just those workers reporting management's emphasis on the non-quality aspects of their work, workers in low-level tasks were more frequently bothered by that emphasis than the workers performing positive tasks. Nearly two-fifths of the first group, but only one-fifth of the latter group, said this lack of emphasis on quality work bothered them very often, or nearly all the time.

Overall Job Satisfaction

Some researchers in the field of job satisfaction studies criticize the use of such direct questions as, "Are you satisfied with your job?" and variations of that type of questions (including "How satisfied are you?"). Despite such skepticism, we used the following version of this type of questioning and found it worthwhile. "How much of the time are you satisfied with your job? Most of the time? A good deal of the time? About half the time? Occasionally? Hardly or never?"

The answers are very closely related to the workers' own ratings of their job tasks. That is, Pennsylvania workers who rate their job as high in variety, autonomy, and/or responsibility—regardless of age—are much more frequently satisfied with their jobs than those reporting less positive ratings.[13]

Relationship of Job Satisfaction Frequency to Job-Task Levels

	Most Positive			Most Negative
	1	2	3	4
A. Percent satisfied most of the time	75%	55%	37%	25%
B. Percent satisfied occasionally, or hardly ever; never	2	5	14	29
A/B (Composite Job Satisfaction Index)	37.5	11.0	2.6	0.9

The main point, however, is that regardless of whether we ask the indirect or direct kinds of questions designed to tap favorable or unfavorable orientations of workers toward their job, they will tend to be related to the ratings the workers have of the intrinsic nature of their job tasks.[14] The measurement and analysis of selected aspects of this intrinsic nature yield some critical findings that should concern responsible leaders in management, labor, government, and organizations interested in the quality of work-life in modern America.

Saliency of Task Attributes

If I had to indicate which of the several dimensions about their jobs was the most salient one, I would have to reply, first, that the presence or absence of promotion opportunities (a dimension not included in the intrinsic task measures) was the most critical one. The details concerning this question in the interview are discussed later. Nearly two-fifths of the Pennsylvania sample said they had little or no real chance to get ahead on their jobs and were bothered sometimes, very often, or nearly all the time by this lack of advancement chances.

Given the basic stress in American society on success and getting ahead (it is questionable that the "Greening of America" will make a revolution about work attitudes deep enough to affect the mainstream of American workers), this pressure of job life cannot be neglected.[15] *The challenge is how to build into the total system of the world of work greater opportunities for some form of advancement meaningful to the employee.*

But concerning the intrinsic task aspects, apparently the degree of opportunity to learn more about the work and enable a worker to improve his knowledge about the process and his skill is the most salient. Forty-two percent of the Pennsylvania workers reported little opportunity to learn more about the process or to increase their skill, and among these, 60 percent—or about one-fourth of the total Pennsylvania sample—were bothered by this lack of opportunity sometimes, very often, or nearly all the time.

The striking feature of this facet of workers' jobs emerges from other questions in the interview, including the one asking about chances for advancement. The relationship of the presence or absence of a training program to improve skills as a possible fringe benefit to the workers' job task perception also reveals the importance of this side of life and work. It is clearly an unmet need in this group of workers. Only one-fourth of the workers in the most negative job tasks indicated they had a training program of this nature (to improve skills), in contrast to more than half in the most positive tasks. On another question, asking whether they would take a training or education program aimed at a better job, more than 80 percent of the total sample said they would enroll in such a program.

DEMOGRAPHIC AND ECONOMIC ASPECTS

In the previous chapter, we reported that older Pennsylvania workers (50 and over) with at least a high school education were more likely to have the "blues" (those having a high discrepancy between early life or job aspirations and current achievements, plus the belief that there are little or no advancement opportunities in their current job situation). Conversely, workers who were young and with at least a high school education had the lowest percentage with the "blues." Age and education, in other words, must be combined, and not examined separately, in the search for relevant explanations about behavior and attitudes.

The question here is: Does the same finding prevail when we consider intrinsic job tasks instead of the "blues" as a possible correlate to the age-education variable? We think it does.

If we take a look at the Pennsylvania and Kalamazoo workers and isolate those with at least one year of college, workers 40 and older (only eight of them) have by far the greatest percentage with negative job task ratings. But those under 40 have by far the lowest percentage (33 percent) with a negative task rating! Despite the small number of college-educated workers involved in each of the two age groups, the odds that these differences are due to chance are less than 5 out of 100.

	Percent with Negative Job Task Ratings	Number in Sample
40 and older, 1 year of college or more	75%	8
Under 40, high school or less	52%	117
40 and older, high school or less	46%	194
Under 40, 1 year of college or more	33%	33

Migrant Status

In recent years, interest has developed in the possible impact of the broader social structure within which men and women live and act out their work roles. One aspect of this social structure is the size of the population area of their residence, or their migrant status—whether they were born in the urban area in which they now work, or migrated there from a variety of other types of areas. In this study we were able to differentiate between "native urbanites," workers born in the urban area in which they were working; migrants from other urban areas of at least 50,000 population; migrants from small towns, areas with populations between 2,500 and 50,000; and migrants from rural areas—smaller towns, villages, or farms.

The larger the area of the worker's origin (or the more urbanized that area), the greater the likelihood that the worker had a less positive job task rating. This may be only a descriptive finding; that is, due to other factors, such as age or one's actual occupation.[16] A more technical and sophisticated statistical analysis is needed to determine whether this reported relationship is spurious or genuine. It does, however, fit with the findings of other researchers in the field of work attitudes and job satisfaction[17] who have found some degree of influence of the urban–rural (or small town) environment on worker responses. Here, we are dealing completely with urban-dwelling workers, who are classified according to their migrant status.

If we take age into consideration, we find that the relationship reported here holds true only for those 40 and older. In this age group, the relationship between size of birthplace and job-task perception is quite definite: Among older workers, those born in urban areas with at least 50,000 population are less likely to have positive job-task ratings in contrast to those born in small towns, villages, and farms. The odds that this difference is due to chance are about 2 out of 100.

Adequacy of Take-Home Pay

For special reasons, we will present, in the next chapter, data on hourly wage and task levels. Workers were also asked if their individual take-home pay was good enough to take care of the family's usual bills and expenses. While two-thirds of the total sample said it was good enough, the response varied by job task. The proportion of each of the four worker categories by job-task ratings indicating adequacy of take-home pay was as follows:

		Take-Home Pay Is Adequate
Most Positive Task Rating	1	80%
	2	71%
	3	62%
Most Negative Task Rating	4	60%

This question deals with how adequate take-home pay is as a source of meeting the family's usual bills and expenses. But a further question asked the following: "Do you feel that this total income [including other income if take-home pay considered inadequate] is enough to live as comfortably as you'd like to?"

Here, too, the answers are related to total task rating, and the more positive the task rating, the more likely the worker answering this question will report his total income enough to live as comfortably as he'd like to—from 49 percent among those with the most positive scores to only 28 percent for the workers with the most negative scores. The overall average was 37 percent. But this relationship is no doubt explained by the differences in wages according to task levels.

By age, the percentages of the Pennsylvania and Kalamazoo workers reporting enough total income to live comfortably were: Under 30: 40 percent; 30–54: 47 percent; 55 and older: 51 percent. This response does not confirm the popular notion that the middle-aged worker is experiencing the greatest "economic squeeze"—from *his* point of view—more than other age groups. Instead, it may suggest that younger white male workers have higher expectations or standards as to what is meant by "comfortable" living, and that their total income is inadequate relative to those standards. A special chapter on the young worker will go into greater detail on this and related issues.

Future Income and Employment Expectations

The nature of the worker's job tasks affects his estimates of his future "income career." The question on this topic was worded as follows: "As you look to the years ahead, do you expect a steady rise in your income before retirement?

Some rise and then a decline before retirement? Or do you expect many ups and downs in your income before you retire?"

The degree of uncertainty about income future (as indicated by the second two possible answers to the above question) is related to the worker's job-task rating; the more negative the rating, the greater the uncertainty—from 25 percent with the most positive perception to 44 percent with the most negative. Even when age is considered, the basic relationship tends to hold.

Such uncertainty and lack of optimism repeat themselves in the answers to a question asking the worker how many out of 100 workers like himself could find new jobs within one month, if they lost their present jobs. Regardless of age, the more positive the worker's job-task level, the higher his estimate of re-employment. Only one-fourth of the total sample, however, is optimistic enough to estimate that 50 or more out of every 100 workers like themselves would find a new job within a month. Even for workers with positive task ratings, the "optimistic" estimate[18] rises only to 32 percent, and is as low as 19 percent among those with negative ratings of their job tasks. Could this be one reason why many workers, despite the negative ratings they attribute to their job tasks, cling to what job they have?

While the percentages may have changed over the decades, this type of finding is in keeping with Selig Perlman's description, as far back as 1928, of the relatively pessimistic outlook of workers compared to that of businessmen, as far as economic opportunities are concerned.[19] For workers, to paraphrase Perlman, there are always more job-seekers than job openings, and their underlying motivation is a *job-security consciousness*.

As long as such insecurity troubles the American worker, he and/or his representatives understandably will place a greater priority on those measures aimed at protecting his rights to a job and reducing the risks of job loss. The degree to which unions can reduce the conditions engendering such insecurity will affect the priorities they place on the nature of the problems receiving the brunt of attention in this book; that is, the intrinsic content of their members' job tasks. (We will have more to say on this issue, in Chapter 5.)

Thus, the degree to which job security and income adequacy problems are conquered will affect the interest of unions in such matters as the degree of variety or autonomy a worker has in his job assignments. But job security and income adequacy are not so easily achieved through employer and union actions alone. They may also require decisions and policies that transcend the workplace and the collective bargaining table.

Nevertheless, several things still need saying. For example, compared to the past, today's job security and income adequacy problems are not as precarious (nor as universal). We say this despite the unhappy employment picture of 1971 and 1972. More to the point, the new worker—the one who did not experience the long-term and widespread deprivations of the Great Depression of the 1930s—may be more concerned than his father or grandfather with some of the intrinsic task attributes of his job. This does not always mean that he places greater priority on the nature of these attributes than he places on job security and income adequacy. But they may be more important to him than to workers of earlier generations still in the labor force.[20] Professor Fred Foulkes argues in his *Creating More Meaningful Work* that "it should be of great interest to unions five or ten years hence."[21] He goes on to write:

> Although unions should be interested in participating in programs designed to satisfy their members' psychological needs as well as their physical needs and, thus, should be bargaining for more meaningful work, there is little evidence that they are doing this in any organized fashion or to any meaningful degree. (p. 32)

Few significant shifts in organizational interests emerge full blown or overnight, however. It is doubtful, furthermore, whether most employers or personnel officials have yet been persuaded that intrinsic task attributes are worth paying any attention to on any substantial scale. Much more to the point, the very fact that a union official is partly responsible for the survey forming the basis of most of this report is one concrete indication that some steps are being taken to increase the interest on the part of the American labor movement.

Finally, it should be of more than passing interest to union leaders that the actual content of their members' jobs may affect how those members evaluate their union—a topic discussed elsewhere.

Unemployment Experience

Overall pessimism about re-employment after a lay-off is not necessarily related to the immediate pre-interview unemployment experience of the Pennsylvania workers we interviewed—at least in the 20 months or so prior to being interviewed. But it is true that, in the group of workers with the very highest positive tasks, only 12 percent had any kind of unemployment experience in all of 1969 and in the approximate eight months preceding the 1970 interview (and half of these were unemployed altogether less than one month). For the rest of the sample, the proportion with any unemployment during the same period was 28 percent, considerably greater than for the workers in the highest tasks. The vast majority of these were unemployed altogether for more than one month.[22]

In other words, workers in more negative job tasks tend to be in jobs with greater real risks of unemployment (judged from their past experience), and these workers might be expected to be less optimistic about their re-hiring success in the event of any lay-off. But there are some other noteworthy findings. Older workers, as a whole, had the best employment status both at the time of, and in the 20 months prior to, their being interviewed. When interviewed, every one of them was employed, and, prior to that time, had the highest proportion without any weeks of unemployment in 1969 and 1970 of any of the three age groups—85 percent vs. 63 percent for the youngest and 81 percent for the middle-aged. Nevertheless, these older workers revealed the most pessimistic estimates for finding a new job if ever they became unemployed. Only 14 percent of them could be called "optimistic," in the sense defined earlier, in contrast to 28 percent for the younger age groups.

This sharp difference between the workers 55 and older and the younger groups is subject to at least two complementary interpretations. The first is that older workers, in general, are aware of the widespread belief (based on a great deal of truth) that once unemployed, the older worker has a much more difficult time finding a new job.[23] The second and equally plausible explanation, implied earlier, is that workers now in their mid-fifties or older were at least 20 years old in the midst of the Great Depression, and that such experience has become indelibly etched in their memories and psyches. To repeat, job security for that generation is a much more salient and anxiety-inducing notion than for the younger workers of today. Hence their greater pessimism about re-employment success. Even the older workers in positive job tasks are more pessimistic than the younger ones in the same categories. Only 20 percent are optimistic, as compared to 35 percent of the younger workers. In Kalamazoo, only 7 percent of the older workers in positive job tasks were optimistic, in vivid contrast to 35 percent among the younger workers who were also in high-level tasks.

MOBILITY CHANCES, THE DESIRE FOR UPGRADING, AND ENTHUSIASM FOR JOB ROTATION

This section of the report is devoted to a presentation of the findings on the relationship of job tasks to other job features and job improvement proposals that may affect worker satisfaction. One of these is the question that asks how much opportunity to get ahead their job offers them. More than two-thirds of the total sample told us that on their jobs there was little or no chance to get ahead, but this varied according to their job-task ratings:

Job Mobility Chances, by Workers' Job-Task Ratings
(Pennsylvania Only)

	Most Positive			Most Negative
	1	2	3	4
Percent reporting little or no chance to get ahead on the job	41%	62%	80%	84%

The range in low-mobility estimates is extreme, from 41 percent in the case of the workers with very positive job-task perceptions to 84 percent among those with very negative perceptions.[24] The differences, of course, reflect in part the skill level of their jobs. Workers with the greatest need for upward mobility (those in the lower task levels) apparently have the least expectations of moving up. Even two-fifths of the first group (the workers with the most positive ratings of their jobs) feel that they have little or no chance for getting ahead in their current jobs. The two phenomena are not completely connected: that is, it is possible to have a job with a great deal of variety, autonomy, and responsibility which, nevertheless, contains little chance for upgrading or promotion. But all in all, the odds for advancement, as reckoned by the workers themselves, are related to the nature of the jobs themselves.[25]

More important, the degree to which such lack of mobility chances bothers or is critical to workers is related to the nature of their job tasks. Among workers in the two most positive task levels who cited little or no chance for getting ahead in their jobs, 47 percent indicated that this bothers them sometimes, very often, or nearly all the time—in contrast to 68 percent of the corresponding group of workers with negative tasks (p. < .05). The more negative the job tasks, the lower the reported chances for getting ahead; and the more negative the tasks, the more salient these reduced chances are to the worker. Putting this another way, about one-ninth (11 percent) of the group with the most positive job tasks report very little or no chance to get ahead and are bothered by that, in contrast to nearly three-fifths (58 percent) of the workers with the most negative job-task ratings.

Poor Jobs and Poor Promotion Chances

There were 70 workers with negative ratings of their job tasks who were also bothered by the low chances for getting ahead on their jobs—about one quarter of our total Pennsylvania sample. A group like this may be a source of white-worker discontent, and ripe for political exploitation. Since the corresponding percentage for the Kalamazoo workers was identical, it suggests that the proportion of white male manual workers who have similar characteristics is a sizeable minority that cannot be ignored. In what ways are they unique, and do they exhibit any specific attributes that unions, management, government and other organizations interested in the quality of work should be concerned about?

In the first place, they are not any younger or older than the total Pennsylvania sample. Age by itself does not appear to be related to whether or not a worker will have negative perceptions of his job tasks and at the same time be bothered about his slim chances for getting ahead in his job.

Second, they do seem to be different in educational backgrounds. More than half of them never finished high school, in contrast to slightly more than two-fifths of the total sample.

Third, participation in voting is much less than that of the total sample. As a corollary, it is not surprising, therefore, that their feelings of political effectiveness are far below that of the general sample.

Fourth, they are also more alienated. This concept will be discussed at greater length in the following chapter.

Fifth, despite the fact that they are in lower skills, with negative task ratings, and are bothered by their slim chances for upward mobility in the job situation—as well as being less educated, more alienated, and feeling less politically effective—these workers appear to be no more anti-Negro than the general sample. The race attitude of white male workers appears to be related to something apart from, or in addition to, skill levels and mobility frustrations.[26]

Finally, when asked how helpful their union has been, they are not as favorably inclined as the general sample. While slightly more than half of them say their union is very or fairly helpful, the corresponding proportion for the total sample is higher—more than three-fifths.

Desire for Job Changing

If the workers' ratings of their job tasks have any importance to them, these task ratings should have some effect on a willingness to change to new types of jobs. Workers with negative ratings should be different from those with positive ratings in this regard.

We have already reported some of the findings on this proposition. But in addition, workers with negative ratings are twice as likely to have thought very often about seriously making an effort to enter a new and different type of occupation (22 percent vs. 11 percent of all other workers). The contrast is especially great among the young workers: For those under 40 and with negative task ratings, the proportion having thought very often about a change in occupations is 42 percent, as compared to only 17 percent for those young workers with a positive job task score. We have more to say about even younger workers in our sample in a separate chapter.

How do task ratings affect the workers' responses to a proposition that offers them an opportunity for a promotion with their current employer or for a better job somewhere else, for example, as a result of a training program? We should expect to find that workers in low-level tasks would be much more likely to jump at such an opportunity than those with a positive perception. But the results do not clearly show this tendency. Task levels make little difference in affirmative responses to a question worded as follows:

"Suppose your employer, the government, your union, or some other organization offered you a training and education program, with enough money to support yourself and family, to make it possible to get a promotion with the employer you have now, or to get a much better job somewhere else."

"Would you choose the program leading to a promotion with your present employer? Or the program leading to a better job somewhere else? Or would you just not take any program like that?"

But this is not the end of the story. There is one major effect of job tasks on the workers' answers to this question that cannot be ignored. The effect of variations in job tasks shows up in *where* the worker would want that training program to take him—towards a promotion within his company, or to a much better job somewhere else. If a worker does say he would choose a training or education program for a promotion or a better job, his job task does determine whether he would take the program for (1) a promotion with his present employer, or (2) a much better job *somewhere else*. The lower the task, the greater the proportion of both the Pennsylvania and Kalamazoo workers opting for a "much better job somewhere else." Excluding workers saying they would not take any program, the proportions choosing a training program for a better job somewhere else are as follows:

	Job Task Level	Percent Choosing Training Programs for Better Jobs "Somewhere Else"
Most Positive	1	14% ⎫ 23%
	2	30% ⎭
	3	48% ⎫ 46%
Most Negative	4	46% ⎭

Among the oldest workers (55 and older), none in positive task levels would choose programs leading to jobs somewhere else, but among the oldest workers in negative tasks, exactly half would do so.[27]

First, these statistics indicate that regardless of task level, the vast majority of the workers in our sample (more than eight of every 10) are anxious to have a meaningful upgrading training–education program. Even among the oldest workers, the proportion is still high, and only declines to three-fifths indicating a desire for such a program. Second, the figures show that workers with negative job tasks would be more likely than others to want a program of this sort for the purpose of getting a better job outside of their current place of employment. One might argue that these are the workers who may constitute the key target group for government, management, and union efforts for effective training and education programs with an upgrading content. Congress, for example, has recently been considering a "Middle Aged and Older Workers Employment Act," which would provide for such a program. The fact that they register much higher preferences for programs leading to better jobs *elsewhere* is also a symptom of their dissatisfaction with their current jobs.[28] In a separate chapter, on the emerging pattern of second careers, there is a more intensive analysis of the 40-plus adult workers whom we have labeled as "candidates for second careers," which presents a more extensive discussion of the role of the job as an influence on the desire for occupational change.

Evaluation of the Union and Task Levels

It is also significant that, when asked if they thought their union could be doing more for improving members' skills or getting a promotion to a better job than it is now, 70 percent of both the Pennsylvania and Kalamazoo samples said yes, their unions could be doing more. But more to the point, the workers' job tasks affected their answers to this question. The more negative the rating, the higher the proportion stating that their union could be doing a better job on improving members' skills or promotion to a better job. Unions, it appears, are not relieved by their members of the responsibility of creating opportunities for better jobs.

On a more general question, asking how helpful they feel their union is to its members, there is a very strong relationship among the Pennsylvania workers between their answers and their job task ratings. (No such relationship was found for the Kalamazoo workers.) Among Pennsylvania workers in the most positive tasks, half said their union is very helpful, but this proportion declines sharply to one-fifth among workers in the most negative tasks. The more negative the task, the greater the proportion of workers saying their union is mostly not, or not at all, helpful (from 4 percent of the most positive group to 11 percent of the most negative one).

Workers' Reactions to Job Rotation Proposal

As stated in the recent book by Fred Foulkes, *Creating More Meaningful Work*, "monotonous, mechanical labor reduces even the brightest employees to dullards on the job. . . . In a highly competitive environment causing more and more pressure on profit margins, management simply cannot afford this kind of waste." But one need not be concerned merely with improving worker efficiency for the purpose of increasing profit margins, in order to take notice of the human impact of certain types of job tasks. Professor Foulkes reports on company experiments in job rotation, in which workers are given changing work assignments without having to re-design any jobs.

Many years ago, the pioneer French industrial sociologist, Georges Friedmann, in his *Anatomy of Work* (French title, *Travail en Miettes*),[29] also took up the issue of boring and unchallenging work and such possible solutions as job rotation. In this book, Friedmann once again (as in his many other attacks on the dehumanizing aspects of certain types of work) calls attention to the impact of job specialization in industry, and how workers' satisfaction generally increases with the complexity of the work performed.

This does not mean, of course, that there is no limit to how complex a job may become before satisfaction is adversely affected. Friedmann's description of one plant (from p. 14 of his book) is worth noting in the context of the need for job rotation:

In a highly rationalized watchmaking factory [in Switzerland] the work, which was minutely subdivided, was particularly tiring, an industrial psychologist told me, *because* it could not give any satisfaction. The jobs many of the workers were forced to perform were, he thought, definitely below those they were capable of doing, had they been given the opportunity. That was one of the chief reasons for their aging prematurely, he added. "Much of the work done in our factory," he continued, "could and should be done by half-wits . . ." This view of the kind of work for mental defectives hardly agrees with the successful experiments recently carried out by occupational therapists in many lands.

How do the workers in our sample respond to a suggestion that they be trained to quality for changing job task assignments—job rotation? They were asked the following: "If you could be trained to rotate, where you work, between 2 or 3 really different jobs over a period of a year, do you think that would be a very good idea, or not a very good idea?"

Do workers in negative job tasks see in job rotation a partial solution to their apparent negative evaluations of their jobs? In other words, are they (compared to workers in positive job tasks) more likely to say that the suggestion for rotation training is a good idea?

The answer to that question is paradoxical. Contrary to what one might expect, workers in negative job tasks are less likely to think that training for job rotation is a good idea; only 46 percent vs. 55 percent of those with positive ratings. This is quite a contrast from the findings regarding their interest in changing jobs altogether.

Age, more than job task, seems to be one of the major correlates to a preference for job rotation training. Among workers under 30, in Pennsylvania and Kalamazoo, 73 percent said the suggestion was a very good idea. Among the oldest workers, only 42 percent.[30]

But age alone is never a satisfactory explanation of human behavior and choices. What are the differences, then, between those workers saying that job rotation training would be a good idea and those who don't, apart from, or in addition to, age?

A good part of the explanation brings us to the role of authoritarianism, and also to achievement values, concepts to be explained and discussed later in this report. The authoritarian personality is rigid in many respects, including a reluctance to change, which training and the very performance of job rotation itself would entail. This may explain why a higher proportion of the less authoritarian workers than of the more authoritarian ones gave favorable responses to the idea of job rotation training (57 vs. 42 percent). This difference is statistically significant, at less than the .05 level.

When age and authoritarianism are both taken into consideration, we find that young workers with low authoritarianism have the greatest proportion in favor of the job rotation idea, while their opposite numbers—older workers with high authoritarianism—have the lowest proportion in favor of job rotation. Older workers who are non-authoritarian were no different in their reaction to the job rotation notion than authoritarian younger workers. Older age seems to offset the otherwise favorable responses of the non-authoritarians, and authoritarianism offsets the otherwise favorable responses of the young.

When job task and authoritarianism are considered jointly, non-authoritarians in positive job tasks are by far the most favorably inclined toward job rotation (67 percent vs. 50 percent for the Pennsylvania sample).

While it is true that the overall job task ratings showed little relationship to the job rotation proposal, this does not mean that none of the job task components used in the construction of that overall index has any relationship to how the workers feel about the job rotation proposal. There is some evidence, for example, that the following job-task-related factors may be related to how the worker tends to judge the desirability of a job rotation proposal:

1. How important or salient the absence of variety in job methods is to the worker.
2. How much of the worker's potential ideas and skills are used on the job.
3. How important the quality of his work is to the worker, compared to quantity or speed of work.

The first point suggests that the comparison should not be between workers in high task levels and those in low task levels, but rather between those workers in low levels who are bothered by being in such jobs. That is, saliency needs to be taken into account. If we analyze the workers' evaluation of job rotation training in these terms, we do get results in the expected direction. Among workers with low task ratings who are bothered at least sometimes by having little variety, 56 percent say that job rotation training would be a good idea, in contrast to only 43 percent of all the others with low task ratings.

Another finding in this type of comparison supports the analysis by Turner and Lawrence in their *Industrial Jobs and the Worker*. It also tends to reinforce some of the conclusions by Hulin and Blood from their research concerning the role of such factors as urban size and community characteristics in "job satisfaction" and the effectiveness of job rotation efforts. As stated earlier, we were able to ascertain whether the worker was born in the urban area where he was interviewed (a "native urbanite"), or a migrant to that area. Among the Pennsylvania native urbanites, only 46 percent approved of the idea of job rotation training, as compared to 57 percent of the migrants.

Native urbanites are not only less receptive to the idea of job rotation, they are also less positive in their overall job task ratings compared to migrants in our sample.[31] This is especially true among the older workers.

Nevertheless, there are some native urbanites in favor of job rotation— 46 percent of them. As our working force becomes more and more urbanized, and as more and more of our workers become native urbanites (people born in large urban areas and *not* moving from them), resistance on their part to possibly innovative ideas should warrant serious attention on the part of analysts and policy makers dealing with work-related problems.

Our analysis reveals that young native urbanites in our sample, those under 40, are as much in favor of the idea of job rotation as all the other migrants. Perhaps this is a portent of how the new generation of urban workers—those already in the labor force, and those entering in the near future— will react. In other words, there is the possibility that the Turner and Lawrence conclusions, and those of Hulin and Blood, on city-town differences in job satisfaction and in response to job rotation efforts, may turn out to have a time dimension. That is, as older workers in the native urbanite population move out of the labor force, the next generation of native urbanite workers may be different with respect to new proposals for improving the nature of work.[32]

When we combine the variables of authoritarianism and achievement values, we find that among the native urbanites with low authoritarianism and high achievement values, 58 percent are in favor of job rotation compared to only 41 percent of all other native urbanites.[33]

What all this amounts to, then, is that approval of the idea of job rotation is virtually the same for native urbanite and migrant workers, *if* they are characterized by low authoritarianism and high achievement values.

Perhaps the real challenge is how to persuade workers on jobs with little variety, autonomy, and responsibility to *volunteer* for such innovative efforts as job rotation. Given the fact that they apparently may be the ones with the greatest need for such experiments but simultaneously the least willing to volunteer, it seems the challenge is to develop effective incentives and arguments for them to try out the idea. Obviously, some types of workers have less need for job experience variety. The fact that they may accurately describe their tasks as allowing for little or no variety does not mean that this objective fact bothers them. As stated at the outset of this discussion, workers in favor of the job rotation idea have a dramatically higher percentage indicating that the lack of variety bothers them—74 percent vs. only 48 percent of those against the idea. Again, it is not the lack of variety that explains the preference for job rotation; it is rather the saliency of such a lack that is the vital element.

"HOW TO GET AHEAD" AND THE DISCREPANCY BETWEEN WORKER ASPIRATIONS AND ACHIEVEMENT

While success, or getting ahead, is considered a major cultural theme in American society, a wide-range of beliefs are held regarding how success is achieved. Differences in these beliefs are related to the nature of the worker's job. In our study, we asked workers: "Do most people get ahead more as a result of luck, or education, or knowing the right people, or through working at it?"

The more positive the worker's job tasks, the more he is likely to believe that most people get ahead as a result of education and/or through working at it.[34] The more negative his tasks, the more likely the worker is to state that the way most people succeed is rather through luck and/or knowing the right people. Among Pennsylvania workers only, the proportion in the most positive job tasks, claiming education and/or hard work as the way to success is more than three times the proportion that believe luck and/or knowing the right people are the ways to get ahead. Conversely, among workers in the most negative job tasks, education and/or hard work are mentioned less frequently than luck and/or knowing the right people.

As discussed later, these two different outlooks are related to alienation. Alienated workers are more likely to reject education and/or working at it as the best ways of getting ahead. They might even be said to reject achievement as a value or goal in life. Alienation may be a situational factor which, in this case, would mean that workers who feel they have not become successful tend to place less emphasis on persistence or striving, as exemplified through education or working at it.

These differences in beliefs about how people succeed, according to job task ratings, are most prevalent among the under-55 workers in the Pennsylvania sample. Among the older workers, it must be pointed out, the belief in education and/or working at it is quite strong and is not really related to their job tasks. Regardless of task rating, three-fifths of the older workers assert their belief in this way-to-success theme.[35] Among the under-55 workers, such belief is lower and varies according to their task rating:

Education and Working at It as Ways of Getting Ahead,
According to Under-55 Workers, by Job Task Rating
(Pennsylvania Only)

	Most Positive			Most Negative	All under 55
	1	2	3	4	
Education and/or working at it	71%	52%	49%	38%	52%

If alienation as a concept includes the notion of the individual's estrangement from the dominant value themes of his society, our Pennsylvania interviews and the questions used to measure alienation tend to confirm that notion. In saying that, we assume that a major theme of our society continues to be a stress on the value of education and working hard, although some social critics assert that we are witnessing a decline in this ethic. The alienated worker in our sample accepts this theme much less than does the non-alienated worker.

When asked if most people get ahead more as a result of luck, education, knowing the right people, or through working at it, 45 percent of the highly-alienated workers in the Pennsylvania sample chose education and/or working at it as the way or ways most people get ahead. But among the workers with lower alienation scores, the proportion was 60 percent (a difference significant at the .02 level).

The alienated workers in the lower task levels are thus the least likely to believe in the value of education and/or working at it as one of the ways to get ahead. This raises the intriguing question as to whether such individuals are rationalizing their relatively lower socio-economic status or, instead, are in such a status because of their life orientation that is dominated by a belief in chance and fatalism—thus indulging in a type of self-fulfilling prophecy.

Aspiration-Achievement Discrepancy

One of the major orientations in the analysis of the interviews with these white male union members has to do with aspirations pertaining to the job and to life in general, on the one hand, and the extent to which the worker feels he has actually attained those goals. We have called this an Aspiration-Achievement Discrepancy measure. As reported in the previous chapter, three questions were used to ascertain the degree of discrepancy between aspirations and achievement—dealing with the job, achievement since leaving school, and progress over the past decade in the things wanted out of life. Their combined answers were used to construct a continuum of aspiration-achievement discrepancy, and the extent to which Pennsylvania workers have achieved as much as they had aspired to is without any doubt related to their job task ratings. To a lesser extent, the same is true of the Kalamazoo workers.

Proportion of Workers with High Discrepancy between Aspirations and Achievement, by Job Task Rating

	Most Positive Rating			Most Negative Rating
	1	2	3	4
Percent with high aspiration-achievement discrepancy	26%	27%	46%	66%
Number of cases	(53)	(71)	(56)	(53)

On each of the separate measures used to construct this discrepancy index, its relationship to job task rating is indisputable.

Aspirations and Income Adequacy

In the previous chapter, the major focus was on the significance of the Aspiration-Achievement Discrepancy Index in connection with the recent flurry over workers with the "blues." That discussion attempts to provide an argument for concern—on the part of public leaders and responsible organizations—with workers' aspirations, and the degree to which they do or do not achieve them. Here we want to present some results of a slightly different analysis—of the characteristics of the workers with a high Discrepancy Index—but with a different wrinkle, having to do with whether or not they also feel their individual take-home pay is adequate to meet their family's usual bills and expenses. One out of every seven workers in our Pennsylvania sample was found to have a high Discrepancy Index and also stated that his take-home pay is not enough. The comparison here is between (1) that group of workers with a High Discrepancy Index and who say their take-home pay is not adequate, and (2) the total sample of Pennsylvania workers. Each of these measures taken separately is related to the workers' job task ratings. That is, the Discrepancy Index by itself, and adequacy of take-home pay by itself, are related separately to these task ratings.

In what ways are these Pennsylvania workers with a high Discrepancy Index and inadequate take-home pay different from the rest of their fellow workers?

The workers with a high discrepancy between aspirations and achievement, and who also judge their take-home pay as inadequate—compared to the total sample:

1. Are less educated, with lower hourly wages, and lower family income
2. Have more dependents and, at the same time, are more likely to have two or more wage-earners in the family.
3. Receive lower family incomes despite the fact that they have twice the average proportion with two or more earners.
4. Are also more likely to be middle-aged (40–54) than the total sample (but this is not the same thing as saying that most middle-aged workers are of this type).
5. Have experienced more unemployment.
6. Participated less in the 1968 election; but if they did vote, they voted disproportionately for George Wallace, by more than 2 to 1.
7. Are slightly more alienated. On one of the items used to measure alienation, they are clearly far more alienated: nearly half of them do not believe that the lot of the average man is getting better (in contrast to only one-fourth of the total sample).

8. Appear to be no more, and perhaps less, prejudiced than the general sample, despite what might otherwise be expected.

Finally, on the main topic of this general report on how workers rate their job tasks, the workers with a high discrepancy score and inadequate take-home pay are definitely in more negative job tasks. Seven out of every ten rate their tasks at the negative end of the variety-autonomy-responsibility continuum, in contrast to only half of the total sample. In other words, the more negative the worker's rating of his job tasks, the more likely he will also have a higher discrepancy between his job-life aspirations and achievements, and judge his take-home pay as inadequate.

IMAGE OF MINORITY WORKERS AND OF UNION-MANAGEMENT PROGRAMS TO HELP THEM

Because of widespread reports about the reactions of white workers to the efforts on the part of some government agencies, employers, and unions to employ at a more rapid rate members of minority groups, or the "hard core" unemployed and underemployed, we deliberately included in our interviews a carefully worded question to gauge the degree to which such reactions were prevalent. The question was restricted to just those workers with five or more years' experience in their current occupation or with their current employer: "What about the new people that have come on the job over the past year or so—how would you rate them? Have they been just as good on the job as you were when you first got it, better, or not as good?" Among the 200 Pennsylvania workers answering this question, two-fifths replied that such new workers were not as good as they were when they first took their own jobs. If we add those who were uncertain about how they feel, the proportion rises to half. At the other end, 46 percent stated that the new workers on the job were just as good as they themselves were.

The first relevant point here is that such answers appear not to be related to the workers' job task. One factor that is clearly related, however, is age. The older the worker, the greater the proportion indicating that new workers are not as good as they were when they first entered their current jobs. That type of answer ranges from 28 percent of the under-40 workers, to 37 percent of the middle-aged group, and jumps to 52 percent of the workers 55 and older.

As indicated above, this question did not refer explicitly to minority group employees at all. If there is any racial connotation in the answers, it can only be inferred from how these experienced workers answered three additional questions that *deliberately* asked about the race issue:

1. "Do you agree or disagree with this statement: Most Negroes want to get ahead using the same ways other Americans have used to get ahead."

2. "Some people say that employers have been helping minority groups like Negroes and Puerto Ricans too much in getting good training or good jobs for them. Other people say that employers are not helping them enough. What do you think—are they helping too much? Helping in just about the right amount? Or not enough?"

3. "How about unions? Are they helping Negroes and Puerto Ricans too much? Helping in just about the right amount? Or not enough?"

These three questions were asked of all the workers in the Pennsylvania sample, but the analysis here refers to replies of only those 200 experienced workers who were asked the open-end question about new workers. We want first to compare (1) the respondents who believe that new workers in their workplace are not as good as they were when they first took their own jobs, with (2) the respondents saying that new workers are better or just as good, according to how they reply to the questions directly asking about the race issue. And second, we want to see if job tasks are related to these comparisons.

In the first place, there is a connection between negative judgments of new workers and anti-Negro attitudes. For example, 65 percent of the men in our sample saying that new workers are not as good as they were also disagreed with the statement that "Negroes want to get ahead using the same ways other Americans have used to get ahead." In contrast, only 43 percent of those saying that new workers were just as good (or better) disagreed with the statement ($p < .01$). On the second two questions—asking about management and union actions on behalf of Negroes and Puerto Ricans—29 percent of the men with negative evaluations of new workers, but only 16 percent of those with positive evaluations, felt that management and/or unions were doing too much for these minority groups.[36] This difference, too, is significant.

In other words, experienced workers expressing negative evaluations of new workers coming into the workplace in recent years are likely to be expressing some negative attitudes toward Negroes in particular, even though they may make no explicit reference to race when commenting about new workers in general.

But to return to the central theme of this analysis, dealing with job tasks, the data reveal no relationship of workers' tasks to their race attitudes (nor to the more general question about new workers).

NOTES:

1. Wickham Skinner, "The Anachronistic Factory," *Harvard Business Review*, January–February, 1971.

2. *Op. cit.*

3. Furthermore, unlike the Turner and Lawrence project, our study covered nearly 400 workers in several dozen companies in five urban

areas; the feasibility of doing our own direct observational confirmation attempts was very low. A more recent study, *Employee Reactions to Job Characteristics* by J. R. Hackman and E. E. Lawler III, of Yale University (published in 1971 as a *Journal of Applied Psychology* Monograph), also cites the close relationship between workers' own descriptions of their job characteristics and "objective" descriptions.

4. In the Kalamazoo survey of 101 workers, a slightly higher proportion, 53 percent, report a lot or a fair amount of task variety. Thirty percent said they had little or no variety.

5. In Kalamazoo, only 29 percent reported little or almost no opportunity to learn more, but the extent to which this group was bothered by this lack of opportunity was *identical* to the 60 percent found among the Pennsylvania workers.

6. See Turner and Lawrence, *op. cit.* pp. 148–58, for a description of the various weightings given to these separate questions.

7. Using the same cut-off points for the 101 Kalamazoo workers, we found that they were distributed as follows:

$$
\begin{array}{ll}
\text{Most Positive} & 24\% \\
& 32 \\
& 27 } \\
\text{Most Negative} & 17 \left.\phantom{\begin{array}{c}27\\17\end{array}}\right\} 44\% \\
\hline
& 100\%
\end{array}
$$

8. For the Pennsylvania sample, 37 percent would want to hold onto their current jobs. In Kalamazoo, the proportion was 42 percent. The University of Michigan's nationwide survey of all types of workers in late 1969 (for the Department of Labor) revealed a higher proportion, 49 percent. This suggests that for white male blue-collar workers, job attachment as a measure of job satisfaction is lower than for the labor force as a whole.

9. For the sample as a whole, the ratio of workers with favorable judgments about how well their current job measures up to what they originally wanted, to workers with unfavorable judgments is 1.75 to 1. By contrast, the nationwide sample of the University of Michigan (encompassing all occupations, sexes, and races) indicates a ratio of 4.71 to 1. It should be obvious that we are dealing with a much more disappointed group of workers as a whole. The corresponding ratio for the Kalamazoo group was also lower than the national one— 2.63 to 1.

10. If the worker did not say he would retire right away, he was offered

the following alternatives as to how many years he would wait before retiring: less than one year; more than one; less than three years; three years, but less than five; five years, but less than 10; 10 or more years.

11. In the Kalamazoo sample, a much younger group on the whole (only 11 percent are 55 or older), 36 percent would retire right away.

12. Turner and Lawrence used this item to measure the workers' "perceived opportunity to contribute."

13. In Kalamazoo, the percent of workers satisfied with their jobs most of the time ranged from 92 percent in the most positive task level, to 74 percent in next highest level, 73 percent in the third highest level, to only 35 percent in the lowest task level. Corresponding percentages indicating satisfaction only occasionally, hardly ever or never were: (a) 0 percent; (b) 13 percent; (c) 8 percent; and (d) 29 percent.

14. Incidentally, the greatest degree of frequency of dissatisfaction is among younger workers in negative tasks; the greatest degree of satisfaction, among older workers in positive tasks.

15. If concern with success is diminishing amoung younger Americans, as suggested by Charles Reich, our own limited empirical data appear to be out of step with his armchair speculation: the saliency of lack of advancement on their jobs is no weaker than for the older workers. Indeed, it may even be stronger; 27 percent of young (under 30) workers in jobs with little or no chance for getting ahead are very often, or nearly all the time, *bothered* by this restriction, as compared to only 8 percent for the 55 and older workers in the combined Pennsylvania and Kalamazoo samples.

Reich's footloose theorizing may apply to the upper-class youth of today. The presumed differences between such young people and their white working class peers may, of course, form the basis for new opportunities of upward mobility for this working class—a point which is the major theme in Peter and Brigitte Berger's "The Blueing of America," *The New Republic*, April 3, 1971.

16. Migrants to the four Pennsylvania areas reported higher hourly wages, on the average, than native urbanites, for example.

17. Turner and Lawrence, *op. cit.*, and Charles Hulin and Milton Blood, "Alienation, Environmental Characteristics, and Worker Responses," *Journal of Applied Psychology*, Vol. 51, No. 3, 1967, pp. 284–90.

18. "Optimistic" estimates are those with at least a 50 out of 100 expectation of re-employment within a month.

19. *A Theory of the Labor Movement*, 1928. Reprinted by Augustus Kelly Publishers in 1966.

20. In Chapter 5, we will report on the importance of intrinsic job tasks

to workers who have had job security and who enjoy a relatively high wage.

21. Published by American Management Association (New York, 1969). In connection with this issue, see M. Scott Myers, "Overcoming Union Opposition to Job Enrichment," *Harvard Business Review*, May–June, 1971.

22. At the time of the interview, however, 5 percent of the first group (with the most positive task ratings), and only 3 percent of the others, were employed.

23. While this is not exactly the place to discuss the issue, it is highly probable that the lower the age of retirement now being negotiated through collective bargaining, or gained through unsolicited management decision, the lower the age of hiring job applicants. This possibility has been discussed at recent meetings of the Organization for Economic Cooperation and Development. On the facts concerning the fate of older unemployed workers, see Aiken, Ferman, and Sheppard, *Economic Failure, Alienation and Extremism* (University of Michigan Press, 1968); and H. L. Sheppard, ed., *Industrial Gerontology*, (Cambridge: Schenkman Publishers, 1970), and *New Perspectives on Older Workers*, by the same author (Kalamazoo: W. E. Upjohn Institute for Employment Research, 1971).

24. The corresponding Kalamazoo percentage range was from 33 to 88 percent.

25. If we return to an analysis of mobility chances according to wage levels (as a rough index of skill levels), we find that even among workers at the $4.50+ per hour scale, 56 percent of the Pennsylvania workers, and 44 percent of the Kalamazoo workers, say they have little or no chance to get ahead.

26. One provocative finding on this point, dwelt on below, is that workers—at least those 40 and older—anxious to enter new and different occupations and who would take advantage of an upgrading training program are about twice as likely to feel that unions and/or management are doing too much for Negroes and Puerto Ricans.

27. Percentages exclude those not choosing any training program.

28. We have already reported that more than two-fifths of the Pennsylvania workers indicated that their jobs offered little or no opportunity to learn more about their work and to enable them to increase their knowledge of the process and skills associated with their jobs— and also that the saliency of this lack of opportunity was related to their overall job-task ratings. This, too, is another indication of the apparently unmet desire among workers for skill improvement.

29. Published in English by the Free Press, New York, 1961. See also his *Problèmes humains du machinsme industriel*, published in English as

Industrial Society, edited and co-translated by H. L. Sheppard (The Free Press, 1955).

30. Among all the respondents, only half of the Pennsylvania workers, but nearly three-fourths of those in Kalamazoo, thought the suggestion was a good idea.

31. They are also less frequently satisfied with their jobs.

32. But perhaps something else is responsible for the difference between young and old Native Urbanites regarding the job rotation notion. For example, over time, ambitious young workers born in the urban areas may move up and out of the working class, and those left behind become the older workers still to be found in union samples such as this one. We do know that younger workers (under 40) born in the urban areas of our interviews have higher achievement values than the older ones. But within the native urbanite group, the group with the highest proportion in favor of job rotation consists of the under-40 workers with high achievement values (62 percent); and the group with the lowest proportion in favor of the proposal are the older workers with low achievement values (31 percent for the middle-aged as well as for the 55-and-older group).

33. The corresponding proportions among the migrants are 63 percent for those with low authoritarianism and high achievement values in favor of job rotation, but only 52 percent for all the others.

34. Education and working at it have been combined in this analysis because they both imply an active effort on the part of the individual, a certain degree of persistence in reaching a goal or in overcoming obstacles (akin to what is measured in the achievement values scale), which certainly is not as readily associated with the concepts of luck and the right contacts ("pull"). These notions imply much more of a fatalistic, passive, and fortuitous outlook.

35. In Kalamazoo, 90 percent of the 55-and-older workers chose education and/or working at it.

36. In general, the workers in both Pennsylvania and Kalamazoo singled out management more than unions as doing "too much" for minority workers.

Chapter Four

Tasks, Authoritarianism, Alienation, and Political Attitudes

> *Americans highly approve of authority*
> *over things, but they highly disapprove*
> *of authority over people.*
> *—Geoffrey Gorer*

Alienation is a much used and abused word. It can and does mean many things to many people, and sometimes it means many contradictory things. This is not the place to trace its intellectual roots in sociological and philosophical writings and research.[1] As indicated earlier, this study was stimulated in large part by popular discussions about the worker with the "blues," and equivocal references to the middle American white worker, who presumably feels left out, resentful, and distrustful of the social order, has little faith in the responsiveness of the general community and his government to his needs, problems, and status desires—that is, the alienated worker. In our study of the white blue-collar males, we sought to "catch" that alienation syndrome—admittedly in a limited fashion—by asking the workers their degree of agreement with three questions, already described (Chapter 2). "Alienated" (or high alienated) workers in this book are those whose total scores on the three questions placed them in the upper half of the total score range.

The question here is whether there is any relationship between the workers' job tasks and alienation.

Before reporting the findings on this complex subject, we should say first, that alienated workers are less frequently satisfied with their jobs than the non-alienated workers (a difference significant only at the .10 level). To some extent, then, alienation is related to job dissatisfaction.

Second, we asked these men how well their job measured up to the kind they wanted when they first took it. The proportion of the high-alienated workers indicating that their jobs were not very much like the kind they wanted was somewhat higher than among the low-alienated workers (25 vs. 17 percent), but the difference is probably due to chance.

ALIENATION AND JOB TASK RATINGS

To repeat the earlier question, is there a relationship between alienation and the way in which the worker judges various attributes of his job and work situation? As already indicated, a number of questions about the job were asked to determine job task rating and related job attributes:

1. How much opportunity the worker feels his job provides him to learn more about the work and to increase his knowledge of the process and his skill.
2. The degree to which the worker's management puts emphasis on the worker's doing quality work, as opposed to quantity of output.
3. The amount of variety the worker feels he has on the job (in other words, can he do different things, change methods, location, speed of working, and so on).
4. How much freedom he has to do his work as he wants to.
5. How much of his potential ideas and skills the worker feels are used by people on the same kind of job as his.
6. The amount of responsibility the worker feels he has on his job.

Opportunity to Learn on the Job

The workers' responses to this question were unmistakably related to the degree of alienation. Among workers with low alienation, 35 percent said they have little or no opportunity to learn from their jobs. But among those with high alienation, the proportion was much higher—52 percent, a difference significant at less than the .01 level.

Management's Emphasis on Quality Work

Slightly less than one-fourth (24 percent) of the Pennsylvania non-alienated workers, but nearly two-fifths (39 percent) of the alienated ones indicated either that management emphasizes other things such as quantity more than they do the quality of their work, or that management puts almost all the emphasis on things other than quality. This difference, too, was significant ($p = .01$). In Kalamazoo, too, alienation was also found to be related to worker judgment about management emphasis on quality of work.

Variety on the Job

On this job attribute, the workers' answers are not clearly related to alienation, although the difference in responses was in the expected direction. One-third of the low-alienated, and two-fifths of the high-alienated, report that they have little or no variety on their jobs. Nevertheless, the saliency of little or no variety (how frequently the lack bothered the worker) does appear to be greater among the alienated workers.

A major exception exists in the case of alienated Pennsylvania workers who were also low in authoritarianism. More than half of these high-alienated but low-authoritarian workers told us that they have little or no variety on their jobs. Compared to all the other workers—33 percent of whom said the same thing—this special group was clearly different (p = .02). We will discuss below this group of workers and how their unique responses on a number of questions may contribute to a better understanding of worker adjustment to different kinds of jobs (or of better selection for different types of jobs).

Freedom on the Job

We asked the workers whether they had no freedom at all to do their work as they want; little freedom; or were fairly free, or completely free. Here again, their responses were related to degree of alienation. Among the non-alienated, 22 percent, and among the alienated, 32 percent, felt that they had little or no freedom to do their work as they wished (p < .10).

Use of Potential Ideas and Skills

Here, too, the workers' replies were related to degree of alienation. Among the workers with low alienation, 22 percent feel that none or about one-fourth of workers' potential ideas and skills are being used on their jobs, in contrast to 37 percent of those with high alienation scores—a difference that is significant beyond the .01 level of significance.

Responsibility on the Job

This job attribute was probed by two questions, one asking whether the quality of the individual's work was the most important thing, or less important than quantity, speed of working, and other things; the other question, asking the worker whether almost anyone, a good many people, only a limited number of people, or very few people could do his job.

The proportion of alienated workers reporting that quality is not emphasized as much as quantity or other things (or that it is given very little importance) is higher (25 percent) than the proportion of the low-alienated (16 percent)—a difference significant at the .08 level of significance. But on the second question, 52 percent of both groups replied that a good many people, or almost anyone, could do their jobs. This is a high proportion of the total sample, and is by itself a critical finding. Slightly more than half of the workers in this sample apparently have jobs which, in their own estimation, are unchallenging. This lack of any difference between the high and low alienated workers, however, does not mean that social-psychological attitudes are unrelated to the workers' responses to this particular question. Again, it may be related to degree of authoritarianism—to be discussed later.

Total Job Task Rating. The alienated workers are more likely to rate their jobs at the lower, more negative task levels: 53 percent of all our alienated workers (in Pennsylvania and Kalamazoo) are at these levels, compared to 43 percent of the non-alienated (p = .06).

Alienated workers have a very high proportion of negative task individuals who are bothered frequently by being in unsatisfactory jobs—and thus proves to be significantly higher than for the non-alienated workers who also are in negative tasks.

Once again, however, the low authoritarians among the alienated workers stand out as a distinct type. This fact forces us to a consideration of authoritarianism as a variable involved in workers' ratings of their jobs. The non-authoritarians are unique in that their task levels dramatically affect their degree of alienation.

WORKER AUTHORITARIANISM AND JOB TASK RATINGS

Analysis of our interviews suggests very strongly that there is a relationship between the nature of the worker's job and his degree of authoritarianism, but not in the direction implied by Erich Fromm. By authoritarianism we mean, briefly, a person's basic preference for, or tendency toward, strong, strict leadership if in a *follower* position; and if in a *leadership* position, a preference for, or tendency toward, behavior with subordinates characterized by little tolerance for discretionary behavior on their part, and by impatience with prolonged discussion by others about his wishes or commands. Authoritarians tend to be more comfortable in order-taking (or in order-giving) situations. Authoritarian individuals also tend to be characterized by less acceptance of, or readiness for change.[2] In the present study, we used three basic statements, asking the worker how much he agrees with them:

> "The most important thing to teach children is absolute obedience to their parents."
> "Any good leader should be strict with people under him in order to gain their respect."
> "A few strong leaders could do more for this country than all the laws and talk."

But the relationship among the Pennsylvania workers between task level and authoritarianism is not the sort that one might predict on the basis of Erich Fromm's theory expressed in the following statement:

> If . . . a bored and angry blue-collar worker on a repetitive job develops traits of violence, anger, sadism, slight depression and indifference . . . he will some-

times be a bad citizen in the sense that he will be easy prey for demagogues who appeal to his resentment and his desire for revenge.[3]

If such a proposition were correct, we should expect the workers in our sample who report the least variety, autonomy, and responsibility on the job to be more authoritarian, at least as measured by the questions used in our interview. But that is the very opposite of what we found. Instead, workers in the highest task levels are the most authoritarian, and those in the lowest levels, the least authoritarian.[4]

It is important to note that one of the three items in the measure of authoritarianism has to do with a preference for strong leaders as opposed to "all the laws and talk." This measure should bear directly on the proposition suggested by Fromm. On this one separate statement, its relationship to negative job tasks is even stronger than is the overall response to the three statements combined. Among those agreeing with this one statement (the authoritarians), only 41 percent had negative job task ratings. Among those disagreeing (the non-authoritarians), the proportion with lower ratings was considerably higher—58 percent (p < .01).

Fromm's theory would lead us to believe that the negative nature of a job (such as boredom and repetitiveness) operates as a determinant of a worker's basic political-psychology orientation, leading him, for example, to be attracted to demagogues. But our own findings suggest an opposite and equally provocative interpretation—that authoritarianism is much more likely to be a determinant and not a result in this situation. Our results suggest that authoritarian workers will be the most likely to accept and tolerate jobs with little variety, autonomy, and opportunities to use their potential.

Could this observation also help us to understand the contemporary job behavior of today's young workers who, partly because of their better education, are less authoritarian and hence more antagonistic to the nature of so many jobs as structured today? (A separate chapter on the young workers documents this in greater detail.)

Putting it another way, workers with authoritarian personalities apparently have less need to be in jobs with some degree of discretion to do the job the way they want; they more readily accept jobs that do not challenge their imagination and creativity. Instead of the job being the cause of their basic political tendencies, it could well be that their personalities (of which authoritarianism is a part) are among the causes of the way in which they rate their jobs. This is completely opposite to Fromm's theory. If authoritarianism is a basic personality characteristic—part of the individual's social character—it means that it is developed long before the individual enters the world of work. And if it is basic, it also means that work experience may have little effect on degree of authoritarianism among workers.

If my interpretation is correct, we should also expect to find that among the few authoritarian workers who *do* report less variety, autonomy, and use of potential skills and ideas on their jobs, fewer of them will be bothered by such things, when compared with the non-authoritarian workers who also attribute negative characteristics to their jobs. And this is precisely what we find. Authoritarian workers are less likely to report that their jobs have little variety, and so on, but if they do, they are not as frequently bothered by the lack of such job attributes. Conversely, non-authoritarian workers are less likely to see positive features in their jobs, and more likely to complain about the lack of such features. In other words, the non-authoritarians turn out to have a higher "job complaint score" than the authoritarian workers—38 percent as compared to only 24 percent (p = .05).[5] The non-authoritarians in high level tasks who do not have a high complaint score will probably be the least alienated. But if they are in low-level task and complain a lot, their alienation may be as high as among all the other workers.

THE JOINT EFFECTS OF JOB TASK AND AUTHORITARIANISM ON WORKER ALIENATION

Part of the search for such a reformulation of Fromm's proposition leads us to the following question: Is alienation, like authoritarianism, something that affects how a worker will respond to the nature of his job? Or is it actually something that might, in part, result from the interaction of the other two factors: (1) the worker's personality (at least his degree of authoritarianism), and (2) his job?

My belief is that it is more likely to be the latter, that alienation is situational. That belief emerges from many tabulations, cross-tabulations, and dissections of the answers in our interviews. The belief is that alienation is partly (not completely, of course) affected by the fact that authoritarianism influences how the worker defines his job. In other words, job task ratings as influenced by the "intervening variable" of degree of authoritarianism are involved in the development of a worker's alienation. Authoritarians are more likely to be alienated than non-authoritarians, but among the authoritarians, the worker's task level makes little difference as to whether or not a worker is alienated. Whether a non-authoritarian has a positive or negative rating of his job tasks, however, does make quite a lot of difference in how alienated he is.

Authoritarian workers who say their jobs allow for little variety or freedom as to how to perform them are hardly more alienated (55 percent) than the authoritarians who say the opposite (50 percent). But consider the non-authoritarians: Those who say they have little or no variety or freedom are more likely to be alienated (42 percent) than those who report more freedom and variety (only 24 percent).

What I'm suggesting is that job task rating seems to be affected partly by how authoritarian a worker is, and in turn, his alienation is partially a joint effect of authoritarianism and job task. Workers can be alienated by the nature of the job they perform, especially if they are low in authoritarianism. The job does not determine whether or not they are authoritarian. Authoritarianism is apparently a factor more related to the nature of the worker's personality. But alienation, on the other hand, may be much more situational; in this case, something emerging directly or indirectly from the nature of the job, as mediated by how authoritarian he is.

Regardless of workers' job tasks, authoritarians are bound to be much more alienated than non-authoritarians, but taking only the non-authoritarians, variations in the nature of the job task do affect their chances of becoming alienated.

Instead of presenting more examples, let us simply show variations in alienation between workers with positive and negative Total Job Task Ratings (based on the six questions relating to variety, autonomy, and use of potential skills and ideas), depending on whether or not they are authoritarian. (The following table includes the Kalamazoo as well as the Pennsylvania workers.)

Proportion of Workers with High Alienation, by Authoritarianism and Total Job Task Ratings

	Non-Authoritarians		Authoritarians	
	Positive Tasks	Negative Tasks	Positive Tasks	Negative Tasks
Percent with high alienation	23%	41%	48%	51%

This table shows that the workers with the least alienation (23 percent) are the non-authoritarians employed in high-level tasks. Among non-authoritarian workers who indicate that their jobs contain attributes that provide for variety, autonomy, and responsibility, the proportion with high alienation is only about half that among non-authoritarians who indicate otherwise. Among the authoritarians, however, job ratings make hardly any difference in degree of alienation.[6] This proposition holds true even when we consider separately the native urbanites and the migrants in our sample. (This point needs to be made since native urbanites, in general, tend to be most alienated). The personality and work variables associated with low alienation, therefore, are non-authoritarianism and meaningful job tasks.

AUTHORITARIANISM, JOB TASK RATINGS, AND SKILL LEVEL

As already indicated, workers who are non-authoritarian tend to rate their tasks negatively—as having less autonomy, less variety, and so on. But this generalization may leave the reader with the impression that perception or rating of job tasks is essentially or only a function of the worker's personality; that the variations in such ratings are merely in accordance with variations in the way workers psychologically respond to work conditions and situations—irrespective of the variations in the objective job tasks as such.

We do not want to convey this sort of unqualified impression. There are certain aspects about the nature of the job itself that affect the worker's reaction to it. The reader should also be reminded of Turner and Lawrence's own objective confirmation of the workers' "subjective" ratings of their job tasks.

Using hourly wages as an index of skill-level, we find that there is a clear relationship between hourly wages and job task ratings among the Pennsylvania workers:

1. Among workers earning under $3.00 per hour, only 10 percent were in the most positive rating category.
2. Among those earning between $3.00 and $4.00, the corresponding proportion rose to 17 percent.
3. Among those earning above $4.00 per hour, the proportion with the most positive job task rating climbs to 27 percent.

In other words, the higher the hourly wage, the greater the proportion of workers in positive tasks. Personality, in other words, is not the only factor associated with job task rating. The following table presents the data according to wage distribution for each of the four task groups among the Pennsylvania workers:

	Most Positive Tasks			Most Negative Tasks
	1	2	3	4
A. Percent earning $4.01+	46%	38%	35%	19%
B. Percent earning under $3.01	10	16	17	32
Ratio of A to B	*4.60*	*2.38*	*2.06*	*0.59*

It should be quite clear from this table that a worker's job-task level is related to skill level, as measured by hourly wages. But this does not detract from the fact that authoritarianism plays an important role in the worker's rating of his tasks. For example: Within each skill level (or hourly wage level), the authoritarian workers have a more positive task rating than the non-authoritarians. The table below presents the differences in proportions of Pennsylvania workers with positive ratings, holding *both* wage level and authoritarianism constant.

Proportions with Positive Job Task Rating, by Wage Level
and Authoritarianism

	$3.00 or Less		$3.01–$4.00		$4.01 or More	
	High Authoritarianism	Low Authoritarianism	High Authoritarianism	Low Authoritarianism	High Authoritarianism	Low Authoritarianism
Percent with positive task ratings	45%	29%	51%	40%	63%	57%

Only as we move into the highest wage levels (more than $4.00 per hour), do we begin to see little difference in task ratings between high and low authoritarians. The main point is that authoritarianism, even when wages are taken into consideration, affects the rating the worker gives to his job tasks. When taken together, the joint effect of wage level and authoritarianism is substantial: the lowest-paid, non-authoritarian workers have, by far, the lowest proportion with a positive task rating, while the highest-paid authoritarian workers have the greatest percentage with a positive task rating (29 percent vs. 63 percent).

WAGES, FAMILY INCOME, AND MIGRANT STATUS

Wage Rate. The average hourly wage rate of the less alienated workers is higher than that for the alienated ones, $3.87 vs. $3.62 per hour. If we assume that individual earnings should be related to degree of alienation, this finding is in the expected direction, although the difference in hourly wages is not clearly statistically significant.

Total Family Income. Family income, however, clearly does make a difference. Among the non-alienated, 45 percent reported family incomes of $10,000 or more, while among the alienated workers, the proportion with $10,000 or more was only 28 percent—a difference that is definitely significant in the statistical sense (p = .02).

In a separate chapter we will return to the issue of the relative importance of job tasks to the worker, as compared to his problems of job security and wage adequacy. For many people these latter problems are the only ones worth worrying about. Suffice it to say at this point that even among the workers who have attained some modicum of job security and who work at relatively high wages that differences in job tasks still make a difference in how alienated they are.

Migrant Status. Alienation as measured in this study seeks to tap more than individualistic, psychological moods of human beings; that is, there are some social, situational dimensions to such moods. Sociologists might put this more grandiosely by talking about the "social structure" within which various degrees of alienation or anomie are engendered. As mentioned before, one such social variable in our data is the worker's migrant status—whether he is a native of the urban area in which he lives, or a migrant from another urban or a rural area. Apparently, high alienation among the workers in our Pennsylvania survey is related to the status of being a non-migrant (a native urbanite). Among the native urbanites, 44 percent had high alienation scores, in contrast to only 32 percent of the migrants (p = .05).

POLITICAL EFFICACY AND ALIENATION

Alienation is not merely a matter of personal futility feelings. Workers with high alienation, for example, believe much less than those with low alienation that political change is possible and that the individual citizen can play a part in making that change possible. Among those with high alienation scores, only 39 percent had a high degree of political efficacy, as compared to 63 percent of the low alienation workers (p < .001).

High-alienated workers are strikingly unique in their agreement with the first two of the following three statements used to assess the workers' feelings of political efficacy:

	High-Alienated	Low-Alienated
"People like me don't have any say about what the government does."	64%	35%
"There's little use in writing to public officials because often they aren't really interested in the problems of the average man."	67%	42%
"The way people vote is the main thing that decides how things are run in the country."	56%	48%

We have consciously chosen a value position that, in our type of society, we need a citizenry characterized by a feeling of some effectiveness in the broader political process and by a feeling that they are not estranged (alienated) from the general society.

If anyone wants to question this value position, let him consider the following:

1. The non-alienated worker with political efficacy is clearly less authoritarian. For example, he disagrees to a considerably greater extent than his opposite number that, "A few strong leaders could do more for this country than all the laws and talk."
2. He registers the lowest discrepancy between his aspirations and achievements.
3. He participates in elections to a greater extent.
4. If he voted, he was less likely to vote for George Wallace.

5. His acceptance of politics as a legitimate sphere of activity in our society is far greater than that of his opposite extreme.[7]

6. He is less critical of new workers entering his workplace.

7. In this connection, he is also more likely to agree that, "Negroes want to get ahead using the same ways other Americans have used to get ahead."

Therefore, we need to know more about the conditions that make for such a citizenry—of whom the union members studied here are a vital part.

Accordingly, the workers in the Pennsylvania sample were classified by whether or not they were high or low in the scores of *both* the political efficacy and alienation measures used in the interviews. The following table indicates how the overall Pennsylvania sample was distributed according to such a typology (high in efficacy and low in alienation; low in efficacy and high in alienation, and so on):

	Percent of Total Sample
High political efficacy *and* low alienation	38%
Low efficacy, *but* low alienation	22
High efficacy, *but* high alienation	15
Low political efficacy, *and* high alienation	24
	99%

The two critical types in our discussion are the first and the fourth in the table above, for they represent extreme opposites—with the first consisting of workers with the "ideal" attributes for a healthy body socio-politic, and the latter consisting of workers with the least desirable attributes—again from my value standpoint.[8]

But the critical question in this present context is: Are such types different from each other with respect to their job tasks? The overall answer is an unambiguous yes. For example, among all workers with the most positive job task ratings, more than two-fifths are in the "most desirable" classification (in other words, high political efficacy and low alienation). Among the workers with the most negative ratings, only a third are in the same classification. The distribution of the workers with the "less desirable" attributes—those who are alienated and who also feel less effective politically—runs in the opposite direction. While less than one-fifth of the workers with the most positive ratings of their tasks are in the "least desirable" efficacy-alienation grouping, the proportion who are alienated and who have little feeling of political efficacy among the workers with the most negative ratings is more than one-fourth.

This relationship between such efficacy-alienation types and job task level is prevalent in all three age groups dealt with in this analysis. Appendix

A, Table 2, summarizes the differences, within each age group, in the distribution of efficacy-alienation types according to job task rating. Within each age group, workers in positive job tasks are more likely to be characterized by feelings of political effectiveness and low alienation when compared to workers with negative task perceptions. Only in the oldest age group, with negative tasks, does the least desirable type exceed the most desirable type.

POLITICAL EFFICACY AND PERSONAL ACHIEVEMENT VALUES

The previous discussion dealt with the relationship of the workers' job tasks to a typology of political effectiveness and personal futility or alienation. We will return shortly to alienation. There is another but related typology that lays stress not merely on the individual's feelings of effectiveness in the political sphere, but also on the degree to which the individual feels he has some mastery or control over his own personal goals—as measured by a number of questions which presumably deal with what social psychologists (such as Bernard Rosen) refer to as achievement values.[9]

Rosen's concept of achievement values has, to some degree, a component of the economic success facet of human behavior, but it refers to much more than that. It includes an awareness of and willingness to carry out these actions necessary for achieving. These actions involve planning, working, and, perhaps, making sacrifices—all of which are related to orientations on the part of the individual concerning:

1. activism vs. passivism
2. a present vs. future outlook
3. individualism

These achievement values are measured by the extent of agreement with these six statements:

1. "In his work, all a person should want is a secure, not-too-difficult job, with enough pay for a nice car and home."
2. "Nowadays a person has to pretty much live for today and let tomorrow take care of itself."
3. "When a person is born, the success he will have is in the cards, so he may as well accept it."
4. "It is best to have a job as part of an organization all working together, even if you don't get individual credit."
5. "Don't expect too much out of life and be content with what comes your way."
6. "Planning only makes a person unhappy since your plans hardly ever work out anyway."

There is a definite relationship between a worker's job task rating and this joint measure of political efficacy and achievement values. Appendix A, Table 3, indicates the ratio of proportion of workers high on both measures to the proportion low on both, by age and job task rating.

The overall comparison between all workers with a positive job task perception and those with a negative one (2.31 vs. 1.29)—as well as comparison in each age group—suggests quite clearly the relationship of such task ratings to what might be called a *political personality* measure. It suggests that workers with tasks characterized by variety, autonomy, and responsibility are more likely to be the ones to feel some degree of control over both (1) personal lives, and (2) the more external political process.

What is of significance for us is that these different types of human beings are *not* distributed randomly, on a chance basis, in the world of work. Workers with job tasks allowing for greater variety, autonomy, and responsibility are more likely to be men who take an activist orientation toward their lives, who feel that they themselves have something to say in affecting their personal fate, and who also feel their voice means something in the political process of the society.[10]

We are not categorically stating here what the causal direction is— whether the nature of the job affects an individual's degree of personal and political efficacy or whether the latter affects an individual's choice of job. We would at least argue, however, that any effort to improve the degree of variety, autonomy, and responsibility built into a given set of job tasks should increase the probabilities that new workers with high achievement values and political efficacy might be induced to remain with such jobs longer.

Furthermore, the findings suggest the advisability of some type of long-term experimentation in such job changes, with appropriate research design, for the purpose of discovering whether any changes in non-job attributes of the worker occur. Until such experimentation is carried out, the arguments over what is cause and what is effect will go on interminably. Armchair debates and haggling over survey findings will not solve the issue. Finally, we would like to offer the notion that it frequently happens that variables in the social sphere can be both cause and effect, and that effects often acquire a "functional autonomy" of their own.

VOTING BEHAVIOR AND ALIENATION

Alienation also is related to more than other subjective attitudes or values. Voting behavior, too, is possibly affected by, or related to, degree of alienation, by the belief that the lot of the average man is not getting better; that one doesn't know whom he can trust; that, with the way things look for the future, it's hardly fair to bring children into the world.

In our Pennsylvania sample, there was a slight relationship (in the expected direction, but not significant in the statistical sense) between high alienation and not voting at all. In Kalamazoo, nearly half (47 percent) of the alienated, but less than a third (25 percent) of the non-alienated, did not vote.

One specific statement used in the alienation items ("It's hardly fair to bring children into the world with the way things look for the future") yielded a very sharp relationship to the voting choices of our total sample of workers who actually voted in 1968 (including the Kalamazoo group). The following table shows the difference in Presidential choices between those workers agreeing and those disagreeing with that statement:

1968 Presidential Choices, by Agreement or Disagreement with:
"It's hardly fair to bring children into the world
with the way things look for the future."

	Alienated (Agree)	Non-Alienated (Disagree)
Humphrey	33%	53%
Nixon	33	31
Wallace	18	7
Others; refused	16	9
	100%	100%
Number of cases	(94)	(174)

Note: Agreement with the statement indicates an
alienated outlook.

This table reveals that alienation (as measured by agreement or disagreement with the statement) is unquestionably related to the workers' choice of President in the 1968 election. The probability that this relationship is due to chance is nearly 1 out of a thousand.[11] More concretely, it shows that (1) alienated workers (as measured by this one item) are far more likely to have voted for Wallace than non-alienated workers (18 vs. 7 percent), and (2) that the non-alienated workers are far more likely to have voted for Humphrey than the alienated ones (53 vs. 33 percent). Alienation as measured by this one item, however, made no difference as far as the Nixon vote was concerned.

Furthermore, it may not be surprising that the low-alienated worker tends to call himself a "liberal" to a significantly greater extent than a worker with high alienation—49 percent, as compared to only 24 percent ($p < .001$).

ERICH FROMM REVISITED

These last findings bring us back to the earlier discussion of Erich Fromm's theory about boring jobs and the attractiveness of demagogic leaders on the part of workers in such jobs. If we concentrate on the possible effects of the job (as mediated through the degree of a worker's authoritarianism) upon the degree of his alienation, we might be onto a more accurate formulation of what it was that Fromm was trying to say. In other words, low authoritarian workers in jobs with little variety and autonomy are more likely to be alienated, and their being alienated (not authoritarian) may lead to the behavior suggested by Fromm. To check out that broad proposition, let's take a look at the low authoritarian workers in our Pennsylvania sample who rate their jobs as being low in variety and/or autonomy, and see if the alienated workers among them voted disproportionately for George Wallace in 1968. In this particular analysis, we will use as our concrete measure of alienation whether or not the worker agrees with the statement that, "the lot of the average man is getting better, not worse." Workers disagreeing with that statement are defined here as being alienated. But first, workers with these characteristics (alienated, non-authoritarians with little job variety and/or autonomy) had a very high non-voting record in 1968. Second, they stand out conspicuously as having a negative image of the political sphere when asked to give their meaning of "active in politics." And finally, their voting record for George Wallace was way above the total sample average.

Thus, as a result of going through this complicated type of analysis, one could say that Fromm may be correct in that certain types of workers with low job variety and demeaning tasks can be and are attracted to a type of demagogue such as George Wallace. But Fromm's formulation is correct only if we refer to workers in dehumanizing jobs who are also non-authoritarian and alienated. Exactly half of this special group either did not vote at all or voted for Wallace (based only on workers of voting age in 1968). This high proportion should be contrasted with the overall sample percentage of approximately one-quarter not voting at all or voting for Wallace.

The critical point here is that Fromm may be correct in his position that the nature of a man's job affects his behavior and opinions regarding political issues (including attraction to one or another political leader), but only for certain kinds of men—men who, because of their lack of authoritarian tendencies, become alienated as a result of particular kinds of job tasks. Such job tasks are the kind described throughout this book. Finally, it must be made very clear that in none of his writings does Fromm provide us with any hard evidence based on empirical information and facts (nor do the writings of Marx, a major source of Fromm's theoretical and moral concerns).[12]

This does not mean that Fromm is altogether wrong, however. Our own analyses of the empirical facts gleaned from our interviews confirm his general (if poorly articulated) feeling that work does have an effect on man, that such a theory is not just a matter of the projected feelings of intellectuals and other pundits who, in effect, would be and are repelled if they themselves had to engage in job tasks with little variety, little autonomy, and little challenge to their potentials.

At one time in the past, such a charge may have been closer to the truth. But our own evidence suggests that, in this particular respect, the gap between the emerging class of workers (i.e., the young workers, as will be seen in a separate chapter on them) and such intellectuals has been narrowing—that an increasing proportion of workers themselves are repelled by jobs involving low tasks. And it is in this connection that Fromm's concept of "social character" becomes relevant. In this study, we consider our measure of authoritarianism as part of social character. Because the social character of today's working class is different (at least with respect to its orientation toward authority), the impact of the nature of work is beginning to show itself as never before.

The social character of today's workers is different because they have been socialized (have grown up) into a society without mass misery and with a widespread emphasis on a "good life for all." Their social character is also different because they are the children (or grandchildren) of immigrants, and not the immigrants themselves. (Immigrants from European peasantry tend to be more authority-oriented.) Furthermore, their social character is different because they have not known through direct personal experience the dehumanizing, demeaning traumas of mass, long-term joblessness. It is also different because they have come to accept much more seriously their rights and privileges as articulated in our ideology of equalitarianism.

They know or expect, perhaps without too much conscious reflection, that they will not suffer from lack of basic material security. At least they act and make decisions as if this knowledge or expectation is basically correct. What will happen if our government's economic policies fail to live up to the new generation's expectations (and the other demands stemming from the emergence of this different social character) is anyone's guess.

Returning to alienation and the nature of work, the social character of the new worker has relevance within the context of the following statement by Scharr, who otherwise is quite critical of Fromm's general outlook:

> Anyone who deplores alienation from work and who believes in the dignity and worth of the individual must think seriously about [the] contrast between industrial man and free man. Such thought ought to start from the recognition that nothing will replace the individual's need for and satisfaction in the creation of a whole product which he deems worthy and good, or for contributing his best efforts to a common task which he has accepted and which he understands in its entirety. If these goals are not compatible with the profitable, or efficient, operation of a huge industrial enterprise or a massive bureaucratic administrative and business structure, then perhaps the huge factory and the massive bureaucracy ought to be dismantled. . . .
>
> . . . The modern worker works at a task and a pace neither of which he sets himself. He is kept under constant surveillance not by a human warder . . .

but by the nonhuman logics of time and efficiency. His performance is judged and his rewards allotted by intricate computing machines capable of juggling complex performance equations made up of numerous standard terms for energy, cost, time, motion, and the like. (pp. 271–72.)

Scharr goes on to note that the trade unions agree to such a system and that this "is just another index of how far we have come from any real understanding of dignity and freedom in work." To be sure, he gives full credit to the unions for reducing the exploitation of workers and for introducing "something like a constitutional order of fair play in industry." But, he continues,

> when we see the union agreeing to piecework schemes, standard norms and rates of work, duties and rewards determined by time-motion principles, and the like, we must ask whether this is fair play for real human beings, or whether it is fair play for men who are treated as though they were machines which must be handled carefully and maintained properly if they are to perform at their fullest capacity. (p. 272.)

The new element in all this is the development of a social character in America that is clearly anti-authoritarian and which places a greater priority on equalitarianism and on dignity—even in the workplace. In the absence of such conditions in the workplace, the modern worker (especially the young worker who is extremely anti-authoritarian) involved in job tasks that deny his impulse toward equalitarianism and dignity will develop symptoms that are undesirable both to him and to the society around him.[13]

NOTES:

1. See, for example, Dwight Dean, "Alienation: Its Meaning and Measurement," *American Sociological Review*, October 1961; Gwynn Nettler, "A Measure of Alienation," *Ibid.*, December, 1957; Melvin Seeman, "On the Meaning of Alienation," *Ibid.*, December, 1959; Robert Blauner, *Alienation and Freedom: The Factory Worker and His Industry* (Chicago: University of Chicago Press, 1964); and Karl Marx, "Alienated Labor," reprinted in Eric and Mary Josephson, eds., *Man Alone: Alienation in Modern Society* (New York: Dell Publishing Co., 1962).
2. For an extensive and lucid discussion of the meaning of this concept, see Roger Brown, *Social Psychology* (New York: The Free Press, 1965) especially pp. 477–548); and Richard Hamilton, "Working Class Authoritarianism Reconsidered," in *The Personality and Labor*, in Proceedings of 18th International Congress of Psychology,

Moscow, 1966. Reproduced by Bureau of Applied Social Research, Columbia University.

3. From a communication quoted in a 1968 report by the Department of Labor on its December, 1968 conference on Job Satisfaction, chaired by Esther Peterson, Assistant Secretary of Labor, at Airlie House, Virginia.

4. Among the Kalamazoo workers, no relationship whatsoever was found, except among the steelworkers—and this, too, was like the relationship discovered in the Pennsylvania sample.

5. If we concentrate only on those non-authoritarians who are alienated, the proportion with high complaint (saliency) scores climbs to 45 percent.

6. In a "3 x 2" table (combining the workers with positive and negative scores among the authoritarians), a Chi-square test indicates that the relationship being tested here is significant at less than a .001 level. In other words, the odds that this relationship (of low alienation to positive task ratings by non-authoritarians) is due to chance is less than one out of a thousand.

7. The importance of the "legitimacy of politics" to a democratic society has been spelled out by Bernard Berelson, in his "Democratic Theory and Public Opinion" in Eulau, Eldersveld, and Janowitz, eds., *Political Behavior* (Glencoe: The Free Press, 1956), pp. 107–16.

8. In Kalamazoo, 44 percent were in the "ideal" category, while only 16 percent were characterized by low political efficacy and high alienation (ratio = 2.75).

9. See, for example, his "Race, Ethnicity, and the Achievement Syndrome," *American Sociological Review*, February, 1959.

10. Analysis of the data indicates that there is no intrinsic connection between achievement values and political efficacy; there is no difference in political efficacy between high and low achievement value workers. In other words, we are not measuring the same thing when we talk about achievement values and political efficacy. These two attributes are discrete characteristics, and together they make for distinct types of citizens, human beings, and workers.

11. Chi square of 12.64, with 3 degrees of freedom.

12. This issue is posed by John H. Scharr, in his *Escape From Authority: The Perspectives of Erich Fromm* (New York: Harper and Row, 1961), in the following form: "Read strictly, Fromm would seem to be saying that one's mode of work determines his character. To demonstrate that thesis would take far more, and far more systematic, knowledge concerning class differences than we now have." (p. 95).

13. Since working out this type of theoretical proposition we have

found, in Alan Fox, *A Sociology of Work in Industry* (London: Collier–Macmillan, 1971), some recognition of the same role to be played by authoritarianism in fulfillment in one's work:

Should we . . . as Friedmann suggests, set ourselves the long-term goal of redesigning work in directions which lead to self-actualization for everyone? . . . There are arguments on two different levels which must caution us in this apparently admirable aim. Those whose life experience and cultural values have created neither the expectation of, nor the aspiration for, self-actualization may prove remarkably resistant to this treatment, *as may also those whose authoritarian personality structure disposes them to prefer a situation of dependence on, and domination by, others.* (Pp. 11–12, italics mine.)

Chapter Five

Economic Factors and the Impact of Meaningless Work

> *. . . fairness and decency for American workers
> means more than simply keeping them alive and safe
> from injury or disease. It means an effort to make it possible
> for workers to live not just as robots or machines,
> but as men and women who are human beings.
> Additionally, making the assembly line more human and humane
> is a large and difficult task,
> but it is at the heart of anything we mean
> by social justice in America.*
> —Senator Edward Kennedy

It is time we stopped fooling ourselves about the sole importance of job security among blue-collar workers. It is obviously important, but too much stress is placed on this single point alone, as if it were the one and only goal or need. This kind of superficial thinking is reminiscent of some of the Soviet economists and industrial social scientists I met in Moscow who insisted that job satisfaction studies are irrelevant in a society in which the workers own the means of production.[1] Once a worker owns the factory in which he works, he is a happy human being and citizen, or so the ideology insists. This is a comforting myth, especially to fools who wish to believe it.

In the same way, many American cynics and critics—and they include employers and managers, union leaders, industrial engineers (especially the industrial engineers), and many "intellectuals" weaned on the doctrine that all that men want or need is job and income security[2]—are the same breed of "know-nothings" who dismiss any concern with alienation (both on and off the job), or any concern with creating meaningful work. Many of them view such concern simply as distracting and clever ruses to keep our minds (especially those of the workers) off the one and only thing that matters—the solution of unemployment and/or the attainment of decent earnings.

What is the proof of their assertions? The best they come up with are either–or propositions, a few examples of cases in which workers—when forced to make a choice—accept a wage increase or a supplementary unemployment benefit over improvements in the nature of their job tasks. But, examples are not proof. Another argument they conjure up is that workers "find their level of job-tasks" and/or that they "adapt" themselves to jobs that many of us would not suffer very long. This argument smacks of Social Darwinism, and it also ignores the possibly unhealthy consequences of "adaptation."

Unfortunately, it is necessary to point out that no one in his right mind has argued that job security and decent income are irrelevant to any human being. But that is what the critics and cynics seem to be hearing when they read about, or participate in discussions about, proposals to "create more meaningful work."

If such critics are correct, we should expect to find that among workers with no unemployment, on-the-job and off-the-job satisfaction will be unaffected by, or unrelated to, the kind of tasks they perform.

But what does the examination of interviews with those blue-collar workers with zero weeks of unemployment over the 20 months prior to being queried tell us about that expectation? The examination reinforces the general proposition that job security is not in itself a guarantee of worker fulfillment. Neither is it a cure for worker alienation.

We find that for non-authoritarian workers, alienation is twice as great among workers in low-level tasks as it is among workers in high-level tasks. (Remember, we are talking here only about workers without any unemployment for the twenty months prior to being interviewed.) The other part of this analysis confirms the findings reported in the previous chapter that alienation among the *authoritarian* workers is the same, regardless of task level.

One of the arguments being made here is that job security is a necessary but not a sufficient condition for low alienation.[3] Two of the sufficient conditions (obviously not all of the sufficient conditions) are, (1) jobs with high variety, autonomy, and responsibility, and (2) non-authoritarianism. An implication is that as authoritarianism declines in our working population (and it is declining, as forcefully reported in Chapter 7, for the youngest workers in our survey), and when and if we attain very low rates of unemployment, alienation will become a *more* critical issue in our society to the degree that we fail to improve the job-content conditions of that working population. We should not wait, however, for that day when truly full employment is the normal order of things. We should not forget that most workers are not unemployed.

Among these never-unemployed workers, the proportion who are non-alienated and who have high political efficacy is also related to job-task level. The higher the task level, the greater the proportion of workers with both low alienation and high political efficacy. We have already pointed out, in Chapter 4, the importance of having non-alienated human beings with feelings of political effectiveness.

The proportion of never-unemployed workers who say that they would prefer a different kind of job, if completely free to change their vocational careers, is related to job-task level. High employment security is, thus, no guarantee of worker attachment to his current job. The same thing is true when it comes to whether the worker would change jobs even for more money. The better the task level, the lower the odds that the never-unemployed worker would not want to change jobs even for more money because the job he has now is a good one. In this context, "better" refers to the intrinsic content of his job tasks. As part of the same story, less than one percent of the never-unemployed workers in the two highest task levels, as opposed to 23 percent of those in the lowest levels, would quit their jobs immediately if they had anything else to do, or would take almost any other job in which they could earn as much as in their current job.

As one more example, these never-unemployed workers differ in how much their jobs measure up to their original expectations. And these differences depend on the type of job they have—again, as measured in terms of variety, autonomy, and responsibility. The more of these attributes in the worker's job, the more likely he is to consider that job as coming close to the kind he wanted when he first took it. The fewer such attributes, the more likely he is to judge his job as not very much like the kind he originally sought.

These selected findings serve only to tell us that alienation and related issues are still (perhaps *especially*) a problem among workers who have not had any unemployment over many months; that one of the major reasons for these continued problems has to do with the kind of job a man has and the kind of tasks that job demands of him. Solving the unemployment problem will not solve the dilemma engendered by boring, monotonous jobs which allow workers little or no freedom to do the work as they want to do it, and in which they are treated as persons with no desire or ability to take on responsible assignments.

But these findings do not completely resolve the issue originally defined in this chapter—that job security is the only important issue to blue-collar workers. So far, we have reported only on the never-unemployed workers. What about the workers in our interviews who have had one week or more of unemployment in the twenty months prior to the time they were interviewed? The critical need here is to compare them with the more fortunate group—the ones we have just talked about. These comparisons provide us with some concrete, factual proof or disproof about the controversy being discussed.

Workers with unemployment experience are slightly more alienated than those without any joblessness, but only if they are in low-level tasks! Unemployment experience does not seem to make any impact on alienation among workers in high-level tasks. The percent with high alienation is the same for these workers as it is for the never-unemployed, high-task-level workers. In other words, even when they have unemployment experience, workers are more alienated if they are in jobs with poor task contents.

The least alienated workers in our sample are those with steady jobs, without any real fears of being laid off, and who are performing tasks that provide for plenty of variety, autonomy, and responsibility. Only 36 percent of the men with such jobs in our sample are alienated. But take a look at the men who have unsteady jobs and who perform tasks with little, if any, variety, autonomy, and responsibility. They have the highest degree of alienation (53 percent). The other workers in the sample, as expected, are in the middle. Analysis of these two other groups of workers (one with steady employment but unsatisfying tasks, and the other with unsteady employment but satisfying tasks) suggests rather convincingly that alienation is equally affected by unsteady employment and low-level task jobs.[4]

Just in case the reader has forgotten, let us remind him that whether or not a human being is alienated makes a difference in a lot of things that should be of concern to all of us. "All of us" means ourselves as citizens and human beings—not just as union leaders, employers, government officials, or researchers. It has already been indicated that alienated workers have different views and act differently than the non-alienated about off-the-job concerns. For example, among the Pennsylvania workers with some 1969 and/or 1970 unemployment experience, 15 percent of the ones in high-level tasks either did not vote or voted for George Wallace. The corresponding percentage for those in the low-level tasks is much higher—more than twice the percentage for the other workers: 32 percent either did not vote at all or voted for Wallace! If we take only the voters among these sometimes-unemployed workers, the proportion of the low-level task workers voting for Wallace still remains twice that for those in the better kinds of jobs.

Employment Security and Wage Adequacy. Job security is one thing and income adequacy is another. What happens to our argument if we take both of these deeply significant worker needs into consideration? For example, among the 111 never-unemployed, high wage workers[5] in our Pennsylvania sample, do we still find that task-level is important? Without any fancy elaborations, the answer remains a clear "yes." In this group, which has both job security and income adequacy, task-level once again is substantially related to degree of alienation for the non-authoritarians. This means that we do not solve the problem of work alienation merely by full employment and adequate wage policies. Full employment and high wages are top priority goals, but this does not mean that what a man does to make a living has no impact on his total personality, or that it is of little importance to the society as a whole.

Even among these elite workers, task-level also makes a difference when it comes to (1) the proportion of them who are not only alienated but who also feel politically ineffective; (2) whether or not they have thought seriously about looking for a new and different occupation; and (3) their willingness to change to another job in which they could earn as much as in their current job.

This last point cannot be dismissed or considered lightly. Workers in low-level tasks (even though they have relative job security and wage adequacy), to a remarkably greater extent than workers in high-level tasks (with the same degree of security and income adequacy) say they would "take almost any other job in which I could earn as much as I am earning now." One-fourth of the former, in dramatic contrast to less than one fiftieth of the high task-level workers, told us that. This demonstrates beyond any doubt that these workers in low-level tasks prefer to change to jobs even at wages equal to their current ones, not because of any employment insecurity, not because of their earnings—but because of the lack of variety, the low degree of autonomy, and the absence of responsibility and opportunity to contribute and to learn.

These same workers with relative job and wage security but performing low-level tasks are also much more dissatisfied with their jobs as reflected in response to questions about how their jobs measure up to original expectations and how satisfied they are with their jobs. On these and other items, there are vast differences between these men and the rest of the group performing high-level tasks and who also have relative job and wage security.

Among the low-wage, never-unemployed workers, the proportion preferring a different type of job to what they have now was high (67 percent), but only among those in the low-level task jobs. Those in the better jobs (jobs with variety, autonomy, and so on), were no different from the high-wage, never-unemployed workers. The proportion in such high-level task jobs preferring a different type of job was actually slightly lower than among those with higher wages.[6] Analysis of another question asking how the worker feels about changing from his current job reveals the same thing. None of the low-wage, never-unemployed workers in the higher task-level jobs would "quit right now" or take "almost any other job in which I could earn as much as I am earning now." Their preference for their current job is almost identical to the preference among their counterparts among the high-wage, never-unemployed workers.

Only if they were in low task-level jobs would they quit right now or take another job earning the same amount. And their preference for their current job is no different from the preferences of their higher-wage counterparts.

In other words, task-level, and not merely wage-level, among the never-unemployed workers is critical. Task level also seems to affect how much the never-unemployed feel their jobs measure up to their original expectations. And it affects these evaluations much more than do wage levels. Between the high- and low-wage workers in this never-unemployed group who are also in high-task levels, there is very little difference in their answers to the question about how their current job measures up to original hopes—similarly, between the high- and low-wage, never-unemployed workers in the lower task levels: little or no difference in how much their jobs do or do not measure up to original hopes.

To put this differently, (1) never-unemployed workers in low-wage jobs are just as satisfied with their jobs as are those in high-wage jobs, if they perform job tasks with some degree of variety, autonomy, and responsibility. (2) Never-unemployed workers in high-wage jobs are just as dissatisfied with their jobs (relative to their original expectations) as never-unemployed men in low-wage jobs, if they perform job tasks with little variety, autonomy, and responsibility.

Task level, and not wage-level, among these never-unemployed workers also explains how much their jobs measure up to their original expectations. If job tasks were as irrelevant as some of the critics seem to imply, we should expect to find no differences on the question between the high- and low-task level workers in the group of never-unemployed. But as far as our own fieldwork is concerned, such differences were found.

Percent Stating Current Job Measures Up Very Much Like the Kind Wanted when They First Took It, by Economic Factors and Task Level

Never Unemployed—Wages $3.51+		Intermediate*		Unemployed 1 Week—Wages under $3.51	
High Task	*Low Task*	*High Task*	*Low Task*	*High Task*	*Low Task*
49%	18%	50%	22%	50%	12%

* Workers with (1) no unemployment during 20 months prior to interview and earning under $3.51 per hour; or (2) with some unemployment but earning $3.51 or more per hour.

As the previous table clearly demonstrates, as long as a worker is employed at a high-level task, employment experience and wages make absolutely no difference as to how he evaluates that job against his original hopes.

We should expect to find some major differences when we compare the group of workers in low-wage jobs who have some unemployment experience with other groups in the sample. What the data show is that task-level becomes increasingly important as far as alienation is concerned, to the extent that the worker has both employment security and wage adequacy.

Percent with High Alienation, by Economic Factors and Task Level

	No Unemployment—Wages $3.51+		Intermediate		Unemployed 1 Week—Wages under $3.51	
	High Task	*Low Task*	*High Task*	*Low Task*	*High Task*	*Low Task*
Percent with high alienation	28%	44%	41%	40%	42%	56%

Among workers in the best economic situation (long-term uninterrupted employment and relatively high wages), those with the lowest alienation are in the high task-level jobs. Those with the highest alienation, despite being in the best economic situation, are in jobs allowing for little variety, autonomy, or challenge. In fact, their alienation is among the highest in the total sample of workers, but more to the point, much more alienated than their economic peers who are working in high tasks.

At the opposite end of the economic security scale—some unemployment during the previous 20 months and at jobs paying relatively low wages—workers are alienated most of all if they are also in low tasks. Their alienation is the highest (56 percent) in the entire sample—and exactly twice that for their opposite numbers—those in favorable economic circumstances and working in high level tasks.

Once again, the basic point is that task-level does make a difference among workers in secure jobs with high wages. It makes a difference as far as alienation is concerned. It makes a difference as far as other matters are concerned, too.

At the risk of repetition, two other findings in this connection should be mentioned, both of which are directly related to how the worker feels about his job. (1) Just how does his job measure up to what his original expectations were? and, (2) How much of the time is he satisfied with his job? The answers to the first question reveal that, regardless of the economic factors of job security and wage adequacy, workers in low-level job tasks are almost identical to each other in their negative evaluations of how well their current jobs measure up to their original expectations. Job security and wages are not relevant here. At the same time, workers with high-level job tasks indicate much more than the others that their jobs are very much like the kind they wanted when they first took them, regardless of how much employment security and wage adequacy those jobs provide.

Much of this discussion may be confusing to the reader. Let us try to simplify it by referring only to our findings about job satisfaction.

The most pertinent point is that, among workers who are in the most fortunate economic circumstances (no unemployment and earning above-average wages), task level makes a difference as far as frequency of job satisfaction is concerned. Those performing high-level tasks are satisfied with their jobs more frequently than workers performing low-level tasks.

Frequency of Job Satisfaction among Workers with No Unemployment and High Wages, by Task Level

	High Tasks	Low Tasks
Percent satisfied most of the time	65% ⎫ 86%	26% ⎫ 64%
A good deal of the time	21 ⎭	38 ⎭
About half the time	12	20
Occasionally, hardly ever, or never	2	16
	100%	100%
Average job satisfaction frequency score:	49.5	27.2

Thus it is not true that as long as workers have good job security and high wages, they will be satisfied with their jobs regardless of the quality of the jobs they perform.

If we had to choose a single factor among the three considered here—(1) employment experience, (2) hourly wage, or (3) task level—as the best "predictor" of how frequently a worker is satisfied with his job, we would have to choose task level. If we compare the proportions reporting frequent satisfaction with the job (most of the time or a good deal of the time) by each of these separate factors (no unemployment vs. some; high vs. low wages; and high vs. low task level), we arrive at the following differences:

	Percent with Frequent Job Satisfaction		Difference
1. Employment:	None 73%	1 week+ 54%	19
2. Wages	$3.51 or more 73%	Under $3.51 63%	10
3. Task level	High 89%	Low 50%	39

The difference in job satisfaction is greatest (39 percentage points) between workers in high and low task levels, as compared to only 19 percentage points in the case of the employment factor, and still less—only 10 points—between workers earning $3.51 or more and workers earning less than that.

This should be proof enough about the importance of a worker's job tasks—compared to economic factors—in his job satisfaction.

One other insight into all of this that has not been spelled out before: When we take all three factors into account simultaneously, we find that as long as workers are performing high level tasks, economic factors such as unemployment experience and wage level make hardly any difference as far as frequency of job satisfaction is concerned. Their frequency of job satisfaction is quite high. But these economic factors are important in predicting job satisfaction among those workers reporting little variety, autonomy, and responsibility (low-task attributes). The better the economic circumstances, the more frequent the satisfaction among workers in low-level tasks:

Percent with Frequent Job Satisfaction, by Economic
Factors and Job Tasks

	Never Unemployed—Wages $3.51+	Intermediate	Unemployed 1 Week—Wages under $3.51
1. Workers in high tasks	86%	94%	82%
2. Workers in low tasks	64%	45%	22%

The moral of the story is that if a person is employed in tasks with little variety, autonomy, and responsibility, there is at least some "compensation" if he is fortunate enough to be employed in a job that carries little, if any, risk of joblessness and that also pays a decent wage. Job satisfaction among workers performing low-level job tasks, in other words, is positively correlated with their economic circumstances.

Bu to repeat, among workers in high-level task jobs, economic circumstances seem to have little effect on frequency of job staisfaction. Workers with some unemployment experience and employed at below-average wages are satisfied with their jobs almost as frequently as others in such high-level task jobs.

To the extent that job security and income adequacy are achieved by an individual, these are no longer his only major concerns. Instead, new and higher ones emerge as more important or salient to him. Certainly, as workers achieve some modicum of economic security (as measured by relative lack of unemployment and by high-wage levels), it would only seem natural that other issues in his job world become more decisive influences on his psyche and his behavior.[7] On the other hand, workers plagued by chronic unemployment and/or by low wages would only naturally be preoccupied by the search or desire for economic security much more than challenging and satisfying work.

Workers in inferior economic positions and inferior tasks were the most highly alienated. For these same workers, task-level was also important as a determinant of, (a) how much their jobs measured up to what they originally wanted, (b) how frequently they were satisfied with their jobs, and (c) as a determinant of their preference for another kind of job.

To repeat what was said earlier, nobody in his right mind would deny the priority of economic security for human beings.[8] But it is also true that the nature of a worker's job tasks is no less a reality than the level of employment in an economy and the size of that worker's paycheck.

How do these separate elements—job security, wage levels, and task level—relate to two other important matters that go beyond the job itself, namely, (1) workers' evaluations of their unions, and (2) their political leanings? The next two sections take up these critical questions and reveal the "spill-over" effects of the nature of a worker's job characteristics.

UNION ATTITUDES AND THE RELATIVE IMPORTANCE OF WAGES, EMPLOYMENT EXPERIENCE, AND TASK LEVEL

Task levels—the very content of what a worker does during his eight hours or so each day to earn his daily bread—are too frequently neglected (often completely neglected, and even rejected) by union leaders and management representatives. Their trained incapacity (or occupational disease) leads to an almost exclusive preoccupation with wage levels and/or job security. Our position is that, in the new era, and particularly among the new generation of workers, the nature of the job tasks themselves (not merely wage levels and employment security) will become more and more important to workers.

The 1972 strike among young assembly-line workers (all highly paid), in the new, highly modernized GM plant at Lordstown, Ohio, is a concrete, dramatic example.[9] A corollary, of course, is that the various segments of the "Establishment"—which includes unions, government, management, and academia—will lag in recognition of this new phenomenon. Our personal experience (which admittedly is not *proof*) is that it is tougher to interest the average union leader than it is to interest the management world in this necessary shift in thinking.

Statistical analysis, however, if understood, might provoke greater union concern. Take, for example, the question in our interview asking the worker how helpful his union is to its membership. There is very little difference in how the union members answer this question if we concentrate on the hypothesis that wage rates determine the difference in workers' evaluation of their union: 61 percent of those earning more than $3.50 per hour, and 57 percent earning less than that figure say their union is very or fairly helpful to its members—a difference of only 4 percent.

Similarly, if we think that unemployment experience is the most relevant factor in explaining union members' evaluations of their union, we find that the difference in evaluations between workers with zero weeks' unemployment and those with one or more weeks' unemployment (in the 20 months prior to being interviewed) is in the expected direction but still not very great. Among those with no joblessness, 61 percent are favorably inclined toward their union ("very or fairly helpful"), in contrast to only 54 percent of those with one or more weeks of unemployment—a difference of 7 percent.

But consider how great the difference in evaluation is when we take into account the task level of these same workers. The difference is greater, amounting to 12 percent—a difference which is statistically significant (p = .05).

Percent of Pennsylvania Workers Rating Union as
"Very" or "Fairly Helpful," by Task Level

	High-Task Level	Low-Task Level
Union "very" or "fairly helpful" to Members	65%	53%
Number of cases	(132)	(129)

In other words, if one were to ask which one of the three factors—wage levels, unemployment experience, or task-level—is the best predictor of how a worker rates his union, he would have to choose the third one—the intrinsic job tasks performed by that worker, which (in this study) refers to how much variety, autonomy, and responsibility the worker's job entails.

Obviously, when unemployment experience and task level are combined, a greater difference is revealed. That is, if only those workers who enjoy high task-level jobs and who had no unemployment recently are studied, their satisfaction with their union is much greater—69 percent, in contrast to only 53 percent of all other workers—a difference of 16 percentage points. But the main point is that task level is the more vital factor involved in the development of favorable worker attitudes toward the union to which they belong.

This is strong evidence for the argument that unions desperately need to become more concerned with the intrinsic nature of the jobs their members perform. This does not mean that unions should diminish their concern with job security and adequate wages. It does mean, increasingly, that today's members will become more concerned than members of the past with such preoccupations as how much variety and freedom they have in performing their daily tasks.

POLITICAL PARTY PREFERENCE AND THE RELATIVE IMPORTANCE OF EMPLOYMENT EXPERIENCE, WAGES, AND TASK LEVELS

Unions, of course, are primarily interested in their membership's loyalty, but many unions are also interested in the political party loyalties of their memberships. Traditionally, they have been concerned with their members' affiliation with the Democratic Party. How do the three variables of unemployment experience, wage rates, and job task relate to party preferences of the workers we interviewed in Pennsylvania? We asked the workers: "Which political party do you think represents your point of view best of all?"

Taking each of these three variables separately, there is no question that, unemployment experience is the best predictor of how much the workers choose the Democratic Party over the Republican Party, but in a way that may shatter some older patterns. Workers with no unemployment in the 20 months prior to the summer of 1970 were by far much more pro-Democratic than those with at least one week of unemployment—53 percent vs. 40 percent, as the following table indicates:

Party Preference, by Unemployment Experience

Party Choice	No Unemployment	All Others
Democrats	53%	40%
Republicans	16	19
None, all the same, other	31	41
Number of cases	(198)	(63)

Workers in low-wage jobs were slightly less pro-Democratic than those in the higher paying jobs (45 vs. 54 percent); about the same in their choice of the Republican Party; and much more unaffiliated than those in the better-paying positions.

As for job-task level, it made little difference when it came to choice of Democrats, but those in the higher-level tasks were twice as pro-Republican as were those in the lower-level tasks (23 vs. 11 percent). Workers in the lower tasks tended more than those in the higher tasks to be unaffiliated, or to reject both major parties (37 vs. 30 percent).

What comes out of this analysis is that the unemployment experience of the worker is a more important determinant of a worker's choice of the Democratic Party as representing his point of view, when considered separately, than are the two other variables of wage and task levels. But what do we get when we combine the separate variables?

If we combine unemployment experience and wage levels, we find that the most pro-Democratic workers are those who were never unemployed and who enjoy above-average wages (56 percent choose the Democratic Party). Moving away from this most economically favored group toward the least favored one, the percentage choosing the Democrats declines (to only 34 percent of those with some unemployment experience and below-average wages). The proportion rejecting both major parties increases as we move from the most to the least economically favored group:

Party Preference, by Unemployment Experience and Wage Level

Party Choice	No Unemployment		One or More Weeks Unemployment	
	$3.50+	Under $3.50	$3.50+	Under $3.50
Democrats	56%	49%	45%	34%
None, all the same, other	26	37	39	44
Number of cases	(112)	(86)	(31)	(32)

Note: The difference between 100% and the column sums is the proportion favoring Republicans.

One reading of such a table may be posed in the form of a question. Is it possible that adverse economic conditions are no longer the guarantee for a pro-Democratic Party sympathy among workers that they once were? The greatest loyalty to that party is now to be found among the most economically favored group of workers—those having had no unemployment and working at jobs paying above-average wages. The least degree of loyalty prevails among those in the most adverse circumstances.

Analysis of the relationship of the party preference to task level and unemployment experience or wage levels is not as clear-cut as the one above, but analysis does show that unemployed workers or low-wage workers in high tasks are the least pro-Democratic; that the least affiliated (to either the Democrats or the Republicans) are to be found among the ones with some unemployment experience (or in low-wage jobs) in low tasks. This fits with a point made earlier, that workers with some unemployment experience and in low tasks either voted disproportionately for Wallace or did not vote at all.

Taking the three variables of employment experience, wage level, and task levels together, who are the most pro-Democratic workers? Who are the most rejecting of either political party? The answers should be obvious by now:

1. Workers with the best circumstances—no unemployment, high wages, and in high-task jobs—have the highest percentage with pro-Democratic loyalties and the lowest percentage rejecting both parties.

2. The group with the highest percentage rejecting both parties are those workers existing in the *worst* circumstances—they work in jobs with little employment security, low wages, and with poor tasks (little variety, little autonomy, and so on). More than half of this group reject either party as representing their point of view.[10]

A look at the workers who are both pro-union and pro-Democratic—in Pennsylvania and Michigan together—tells us that the members of such a group (which makes up more than a third of the 371 workers) are the most satisfied with their jobs, think rarely of leaving them, are older than the other workers, complain less about how their current jobs stack up against their original expectations, are more optimistic about the progress they have made over the past ten years, and enjoy far higher family incomes than the less-loyal workers.

There can be little doubt that the unions and the Democratic Party enjoy the greatest loyalty among the most favored unionized white workers—the ones in the best jobs, and this means not only economic *security*, but also the very nature of the job as defined in this report. The other kinds of workers feel left out or neglected—hence, alienated—by these two major political institutions in American society.

The reader has been subjected to enough arguments for the proposition that what men and women do to earn money can become as important to them as both the amount of money they earn and the security conditions under which they earn it. The possible paradox is that it might be easier to create full employment under conditions of high wages than it is to create a structure of work that will meet the demands of workers at all levels in a full-employment society. As Mason Haire put it nearly a decade ago, "with job security and reasonable levels of pay, money incentives lose effectiveness and the demand is for satisfaction at the levels at which the needs are expressed. Trying to pay enough to make up for a deficit in social or egoistic needs is likely to be an expensive process of chasing an ever-receding goal."[11]

On the other hand, we see no alternative. The demand for job security and decent wages cannot be evaded, and, as that goal becomes a reality for more and more employees, the need to cope with work itself will simply have to be faced and dealt with in a more effective manner than has so far been the rule. This demand may characterize the new worker who is, in part, the subject of the next two chapters.

NOTES:

1. Nevertheless, at least one such study has been carried out in Leningrad and recently published in English: A. G. Zdravomyslov, V. P. Rozhin and V. A. Iadov, *Man and His Work* (New York: International Arts and Sciences Press, 1970), translated by Stephen P. Dunn.
2. Among some intellectuals, the only exceptions to this theory are, of course, themselves.
3. We are assuming here, of course, that the twenty months of uninterrupted employment for these 200 or so workers is an empirical measure of some degree of job security, relative to the experience of other workers in the sample.
4. Workers in steady jobs but performing "lousy" tasks are no less alienated than workers in unsteady jobs but performing "satisfying" tasks. The percentage alienated in both of these intermediate groups is identical, 43 percent.
5. We have arbitrarily chosen those men earning over $3.50 per hour as "high" wage earners, as having "income adequacy"—relative to the rest of the workers in the sample.
6. This comparison takes into account workers saying they would want to retire. But even here, the group with the highest proportion indicating a preference to retire were those low-wage, never-unemployed workers in the lower-level task jobs.
7. In the 1971 study of Kalamazoo auto and steel workers, a higher percentage of those reporting adequate take-home pay (compared to those saying their pay was not adequate) said it was very important that increased opportunities to do interesting and satisfying work be improved, without also saying the same thing about more pay.

(These questions about opportunities to do interesting and satisfying work, and about the importance of more pay, were not included in the Pennsylvania interviews.)

8. Every now and then, however, some industrial social scientists write and talk in rather incomplete ignorance of economic realities.

9. See Emma Rothschild, "GM in More Trouble," *New York Review of Books*, March, 1972; and Barbara Garson, "Luddites in Lordstown: It's Not the Money, It's the Job," *Harper's*, June, 1972.

10. Curiously, the group with the highest proportion favoring the Republican Party is to be found among those in high-task jobs but with little economic security (some unemployment and earning low wages). More than two-fifths of this group (43 percent) favor the Republicans, in contrast to 17 percent of the total group of Pennsylvania workers in the sample.

11. "The Social Sciences and Management Practices," *California Management Review*, Summer, 1964.

Part Three

The Young Worker

Chapter Six

The Now Generation of Workers

> *Young workers . . . get three or*
> *four days' pay and figure,*
> *"Well, I can live on that.*
> *I'm not really interested in*
> *these material things anyhow.*
> *I'm interested in the sense of*
> *fulfillment as a human being."*
> —*Walter Reuther*

There is some reason to believe that the 22½ million full-time workers under age 30 produced by the communications revolution, Dr. Spock, and nearly 200 years of political democracy are less authoritarian[1] than past generations of young workers, yet are forced into even more frustrating work situations. Because of this, some experts go so far as to say that democratization of the workplace is inevitable.[2] Others believe this to be far from the truth. They say that our total society is hanging in the balance between democracy and repression. If the latter view is correct, the active choice of democracy in the workplace and the avoidance of a "final and active totalitarianism"[3] should be a major national concern. In either case, it should be useful to consider the characteristics and attitudes of young workers since they will provide much of the force and direction for change in the workplace during the 1970s.[4]

This chapter discusses the young work force, its composition, general levels of dissatisfaction, causes of dissatisfaction, work values, and the extent to which work expectations are realized. To keynote this discussion, we would suggest—based on the following table—that young workers do not seem to get much real fulfillment from their work. When asked the question "How often do you leave work with a good feeling that you have done something particularly well?" the following percentages of workers answered "very often":

Age Group	Percentage Answering "Very Often"
Under 20	23%
21–29	25%
30–44	38%
45–64	43%
65 and over	53%

People who rarely feel satisfied about doing something well at their jobs are probably not receiving one of the most important benefits work has to offer: the experience of achieving and growing on the job.

AN OBJECTIVE DESCRIPTION OF YOUNG WORKERS

Young workers 21–29 years of age know more, earn less, and tend to belong to unions. Very young workers, 16–20 years old, tend to be white, female, blue-collar, and non-union.

Education

Even very young workers, 16–20 years of age, had more formal education than those 45 or older. The age group which one would expect to far surpass the other in education—the 21–29 group—did have fewer members with less than a high school education. The percentage of its members with some college experience, however, was the same as for the 30–44 age group. The 45-and-older group, of course, had the least education.

Personal Income

Three quarters of the very young workers earned less than $5000 per year. In each of the three older groups, the percentage of low earners was about the same (25–29 percent). The percentage of workers making more than $10,000, however, was larger in each successively older group, except that it dropped off significantly among workers over age 44.

Sex

The ever-increasing role of women in the labor force is underscored by the fact that, among very young workers 16–20 years of age, women outnumbered men by a ratio of 6 to 4. The percentage of women dropped sharply to 38 among the 21–29 year old workers, to 33 among workers in their middle years, and to 31 among older workers. Evidently, female participation in the labor force is no longer a case of "back-to-work" after child rearing. Higher percentages of women in their child-rearing years than in their after-child-rearing years are now active participants in the work force.

Race

Very young (16–20) and older (45+) blacks were under-represented among employed persons. In other words, unemployment not only affects young blacks disproportionately but is almost equally hard on the older black worker.

Occupational Status

"Grow old along with me, the best is yet to be. . . ." Browning's words ring true when one sees that workers over age 44 were more than 10 times as likely to be self-employed as very young workers, and five times as likely as workers in their 20s. The chances of a worker's being self-employed increase steadily with age: 2 percent of workers 16–20 years of age was self-employed, 4 percent for those in their 20s, 13 percent for workers in their middle years, and 21 percent of workers age 45 and over. Since self-employed people are remarkably satisfied with their jobs, their concentration in the higher age brackets may help explain the fact that job satisfaction is similarly concentrated.

The percentage of white-collar workers steadily increases from 44 percent among very young workers to 50 percent for workers age 21–29, to 57 percent for workers in their middle years. Then, as with income, the older worker (age 45 and over) slips back a few rungs on the ladder; in this case, back to the 50 percent white-collar composition which also characterized young workers 21–29 years of age.

Union Status

Very young workers were only half as likely to be unionized as workers over age 20. Perhaps, they find it difficult to gain entrance to the trade unions because of extreme youth, lack of a high school diploma, lack of training, and so on, and are obliged to take the poorer non-union jobs. Workers in their teens also tend to be less strongly attached to the labor force and often attend school or have other commitments which prevent them from seeking jobs in industries and occupations organized by unions.

WHO ARE THE DISSATISFIED YOUNG WORKERS?

With the exception of young workers who earned more than $10,000 per year, significantly more young workers than workers over 29 years of age expressed negative attitudes toward work. This was true regardless of race, sex, marital status, education, collar color, etc. However, young black workers were even more dissatisfied than their white brothers (37 percent expressed negative attitudes toward work as compared to 22 percent of young whites). Young workers with more than a high school education, females "under 30" and young workers making less than $5,000 per year represented other pockets of high dissatisfaction within a generally dissatisfied age group.

Appendix A, Table 4 shows the percentages of respondents in each of three groups (and for the sample as a whole) who answered "Not too satisfied" or "Not at all satisfied" to the question, "All in all, how satisfied would you say you are with your job?" The percentages are shown by occupational group, race, education, sex, marital status, and personal income. For the work force as a whole, there were many statistically significant differences in satisfaction levels among these groups. However, when the data are further broken down into three age groups, the number of respondents in each subgroup is so small that only the most extreme differences meet the requirements for statistical validity. In fact, the table reveals only one such extreme difference: the substantially higher dissatisfaction level of blue-collar vs. white-collar workers *in their middle years*. This is particularly interesting since blue-collar workers under age 30 and over age 44 reported virtually the same levels of overall work dissatisfaction as did white-collar workers in these age groups. The young blue-collar worker doesn't regard himself as permanently cast in that role, and the worker over age 45 has already made the painful adjustment to reality. The middle-aged blue-collar worker, however, has come face to face with the realities of his occupational life and cannot accept them. Since blue-collar/white-collar dissatisfaction differences diminish when income is held constant, it may also be true that young blue-collar workers make about the same salaries as young white-collar workers, but that income differences become pronounced after age 30. The blue-collar worker reaches a plateau, but the white-collar worker continues to advance.

Even though the other differences within age groups must be taken with a large grain of salt, due to the small numbers of respondents involved, some comments appear warranted.

Race

In the two younger age groups, blacks were less satisfied than whites. Among older workers, the reverse is true. This suggests a greater generation gap among black workers than among white workers. It also supports the notion that, at least among black workers, young workers today are different from young workers of the past.

Education

Young workers with education beyond high school were somewhat more likely to report dissatisfaction than were those without any college. Slightly fewer workers in their middle years who had college experience reported work dissatisfaction and, among workers over age 44, the percentages are exactly identical.[5] Perhaps the more educated workers begin to achieve their goals during their middle years, while the less educated workers (with many of the same aspirations) begin to realize, as they enter their 30s, that their early goals were really only fantasies.

Sex

In general, women workers were significantly more likely to report dissatisfaction than were male workers. This was true among all age groups, but the gap between men and women was least among young workers.[6]

Marital Status

For the total work force, married people were significantly more satisfied with their jobs than were unmarrieds This general trend persisted within the young worker group.[7]

Personal Income

For the work force as a whole, income was a strong and statistically significant predictor of overall job satisfaction. However, young workers appear to be relatively indifferent to income levels. Workers over age 44 seem to share this indifference to some degree, but workers in their middle years were almost twice as likely to report dissatisfaction if they made less than $7500 per year.

The similarities among young workers were more impressive than the differences. In no subgroup of young workers identified in the sample did fewer than 21 percent express dissatisfaction—except the 41 workers age 29 and under who were earning $10,000 or more. Only 10 percent of these workers were dissatisfied. This contrasts with the fact that no middle-aged worker subgroup (ages 30–44) had more than 21 percent dissatisfied, and no older workers (ages 45 and over) had more than 15 percent.

It will become increasingly apparent throughout this chapter that, at least in terms of attitude, young workers are a more homogenous group than are their elders. Young workers with more education did tend to be somewhat less satisfied with their jobs. Socio-economic differences, however, seem to have far more pronounced effects on the job satisfaction of workers over age 29.

WHY ARE YOUNG WORKERS DISSATISFIED?

Early in the interview, all respondents were asked to rate 25 characteristics of work according to whether they considered these characteristics to be "very important," "somewhat important," "not too important," or "not at all important." Then, later on in the interview, they were asked whether the same characteristics were "very true," "somewhat true," "not too true," or "not at all true" of their jobs. For our purposes, the percentage of respondents in each age group who considered an aspect of work to be very important is taken as an index of that item's importance to the group under consideration, and the percentage of each group who reported it to be very true of their jobs is taken as an indication of the quality of the jobs held by that group. Where a larger percentage of respondents in an age group considered a specific work characteristic to be very important than reported it to be very true of their jobs, a "satisfaction gap" is assumed: we know for sure that some workers in that group felt they were being "shortchanged."

Work Values

The labor force as a whole considered job content characteristics to be more important than the economic benefits derived from the job. The highest-ranked item among all age groups was interesting work.

Young workers placed even more importance than their elders on the nature of the work itself and far less on the comfort aspects of jobs (such as, transportation arrangements and whether or not one is asked to do excessive amounts of work).

We often suppose that young workers have a different set of work values than do their elders and, indeed, this appears to be quite true. But contrary to the suppositions of many older people, their values appear to be highly responsible. They placed substantially more importance on the interesting nature of the work, on their opportunity to develop their own special abilities, and on their chances for promotion. They were less concerned than their elders with being asked to do excessive amounts of work, whether or not their transportation arrangements were convenient, and whether their jobs allowed them to forget their personal problems. With regard to pay, job security, and fringe benefits, age seemed to make no difference: all age groups seemed to be equally interested in the economics of work. While most differences either increased or decreased steadily with age, the importance placed on the chance to make new friends at work was higher for young workers and for workers past age 44, but lower for workers in their middle years.

Work Realities

If the worker's own view of his job is any yardstick, young workers have very bad jobs indeed!

The differences in work values described above were minor compared to the differences in the extent to which young workers believed certain desirable characteristics to be lacking in their jobs. For 19 of the 25 elements specified, young workers rated their jobs lower than did workers 30 and older.

The differences between workers in their middle years and older workers were not so great. Nonetheless—with regard to every element of work except "the chances for promotion being good"—workers over age 44 rated their jobs as high or higher than did workers in their middle years. The progression was fairly constant, ranging from low percentages of young workers who gave their jobs high ratings, to medium percentages among workers in their middle years, to high percentages among older workers.

The Expectation Gap

When the compounding effects of their higher work values and lower work realities are taken into account, the greater general dissatisfaction of the young worker can readily be understood. The expectation/reality discrepancy among young workers is most acutely felt in matters concerning the work itself.

In order to place in context the answers to the question "Why are young workers dissatisfied?" it is first necessary to describe the principal dissatisfaction of middle-aged and older workers. Using the satisfaction gap[8] as a means of identifying the job features which cause dissatisfaction to large numbers of people, it would appear that most workers in their middle years and older workers had as much comfort as they desired in their jobs, had the resources they required to get their jobs done, were well satisfied with their personal work relationships, and had relatively little fault to find with the content of their jobs. They had two substantial areas of dissatisfaction, however. First, while few workers in those age groups considered chances for promotion to be very important, even fewer felt these chances to be very good. Second, older workers did place a very high premium on good pay. While a high percentage of them also believed they were getting very good pay, there were at least 20 percent who considered good pay to be "very important" but, at the same time, not "very true" of their jobs.

Young workers were also dissatisfied with their pay and with their chances for promotion. In fact, since they rated their jobs very low on these characteristics, far more workers under 30 had pay and promotion "satisfaction gaps" than did their elders. But their prime dissatisfaction centered around something quite different: the *work itself*. While the greatest satisfaction gap among workers over 30 had to do with pay, among younger workers it concerned their lack of opportunity for self-development. (The issue of pay placed second.) The third and fourth areas of greatest discrepancy among young workers (the interesting [or uninteresting] nature of their work, and their chance to do the things they believed they did best) also resulted from high values and low realities in job-content areas.

It is clear from this analysis of the satisfaction gaps that the important difference between the dissatisfaction of young workers and that of their elders stems first, from the high value they placed on challenging work, and second, from the lack of challenge in the work they were actually required to perform.

WHAT CAN BE DONE?

The most significant and persistent differences in work attitudes and values (and, apparently, in actual work situations) are attributable to age. The young worker has different work values than do middle-aged and older workers. Since he also judges his actual situation more harshly than do workers in their middle years and older workers, with regard to many of the work characteristics he most values, there is apparently a general and pervasive discrepancy in the young worker's work life. This discrepancy differs from dissatisfactions in the work force as a whole, in that—while it includes a feeling of being underpaid—it is primarily directed at the work itself. Young workers place high values on interesting work, opportunities to develop and use their abilities, chances to do the things they do best, and chances for promotion. To a greater extent than older workers, they also view their jobs as lacking these opportunities. This creates a difficult and potentially destructive situation—a situation with implications which go far beyond the workplace itself.

One more observation: While young workers do not place any greater importance upon economic benefits than do their older co-workers, the actual benefits available to them are so far inferior that a serious discrepancy—particularly with regard to pay—also exists in this aspect of the young worker's world.

Having concluded that the younger worker is indeed a person of different values, feelings, and aspirations than his older counterpart, and having identified the most pronounced of these differences, at least two possible conclusions can be reached: (1) The structure of work should change to accommodate young people, or (2) young people should change to accommodate the structure of work. The latter is a popular notion among older folk. They recall their own accommodations (and those of their fathers), and feel it is only proper that the young people of today should change.

But this gives rise to two questions: First, is a possibly pathological adaptation to sterile work actually desirable?[9] Second, if it *is* desirable, are the young people of today willing to go that route? My answer to the first questions is an emphatic no! The existence of deadening, numbing, and individually constraining work in the past is no argument for its continuation in the future.

The real potential for change in the 1970s depends far more on the answer to the second question. If young people are willing to adapt and to accept the values of the hierarchical work situation (seeking their place in it and striving to improve their situation step-by-step), we can be assured that little attention will be given to restructuring work. If, on the other hand, young people draw the line and demand that their unions reorder bargaining priorities and that their employers give them a voice in shaping their work lives, then (assuming that the specific forms which the demands take are constructive) we may see at long last an extension of our democratic principles to the workplace.

NOTES:

1. See Harold Sheppard's findings in Chapter 7, which report on young white blue-collar workers.
2. Warren G. Bennis, *Changing Organizations* (New York: McGraw-

Hill Book Company, 1966), p. 32. However, Bennis appears to believe that the system is already becoming less hierarchical. He says, "our position is, in brief, that democracy is the only system which can successfully cope with the changing demands of contemporary civilization." He adds that the inevitability of democratization should not prevent us from "giving a little push here and there to the inevitable."

3. Marcus G. Raskin, *Being & Doing* (New York: Random House, 1971), p. xvi.

   On the other hand, the collapse of liberal authoritarian structures where people are colonized tenderly can result in a final and active totalitarianism in which violence and magic are no longer mediated through education, consumer goods and dreams, but are stated as goals and the basis of life.

4. The data used in discussing these characteristics and attitudes were gathered by the Survey Research Center (SRC) of the University of Michigan under contract to the U.S. Department of Labor. The SRC survey was conducted in November and December of 1969, among a national probability sample of 1,533 employed persons 16 years of age and older who worked 20 hours a week or more.

5. It is noteworthy that the same pattern persists with regard to overall satisfaction with life, except that, during the middle years, a lack of higher education is associated with even higher life than job dissatisfaction, and, conversely, middle-years' workers with some college are extremely unlikely to report negative attitudes toward life in general. After age 45, as with negative attitudes toward work, the percentages of college and non-college people reporting negative attitudes toward life are identical.

6. A statistically significant difference between the general attitude of men and women within age groups was the fact that women in their middle years were twice as likely as men in that age group to report dissatisfactions with life in general.

7. The difference in life satisfaction between marrieds and unmarrieds was so great that it was highly significant even within each age group. Among young workers, unmarrieds were about twice as likely as marrieds to be dissatisfied with their lives. In the middle years, the likelihood of general dissatisfaction was about three times as great and, among workers over age 44, four times as great.

8. The difference between the percentages of workers who stated that a work element was "very important" to them and the percentage in that group who later indicated that it was "very true" of their jobs.

9. On the general topic of the limits and pathology of "adaptability," see René Dubos, "Man Over Adapting," *Psychology Today*, February 1971.

Chapter Seven

Rebels at the Workplace:
A Portrait of Young White Workers

*Labor and Management are failing
miserably in meeting the problems
of young workers. The youth have
little confidence in either of us
finding solutions to their problems.
To cope with the problems will
require a major adjustment in our
thinking.*
—*M. C. Weston, United
Steelworkers Union*

Chapter Six, "The Now Generation of Workers," was based on Neal Q. Herrick's analysis of the University of Michigan survey which included young (under-30) workers of both sexes, all races, and across the gamut of occupations. His group also included non-members as well as members of unions. But in this chapter, we will focus on only one particular group of young workers—white male union members, nearly all of whom are in blue-collar occupations—from our Pennsylvania and Kalamazoo samples.

Much is being written and said about the youth of today, and about the young worker in particular. We will not repeat those observations—the most extreme of which might be found in Charles Reich's *The Greening of America*. In too many instances, these observations have been couched in exaggerated and distorted rhetoric, and too often without the back-up of systematic, factual, or theoretical analysis.

The first point that needs to be made is that there is no such thing as *the* young worker—no more than there is *the* aged, *the* Negro, or *the* female— or *the* youth, in general. In order words, there is heterogeneity within this age group, even within one social class (in our study, one general *occupational* group made up of white males). Nevertheless, we can indicate the differences between the proportions of the youngest workers (under 30) and those of the oldest workers (55 and older) with respect to many of the characteristics and questions probed in our study. In this chapter we will therefore concentrate on these differences:

The nature of the job, especially: (1) Task levels and overall job satisfaction, (2) Fringe benefits, wages, and adequacy of wages, (3) Attitudes toward other aspects of their jobs, including union attitudes, and (4) Their evaluation of training for job rotation, and for "Getting ahead."

Social Psychological and Political Characteristics, especially: (1) authoritarianism, (2) alienation, (3) achievement values, (4) political efficacy, (5) liberal vs. conservative identification, (6) party preferences and voting behavior, (7) campaign issues, (8) discrepancy between aspirations and achievements, and (9) evaluations of new workers and of minority groups.

Demographic Characteristics, especially: (1) migrant status, (2) education, (3) marital status, (4) number of dependents, (5) additional earners in the family, (6) family income, (7) home ownership, (8) religion, and (9) number of organizational memberships.

THE NATURE OF THE JOB

Task Levels and Overall Satisfaction

As an example of what is meant by the heterogeneity referred to earlier, there is no simple generalization concerning the overall Task Level Index of younger workers as compared to those 55 and older. Our findings (based on the Kalamazoo and Pennsylvania interviews) show that the youngest group has a lower proportion in the highest task level than the oldest group (20 vs. 27 percent), and, at the same time, they also have a lower proportion in the very bottom of the task levels (16 vs. 24 percent). In other words, they are more concentrated in the two intermediate task levels:

Task Level	Youngest (under 30)	Oldest (55+)
Highest, 1	20%	27%
2, 3	64	49
Lowest, 4	16	24
	100%	100%
Number of cases	*82*	*78*

The differences that do exist, however, show up in the specific components of the Total Task Index, especially regarding the importance or saliency of these components. And the young workers have higher saliency scores than the oldest, if they report any negative features about their job tasks. For example, take variety on the job: more older workers refer to their job tasks as having little or no variety (40 vs. 27 percent), but when asked how frequently this bothers them, the younger workers answered "much more frequently" by a ratio of nearly 8 to 1. (Twenty-three percent of the young workers, but only 3 percent of the oldest, indicating little or no variety are bothered by this very often or nearly all the time.) In fact, only 9 percent of the youngest, but 55 percent of the oldest, say the lack of variety bothers them rarely or never!

Concerning freedom to do their work the way they want to, the youngest workers are only slightly different from the oldest—in the direction of less freedom in their tasks. But once again, the saliency or severity of the lack of freedom is greater among those young workers reporting little or no freedom.

The other component of the autonomy measure that deals with how much of their potential ideas and skills is being used in their kinds of jobs reveals some sharper differences between the youngest and oldest worker. The under-30 group reports less use of their potential. For example, only 19 percent of the young, but one-third of the old workers, say that almost all of their potentials are used in their work.

Responsibility. Three items (detailed in Chapter Three) were used to measure this component of the Total Task Index:

1. How much opportunity is provided to learn more about the job and to increase the worker's knowledge of the process and his skill.
2. How important the quality of his work is to him.
3. His judgment as to how many people can do his job.

While the young group reports greater opportunities to learn more in the jobs they now have, for those who do indicate little or no such opportunity, this shortcoming bothers them more than it does the oldest group. The youngest workers also place less emphasis on the quality of their work than the oldest; and perhaps most important of all, rate their jobs more poorly. When asked whether very few people or almost anyone can do their jobs, a third of the young, but nearly three-fifths of the oldest men feel that only a limited number of, or very few, people can do their jobs.

The overall index for responsibility (based on opportunities to learn, importance of quality of work, and importance of one's job) shows that the proportion of the young workers giving their jobs a low responsibility score is somewhat higher than that of the oldest workers (42 vs. only 26 percent):

Overall Responsibility Index:	Youngest	Oldest
High	34%	36%
Intermediate	24	38
Low	42	26
	100%	100%

This should not detract from the fact, however, that the youngest workers are no different from the oldest in their respective proportions registering a high score (34 vs. 36 percent).

To repeat, young workers are bothered more frequently than the oldest, if they say their jobs lack variety, autonomy, and responsibility. By constructing a total saliency index, we were able to determine that two-fifths of the entire group of under-30 workers, but only one-fourth of the oldest, had high saliency scores. In other words, while the differences in total task levels are not clearly related to age, the degree to which employment in a low-level task bothers the worker *is* related to age—and it is the young worker who is bothered the most.

Overall Job Satisfaction. A larger percentage of young workers rate their job as of little importance (62 percent, but only 45 percent of the oldest say almost anyone or a good many people can do their job). Therefore, it should not be surprising to find that only a third of the under-30 workers say they are satisfied with their jobs most of the time. This is substantially below the proportion of the oldest group (64 percent) who are satisfied most of the time. At the other end of the satisfaction scale, nearly one-fourth of the youngest group of workers say they are satisfied only occasionally, hardly ever, or never, while the corresponding proportion for the 55+ group is less than one-tenth! Our total sample data indicate that the younger the worker, the more frequently he is dissatisfied with his job. (In other words, the middle-aged group is intermediate in frequency of job satisfaction.)

One of the most important points to be made is that this wide gap in job-satisfaction frequency between the young and the old is primarily due to the role of task levels. It is primarily among workers doing these negative tasks that age makes a major difference. In this group, the proportion of young workers satisfied with their jobs most of, or a good deal of, the time, is far below the proportion for workers 55 and older who are also in negative tasks. This finding is a rather strong indication that younger workers today are increasingly dissatisfied with jobs that have little intrinsic content value. It is my hunch that, compared to their fathers and grandfathers, the young workers will *not* adapt themselves to such tasks if they remain in them, and they will not as readily tend to sublimate their dissatisfaction as they grow older. This prediction is based on some theories about the impact of authoritarianism, discussed in an earlier chapter, and to which we will return, in examining further the nature of today's younger workers.

Fringe benefits, wages, and adequacy of income

Workers in the lower age brackets have far fewer fringe benefits than those 55 and older, a fact possibly attributable to the benefits that accrue from gaining seniority on the job. (Recall that these are all union members.) It is important to note that younger workers consider the lack of fringe benefits a serious problem somewhat more frequently than do older workers also lacking these fringe benefits.

Contrary to what might be expected, we found that the youngest and the oldest workers' wage distributions were not sharply different from each other, except possibly at the lowest wage levels. About one-fourth of the youngest, but only one-sixth of the oldest, earned $3.00 or less per hour on their jobs. But at the upper levels (above $4.00 per hour), they were identical, with one-third of each group in that higher wage category. There is some evidence that suggests that the middle-aged workers, however, enjoyed higher wage levels than either the youngest or the oldest.

While the difference may not be significant, young workers—despite their relative similarity in wages to the 55+ group—are less likely to judge their take-home pay as adequate to take care of their family's bills and expenses (73 vs. 80 percent). What is clear, however, is that among those young workers reporting their take-home pay as inadequate, one-third say that, even when total family income is taken into account, they still do not have enough for their bills and expenses—as compared to only 5 percent of the very oldest workers. We have already reported in Chapter 4 that younger workers are far less likely to feel that their total family income is enough to live on as comfortably as they would like (40 percent vs. 51 percent of the oldest). Expectations and aspirations play a major role in this greater discontent among the younger workers. Their greater dissatisfaction with the lack of certain fringe benefits reinforces this point. At the same time, they expect, in the years ahead, a steady rise in their income slightly more than do the oldest workers.

Attitudes toward other aspects of the job

Even when we account for the obvious differences between age groups in their retirement propensity, younger workers, when asked what their job choice would be if completely free to choose, are much more likely to say they would prefer another kind of job than the one they have now. This is backed up by other results of the interviews. For example:

1. Thirty-eight percent have thought very often about making an occupational change—compared to only 10 percent of the oldest workers.
2. Only 14 percent are so attached to their current jobs that they would not change jobs even for more money—compared to 45 percent of the oldest.
3. The younger workers tend less to consider their current jobs as very much like the kind they wanted when they first took them.

This last point is very much in keeping with studies over the years, which show that young entrants into the labor force choose or find their first jobs on the basis of very little rational analysis or adequate knowledge about what such jobs are really like, and that, consequently, they undergo many job changes before settling down.[1]

Young workers also believe that management places little emphasis on the quality of the work they are paid to perform, and they believe this to a far greater extent than the oldest group of workers. While only 28 percent of the under-30 workers report that their employers put heavy emphasis on the quality of their work, the percentage among the older workers is much higher—42 percent. At the opposite end of the scale, 45 percent of the youngest, but only 28 percent of the oldest, indicate that management emphasizes things *other* than quality of work.

What may be more important, however, is that the lack of management emphasis on quality of work is far more serious to these young workers, by a 2 to 1 ratio among those reporting management emphasizing things other than work quality. More than one-third of the total group of under-30 workers report little or no management emphasis on work quality and are bothered by this—in contrast to less than one-fifth of the very oldest workers. This finding goes very much against the widely-held view that the young worker is less interested in work quality. This contradiction between our empirical findings and the popular image calls for more systematic investigation than our own study has made possible. The finding might also seem to contradict our own finding (reported above) that suggests that younger workers *themselves* place less emphasis on quality work than the older workers. But the saliency question (how much the person is bothered by the low priority placed by management on quality) reported here may be a more sensitive measure of this topic, and it supports our opinion that the young worker does have a greater concern about work quality than we ordinarily would believe.

Further confirmation of this opinion is found in the answers to additional questions (designed by Neal Herrick for a separate analysis reported in Chapter 12) asked of the workers in Kalamazoo. The under-30 group considered it "very important" that opportunities to do interesting and satisfying work be increased. Improvements in their *pay* were reportedly less important (51 percent citing need to improve quality of work vs. 38 percent citing more pay). The same was true of the 55+ workers in the Kalamazoo survey, but the gap between their ratings of needed improvements regarding opportunities to do interesting and satisfying work vs. more pay was much smaller than among the very youngest—45 vs. 36 percent.

Furthermore, a much lower proportion of young workers feels that it is not too important, or not important at all, to improve such opportunities—only 14 percent, as compared to 27 percent of the 55+ group.

The greater emphasis among the young workers on interesting and enjoyable work repeats itself in the answers to another question asking how satisfied they are *now* with their opportunities to engage in such work.

Job Advancement Chances. Critical in the life of most, if not all, American workers is their estimate of their chances for getting ahead in the world of work. In this respect, the youngest workers in our sample are very optimistic in comparison to the oldest ones. Forty-five percent of the young, but only 26 percent of the older workers, feel their chances for getting ahead on their jobs are above average or excellent. But once again, if a young worker says his job offers little or no such chances, he is much more likely to be *bothered* by this lack of mobility opportunity offered by his job.

Training for Getting Ahead and for Job Rotation

Young workers are not only more optimistic about their job advancement chances, but they are also more responsive to any opportunity for further training or education that would make it possible either to get a promotion with their current employer or to get a better job somewhere else. More than 90 percent of them said they would take advantage of such an opportunity, in contrast to only 60 percent of the oldest workers. (But even 60 percent among men 55 and older is a substantial figure that shows the widespread interest among workers for upgrading training programs.)

But perhaps even more critical is that, among those saying they would take advantage of such training or education (with enough money to support themselves and their family), the younger worker would opt much more often for a better job *somewhere else*. They want to leave their current jobs much more than do the older workers—by a ratio of 2 to 1. Many older workers feel "locked" or "trapped" in their current jobs, because of the many benefits derived from long service with one employer. Furthermore, although we cannot prove it, the older workers in our sample are probably those who "remained behind." There may be many workers who, before they reached 55, moved up and out—and hence were not "caught" in our sample net. At any rate, the younger workers, as suggested by their responses to these questions, are sufficiently unattached to (or dissatisfied with) their current jobs to make them more interested in taking advantage of such training opportunities as a way out of those jobs. This is especially true of those young workers in low-level tasks.[2]

We have already discussed at length the findings on the notion of job rotation. We will simply mention here that job rotation seems to be more popular among the younger workers: Among the under-30 workers, nearly three-fourths, but only two-fifths of the oldest workers, think favorably of the notion of being trained for working at two or three really different jobs over a period of a year. While earlier studies on this issue have had negative policy conclusions and have tended to downplay such proposals on the grounds that few workers would be interested, we can only suggest that perhaps those older studies were dealing with a generation of workers with greater resistance to change, with greater tolerance of, or satisfaction with, the intrinsic features of their job tasks. Our complete data show that the younger the worker, the greater his willingness to accept the idea of job rotation—especially if he is working at low-task-level jobs.

Unions and the Younger Worker. At a time when trade unions are believed by many to be less fortunate in recruiting new leaders from among its young rank and file members, it is critical to inquire into some of the dimensions and possible roots of young worker attitudes toward the union.[3] Our interviews suggest that the younger worker feels left out of, or neglected by, his union—to a far greater extent than the oldest members. The following table shows how the two contrasting age groups rate the degree of helpfulness of their union to the membership.

Young and Old Workers' Rating of Their Unions

	Under 30		55 and Older	
Very helpful	16%		30%	
Fairly helpful	23	39%	38	68%
Sometimes helpful	47		23	
Mostly not helpful; not at all helpful, don't know	14		12	
	100%		100%	
Number of cases	*(82)*		*(78)*	

The proportion of the youngest workers giving their union the highest rating ("very helpful") is about half that for the oldest members, 16 vs. 30 percent. When combined with those saying "farily helpful," favorable ratings of their union are only 39 percent among the under-30 workers, but 68 percent among the oldest union members. If these evaluations (along with the conditions that engender them) persist, the problem of union leadership in the future may well be a critical one.

The lower regard for their union that young workers have provokes the interesting question, just who are the young workers who feel this way? How do they differ from the other young workers who report that their union is very or fairly helpful to its members?

First of all, it is not a simple matter of wages. Young pro-union workers, if anything, tend to have more among them at the lower wage scale ($3.50 or less) than those rating their union as less helpful. When it comes to fringe benefits, however, we find a different picture. The young pro-union worker enjoys more of such benefits.

Workers with their current employers less than a year are more likely to be found among the less pro-union young.

The pro-union workers are slightly better educated—85 percent have at least a high school diploma, compared to 71 percent of the less favorably inclined.

As for the less tangible features of their jobs, young pro-union workers are more likely to consider their current jobs as matching the kind they wanted when they first took them. Furthermore, they are much more frequently satisfied with their jobs than the young workers giving lower ratings of their union. For example, only 4 percent of the pro-union workers say they are satisfied with their jobs only occasionally—none say hardly ever or never. But more than one-third of the less favorably inclined report they are satisfied with their jobs occasionally, hardly ever, or never.

Young workers who are pro-union are also characterized by a much lower discrepancy between their aspirations and actual achievements. More than half reflect little of such discrepancy, compared to only one-fourth of the workers who rate their unions as being other than very or fairly helpful to the members.

Finally, if we take the two international unions with large representation in our total sample, the young UAW members give higher ratings of their union than do the young members of the United Steelworkers. Among the auto workers, 56 percent say their union is very or fairly helpful, compared to only 37 percent of the steelworkers' members.

To repeat, differences in wage levels apparently are not the explanation for the differences in union ratings among the young workers reported here. But the intangible aspects of the job seem to be more relevant in a search for an explanation. Young workers' expectations as to the kind of job they wanted when they first took their current one, and the frequency of their satisfaction with it, do provide us with better insights into the reasons for the ratings they give to their union, although the tangible feature of fringe benefits also plays an important role.

SOCIAL-PSYCHOLOGICAL AND POLITICAL CHARACTERISTICS

One of the most basic facts of life that we must now accept about the young workers of today is that they are much more anti-authoritarian than their fathers and grandfathers were and are. This one fact provides us with a profound insight into many other dimensions of their outlook and behavior. More than half of the under-30 workers in our sample must be considered as extremely non-authoritarian (53 percent scored in the lower fourth of our authoritarian scale). In dramatic contrast, only 14 percent of the oldest men can be similarly labeled as extremely non-authoritarian.[4] When we combine the two lowest levels of authoritarianism, 75 percent of the young turn out to be non-authoritarian, compared to only 37 percent of the oldest—half the proportion of non-authoritarian among the youngest.

The young workers of today are not like the young workers of yesterday. Their "social character" is the unique feature, and their anti-authoritarianism is part of that character. As a result, they will not be satisfied with jobs of little intrinsic value, especially those allowing for little variety, little autonomy, and little responsibility. And those young anti-authoritarians who now find themselves in such jobs (especially if they are also with at least a high school education) will become highly alienated.[5]

To be precise, authoritarianism is the issue here, not age. This contention is based on the finding that, among the few authoritarians in the youngest group of workers, the frequency of job satisfaction, for example, is identical to that among the older authoritarian workers. It just so happens that fewer of the young than of the old are authoritarian. We must also face the high probability that young workers will remain less authoritarian than most old workers of today. On all three items used in our interviews to measure authoritarianism, the young workers are different from the old ones, especially regarding the first two of the three:

	Percent Agreeing with the Statement	
	Under 30	*55+*
1. The most important thing to teach children is absolute obedience to their parents.	45%	86%
2. Any good leader should be strict with people under him in order to gain their respect.	45%	79%
3. A few strong leaders could do more for this country than all the laws and talk.	55%	68%

The closeness of the two age groups on the last item, however, should warrant some concern among Americans worried about anti-democratic tendencies in the populace. Equally important, these findings relate to the controversy in the late 1950s about the greater authoritarianism of American workers, relative to the middle and upper classes. Without attempting to join that old issue, let us simply say here that a new survey on the question should reveal a closing of the gap in authoritarianism between workers and members of other, higher social classes.

Increased education, the emergence of native-born members in the white working class (or the decline in the number of European-born workers), and the general ethos of the times, have contributed to the increase of non-authoritarianism in that white working class.

On our measure of alienation, here too, the youngest group of workers is less alienated. Nearly two-fifths of these workers, in contrast to less than one-fourth of the oldest workers, have very low alienation scores, for example. There is no claim here, contrary to our arguments about authoritarianism, that level of alienation is likely to persist among individuals as they grow older. Alienation seems to be much more "situational"—subject to change depending on the life situation at any particular time in the individual's life career. In other words, new experiences in the future can change the level of alienation.

On two of the three alienation items, the young stand out in great distinction from the old workers, as the following table indicates:

	Percent Giving "Alienated" Responses	
	Under 30	*55+*
1. These days a person doesn't really know who he can count on.	43%	74%
2. It's hardly fair to bring children into the world with the way things look for the future.	28%	43%
3. In spite of what some people say, the lot of the average man is getting better, not worse.	26%	24%

Note: Disagreement with item 3 is defined as an alienated response. *Agreement* with the first two statements is defined as an alienated answer.

The extent of distrust and of bleakness concerning the future distinguish the two extreme age groups from each other. But on the third statement, it is nevertheless significant that disagreement is the same among the workers, regardless of age.

Authoritarianism and Alienation Combined. But what about the portrait of the young worker insofar as authoritarianism and alienation jointly considered is concerned? The surprising finding is that, even though young workers have few among them who are authoritarian and alienated,[6] they nevertheless have the highest proportion who are non-authoritarian *but* alienated! Twenty-five percent of these men under 30 have such characteristics, while only 8 percent of the oldest men have similar social-psychological attributes.

Types of Young and Old Workers by Authoritarianism and Alienation Combined

	Under 30	55+
Non-authoritarian and alienated	25%	8%
Non-authoritarian and non-alienated	50	30
Authoritarian and alienated	9	39
Authoritarian and non-alienated	16	23
	100%	100%

As already indicated and discussed in greater detail in Chapter 4, alienation must be considered as situational. One of those situations has to do with the nature of the job tasks the workers perform, and, if a non-authoritarian of any age is in a job with low-level tasks, the argument is that he is likely to be much more alienated than if he were in a job with high-level tasks. And at the risk of being repetitive, the young workers are the least authoritarian. Among all the task-level and age categories examined here, the young workers in negative tasks have the highest percentage who are non-authoritarian *but* alienated.[7]

Achievement Values. The young worker is also characterized by higher achievement values which reflect a greater emphasis on activism rather than passivity, a rejection of fatalism, and less concern with material insecurity. In the very highest achievement value classification, the under-30 men in our sample outweighed the oldest by a 3 to 1 ratio (42 percent vs. 14 percent), and at the very opposite end, those with very low achievement values (only 11 percent of the youngest, but 35 percent of the oldest) were very low in such values.

As one example of such differences, agreement with the proposition that, "In his work, all a person should want is a secure, not-too-difficult job, with enough pay for a nice car and home," was much lower among the young workers than among the older ones. Only 37 percent of the youngest, compared with 66 percent of the men 55 or older, agreed. This one finding also confirms the overall impression from our interviews that young workers are interested in much more than mere security and easy jobs.

They are also less fatalistic and have higher expectations than older workers, as evidenced by the fact that few of them (only one-fifth) accept the proposition, "Don't expect too much out of life and be content with what comes your way"—compared to exactly half of those 55 and older.[8]

Political Efficacy. It is surprising, perhaps, to find that the youngest and the oldest workers are virtually indentical in the degree to which they feel they have control over the political processes of our society. This does not mean, however, that there are no age differences whatsoever. The middle-aged workers are higher in their feelings of political effectiveness than either of the two age extremes. This finding suggests that people are less involved and interested in political matters in their young adult lives, but as they grow older, coming into roles and situations that engender greater awareness of the impact of political decisions in their lives, they do become more involved and interested; then in later years, as they grow into their late 50s and older, it may be that their middle-age beliefs and expectations suffer some disappointments. They may become wiser about the difficulties of an individual having any influence in the political sphere.

One specific item in the political efficacy scale reveals a major difference between the youngest and the oldest age groups. The youngest workers are much more likely to disagree with the statement that, "The way people vote is the main thing that decides how things are run in this country" (60 percent vs. only 41 percent of the oldest workers). Thus, in this respect, there is already a greater cynicism among the young workers. It also shows up in the high degree to which they believe that neither of the two major political parties represents their point of view best of all, as reported below.

Political Efficacy and Alienation. Previous chapters have discussed the great significance in our kind of society of having men and women who feel politically effective and who are also non-alienated. Younger workers have a somewhat higher proportion of such persons than do the workers 55 and older—39 vs. 29 percent—and fewer with the opposite characteristics—22 vs. 31 percent. Thus among the young, the non-alienated, politically-effective workers outnumber those with the least desirable characteristics; but among the oldest, the least desirable outnumber the non-alienated, politically-effective citizens.

Political Efficacy and Authoritarianism. The young workers in this case are much more characterized by high political efficacy and low authoritarianism. The contrast between them and the oldest workers is far greater than in the case of political efficacy and alienation: 37 percent of the under-30, but only 17 percent of the oldest, workers are *high* in their feelings of political efficacy and *low* in authoritarianism; and the proportion of the young with the very opposite characteristics is only one-third that among the oldest workers (12 vs. 35 percent are low in political efficacy but high in authoritarianism).[9]

Liberal vs. Conservative Identification. Young workers are more liberal than the oldest workers—at least when asked how they would classify themselves—and less conservative, as one compared to the oldest workers. Among the under-30 workers, 43 percent called themselves liberal, in contrast to only 30 percent of the oldest.

But they were hardly more liberal than conservative by self-designation: 42 percent of the youngest workers chose the conservative label to classify themselves. On the other hand, the 55+ group is much more conservative than liberal by self-designation—52 percent calling themselves conservative, only 30 percent as liberals. Roughly one-sixth of each age group chose neither of these two classifications.[10]

Campaign Issues. While we did not ask the workers where they themselves stood on, or how they felt about, specific issues that are part of the focus in political elections, we did ask them—in order to tap what's on their minds—what were the three most important issues that candidates should be talking about during their campaigns. The answers of the youngest workers and those of the oldest are *not* the same.

Above all, war–peace–Viet Nam, was the most frequently cited issue—regardless of age. But the youngest workers mentioned these matters much more than did the oldest—80 vs. 60 percent. Responses to the issues of inflation, high prices, high taxes, racial issues, poverty, and unemployment did not reveal any major age differences.

But in addition to the war, one other issue stood out, and it seems to show how different the young worker of today is, compared to the oldest ones. The issue: pollution and environmental problems. The proportion of the youngest workers citing this issue as one that candidates should be talking about was more than three times as great as among the oldest. Nearly half of these under-30 white male workers (48 percent) referred to pollution and related terms—in marked contrast to a mere 15 percent of the workers 55 and older. On the two issues of war and of environmental quality, we cannot dismiss as cavalier talk the belief that a generation gap exists—at least among the kinds of white male union members we interviewed in the four urban areas of Pennsylvania and the one in Michigan.[11]

Party Preferences and Voting Behavior. One critical difference revealed in our study is that young workers have very little confidence in either the Republican or the Democratic Party. When asked which party represents their point of view best of all, exactly half said that neither represented their point of view, that both are about the same, or cited a third party. Compare this with the older workers in our sample, only one-fourth of whom feel the same way. In other words, 50 percent of the youngest workers chose one of the two major parties, in contrast to 75 percent of the oldest.

As for the two major parties, 41 percent of the under-30 group and 54 percent of the oldest group prefer the Democrats; 10 percent and 22 percent, respectively, pick the Republicans.

We cannot dismiss the basic implication of these findings, that the young worker—compared to the others—is not convinced that the major parties are concerned about him. Just as in the case of union attitudes, they tend to reject the Establishment—and the Democratic Party and the labor movement are to them part of this Establishment. (Only one-fourth of the under-30 workers in our sample, compared to nearly two-fifths of the remainder, are both pro-union and pro-Democrat.) What significance, furthermore, should we attach to the fact that the young workers call themselves liberal to a greater extent than the oldest workers? (Liberals, in general, were no more pro-union than conservatives in our sample.)

Even if we consider only workers who were registered to vote, a much smaller percentage of the youngest workers actually voted in the 1968 Presidential election—only 57 percent, as contrasted with 86 percent of the oldest workers. If they voted at all, fewer of them—compared to the oldest—voted for Humphrey; *fewer* voted for Nixon—but a much larger proportion chose George Wallace.

1968 Voting Choices of Youngest and Oldest Workers

	Under 30	55+
Humphrey	33%	46%
Nixon	26	36
Wallace	23	4
Others, or refused	18	14
	100%	100%

By a ratio of nearly 6 to 1 (23 vs. 4 percent), the young voters in our sample of white male union workers, compared to the oldest ones, chose the candidate who for them apparently expressed a challenge to that Establishment, and who gave vent to whatever resentments and frustrations such men harbor.[12]

The fact that 18 to 20 year-olds among the white male workers can now vote in Presidential elections is not necessarily a source of optimism for liberals, union leaders, or Democrats—if the bases for the attraction of a man like Wallace among young white union members remain unchanged; and, as far as we can make it out, racism—at least among Northern workers—is not an adequate explanation of this attraction.

More important perhaps is what Irving Crespi in his analysis of Wallace supporters has pointed out: ". . . the older age cohort developed particularly strong party loyalties during the 1930's and . . . those who came of voting age since World War II are increasingly 'Independents.' If the latter interpretation is correct, it emphasizes the significance of a decreasing ability of the two major parties to generate political loyalty as a precondition for future Wallace strength."[13]

Young workers—like other young persons—are increasingly Independents, and their voting choices (even if only slightly different from those of older voters) can affect the fate of a major party's candidate. Furthermore, the decreasing ability of the two major parties to generate loyalty among the young workers will affect the future strength for candidates of parties other than any endorsing George Wallace.

The Young Wallace Voter

In what ways is the young Wallace voter different from others in his same age group? Without going into all the possible comparisons, let's indicate the following:

1. He lives (by comparison to the other young workers) in the smaller urban centers (in other words, *not* in the very large metropolitan areas of our study—Philadelphia and Pittsburgh).

2. He is more likely to have been a migrant to these urban areas from very small towns and rural areas.

3. Compared to the other young workers, he is more likely to be Protestant.

4. He works in occupations paying lower wages, and his total family income is low.

5. Despite this, he feels his job lives up to his original expectations (although he is less frequently satisfied with it), and he feels his take-home pay is high enough to take care of his family's usual bills and expenses.

6. On the other hand, he feels that he is not as well off as he expected when he finished school (the young Wallace voters have a higher percentage with some college education). Compared with what he wanted out of life 10 years ago, he feels he has made little progress.

7. He feels *impotent* regarding the degree to which he has any influence

in the decision-making of government. And he believes that neither of the two major parties represents his point of view.

8. Contrary to what might be expected, he is just as liberal—perhaps more—as the young non-Wallace voters, by his own self-designation.

9. In his opinion, his union is of little help to its members.

10. Contrary to the great interest among young workers as a whole, the young Wallace voter is not much interested in hearing from candidates on the issue of pollution and environmental quality.

Discrepancy between Aspirations and Achievements. Young workers are more likely to consider their current jobs as *not* being very much like the kind they wanted when they first took it. We can expect many of them to shop for better jobs. (They tend to think much more frequently about changing to really different types of jobs.) But when it comes to whether or not they are better off than hoped for at the time they finished school, they are not too different from the oldest workers. For example, 31 percent of the youngest and 29 percent of the oldest, say they are *not* as well off as hoped for.

When asked to compare their current status regarding the things they've wanted out of life as against 10 years ago, 74 percent of the youngest workers, in contrast to 53 percent of the oldest workers, say they are "further ahead." In this respect, the youngest group has a lower discrepancy between what they wanted out of life 10 years ago and their progress to date.

Because of the lack of consistency in replies to these three separate questions, the overall Discrepancy Index[14] reveals no difference between the youngest and the oldest workers in our study.

Evaluations of New Workers and Race Attitudes. Among young workers engaged in their current occupations or employed with their current employers for at least five years, their judgments of new workers coming into their workplace over the past year or so are much more favorable than the judgments made by the oldest workers. More than half of the youngest (55 percent), but only 37 percent of the oldest, rate such new workers as just as good or better than they themselves were when they first took their own jobs. A previous chapter has shown that workers with such judgments are less likely to hold anti-Negro attitudes.

Without seeking to carry out a similar cross-tabulation, let us simply present the responses of the youngest and the oldest workers to the question dealing with blacks and other minority groups. Young workers tend to be somewhat more in agreement than the oldest ones with the statement that, "Most Negroes want to get ahead using the same ways other Americans have used to get ahead." Nearly three-fifths of the under-30, but less than half of the oldest group, agree with that proposition.

On the other hand, the young workers are not very unique when it comes to how they feel about management and union efforts to help minority groups like Negroes and Puerto Ricans in getting good training or good jobs for them, as the following table indicates.

	Under 30	55+
1. Percentage stating that *employers* are doing too much in getting good training or good jobs for minority groups.	19%	22%
2. Percentage stating that *unions* are doing too much.	14%	12%

The major comparison is between the two items and not between the two age groups. Unions are criticized by the oldest workers much less than the employers on this issue (22 vs. 12 percent), but this wide gap of 10 percentage points is not matched at all in the case of the youngest workers.[15]

DEMOGRAPHIC CHARACTERISTICS

Appendix A, Table 5, indicates the differences in selected socio-economic characteristics between the under-30 and the 55+ age groups in our survey.

As should be obvious, the youngest workers—compared to the oldest—are far more educated (a factor involved, incidentally, in the emergence of anti-authoritarianism and higher expectations). Contrary to what may have been predicted, more of them are in the upper-income family brackets.[16] Given their greater proportion of single members, it is not surprising that the young workers also have a high proportion with no dependents; but at the same time, the table suggests that, among those who are married, they have many more dependents than the oldest workers. And they belong to far fewer organizations than the oldest. In fact, nearly half belong only to their union.

SUMMARY

On which specific dimensions, both in their job world and in the world around them, do these young white male workers stand out as relatively unique?

1. The majority of them (unlike the oldest workers) are in intermediate task levels.

2. If they do cite negative features in their job tasks, they are more frequently bothered by them.

3. Very few of them feel their full potentials are being used on their current jobs. And in this connection, the majority (unlike the oldest workers) placed a very low estimate on the value of their job.

4. The majority of the young workers (unlike the oldest) are infrequently satisfied with their jobs—particularly if they are in jobs with negative tasks.

5. The vast majority of the youngest workers rate their employers negatively when it comes to their judgments on how much emphasis management puts on quality work—and this bothers them more frequently than it does the oldest men.

6. While they are more optimistic about their chances for getting ahead on their jobs, the young workers who are not optimistic are bothered by the lack of such mobility much more than the oldest.

7. Very pertinent to one of the major themes of our report, a large majority of young workers (unlike the oldest) are favorably inclined toward the notion of being trained for job rotation opportunities.

8. Similarly, they are much more receptive to opportunities for upgrading training and would take such training to get away from their present employer, for a better job somewhere else.

9. Only a minority of the youngest (compared to a large majority of the 55+ workers) give their unions a highly favorable rating.

10. More important than anything else, the young worker typically is much more anti-authoritarian than his elders, and this one unique feature of his "social character" helps to explain much about his job attitudes and his judgments of economic and political institutions in the society.

11. They are also less alienated. They are much less distrustful of others (only a minority, compared to a large majority of the oldest men); and less pessimistic about "the way things look for the future."

12. Despite these last two points, the youngest workers, nevertheless, have a relatively higher proportion of alienated non-authoritarians—and a good deal of the explanation lies in our overall major proposition that alienation is low only among non-authoritarians (regardless of age) who are in situations such as being employed in unsatisfying jobs.

13. Contrary to some popular images, the younger worker is not satisfied merely with an easy job that pays enough for such material things as a nice home and a car. Simple jobs and guaranteed employment are not sufficient for him.

14. On the political side of life, a majority of them (unlike the oldest) reject the notion that the country is run primarily through the influence of voting on the part of individuals, and this is accompanied by little faith in the two major political parties.

15. They are more liberal by self-designation than the oldest workers, but the proportion calling themselves conservative is just as high as for those young workers claiming to be liberal.

16. They are clearly different from the oldest workers when it comes to the kinds of issues they believe that political candidates should be talking about—pollution and environmental problems being the most glaring example.

17. These young workers constitute the major source of support for candidates such as George Wallace—especially if they live and work in the types of smaller urban areas covered by our research.

18. The majority of the youngest workers (unlike the oldest) feel that blacks want to get ahead using the same ways other Americans have used in

their quest for success. But they are no more or less critical of unions' and employers' efforts to help minority group workers.

The findings discussed in this chapter make a case for the argument that a new type of worker *is* growing up in America. How can anyone deny the existence of a generation gap, at least in this work dimension of life, when we find, for example, that three-fifths of the youngest workers—but less than half of the oldest—state that almost anyone or a good many people can do the kind of work they are employed in? This wide difference between the youngest and the oldest workers cannot be explained by any claims that the younger worker is more likely to be in lower-level tasks to begin with, and, thus, his answer to such a question is bound to be affected by the nature of those tasks. This explanation cannot be accepted because even among workers in high-level tasks, age still makes a difference—with the youngest still claiming to a much greater extent than the oldest that almost anyone or a good many people can do their job.

Job task levels are critical, as we have repeated over and over again in this report. But we cannot ignore the emergence of a "new generation" that judges the quality of blue-collar jobs—and perhaps work in general—in terms radically different from the way in which older workers judge those same jobs.

But recognition of this emergence is growing at a very slow pace. In some quarters the term should be *resistance*—not recognition. It is still rare to find statements by labor leaders such as the one quoted at the beginning of this chapter from M. C. Weston, Jr., of the United Steelworkers.[17]

Another example of such awareness on the part of a union leader is in the remarks by a West Coast UAW International Representative, Neil Manning, concerning the job itself:

> . . . management does not give them proper orientation as far as the job is concerned . . . they don't let them become involved in knowing where the product they are making is going . . . new people make no decisions, have no right to make any decisions involving what you would call the basic management rights in the plant . . .[18]

Manning also points out that if a union leader brings up what the unions were able to do for their members back in the 1930s, the young workers "tune out immediately; they have no interest in what happened thirty years ago."

To repeat, such recognition of the generation gap among workers is, at least today, rare. We hope that the kind of report we have written here, and discussions of it and other studies, will contribute to a growing acceptance, first, of the existence of the change in the social character of young workers of the new era—and most of all, to a search for significant solutions that are in accord with this new social character. We should not waste time or energy in even thinking about changing that social character. The focus instead must be on improving the nature of work, and of creating the conditions and changing our institutions to make that improvement possible.

NOTES:

1. See, for example, the British study of Michael Carter, *Into Work* (Baltimore: Penguin Books, 1966), in which the author states that ". . . much job changing, it is clear, is the inevitable outcome of lack of guidance in choosing work, haphazard ways of finding employment, and the indifferent attitudes of employers, children and parents alike." (P. 158.)

2. For the Pennsylvania workers under 40 and in negative tasks, more than half would opt for training to get a better job somewhere else— compared to only about one-fourth of those workers of the same age but in higher task levels. At the other end of the age scale, about one-third of the 55+ workers in negative tasks, but *none* of those in higher level tasks, would choose such training to get a better job elsewhere.

3. For an interesting and provocative discussion of the "leadership shortage" (either in quantitative or qualitative terms), see, "Why Labor Can't Find Its Young Leaders," *Bhsiness Week*, October, 1970. The article comments on the widely accepted fact that labor in the 1930s and '40s recruited a large portion of its leadership from "some of the most overqualified production workers in history," and from idealists outside of the working class.

4. At the opposite end, only 10 percent of the youngest, compared to 23 percent of the oldest, are extremely authoritarian.

5. Young non-authoritarian workers with at least a high school education, who are in negative task jobs, are not only more alienated, they are also more likely to prefer a different job from their current one. Very few of them rate their job as measuring up to what they originally expected; and they are much less frequently satisfied with the job. They also feel further behind in what they wanted out of life 10 years ago and are much more interested in the idea of job rotation. These observations are in comparison with other young anti-authoritarians with at least a high school education but who are in positive task jobs, and not just in comparison with the sample as a whole.

6. Nine percent vs. 39 percent of the 55+ workers.

7. Among these young non-authoritarians, those in negative, low-level tasks are also characterized by: (1) the least satisfaction with their

jobs, and (2) the greatest preference for a job other than the one they now have.

8. It is not surprising that young workers have the highest proportion who are characterized by high achievement values and low alienation, by nearly a 2 to 1 ratio, when compared with the oldest workers (52 percent vs. only 27 percent), and few of them have the very opposite social-psychological characteristics.

9. Approximately the same findings apply when achievement values and political efficacy are combined.

10. Liberals and conservatives (without regard to any age break-down) differ in several respects. For example, liberals are much less critical of new workers, and they are less anti-Negro. By more than a 2 to 1 ratio, they are *non*-alienated (66 vs. 31 percent); less authoritarian— but feel no more politically effective than conservatives. The liberals respect the right of both unions and employers to support political candidates, and choose the Democratic Party as representing their point of view much more than do conservative workers. While they voted much more for Humphrey than the conservatives (60 vs. 34 percent), the proportion of workers calling themselves liberal who voted for Wallace was almost the same as for the conservatives. But the liberals are no more pro-union than conservatives. This last finding may be a hint that the traditionally close association between liberals in general and the labor movement as a whole is undergoing some significant changes.

11. Since the interviews in Kalamazoo were conducted nearly one year after those in Pennsylvania, there is some reason to believe that these two issues during that year grew in importance (although some of the difference must be attributed to the younger average age of the Kalamazoo workers).

12. In a study of over 9300 persons in 1968 (before the election), it was found that in the East (the major source of our 371 interviews), an *identical* percentage (actually, 24 percent) of the under-30 group of unionized, manual workers indicated a preference for George Wallace. This group had the highest percentage preferring that candidate. And the oldest workers within the group of unionized manual workers had the lowest proportion favoring him. See Irving Crespi, "Structural Sources of the George Wallace Constituency," *Social Science Quarterly*, June 1971, especially Table 6, p. 130. On the basis of the Crespi data and our own, there is some reason to believe that last-minute frantic efforts of the labor movement to reduce the pro-Wallace sentiments among its members succeeded primarily among the oldest workers.

13. *Ibid.*, p. 131.

14. See Chapter 2.
15. Although the above table does not report on the middle-aged group, they turn out to be much less critical of their union on this matter than either of the two extreme age groups.
16 This is true even when we exlude those young workers "living rent-free" (usually with parents).
17. From an address before a conference at the University of Tennessee, 1971.
18. "Experience of Union Officials in Dealing with Young Members," in *The Generation Gap: Implications for Labor-Management Relations* (Institute of Industrial Relations, University of California at Los Angeles, 1970), pp. 24–27.

Chapter Eight

The Pro-Wallace White Worker:
Putting it Altogether

> *"George Wallace gave John Doe a face and a name . . . and the deep estrangement on which the Wallace phenomenon fed is still very much there in Mill Town, U.S.A. waiting to be exploited again. It is only when the worker's* humanum *is honored in the structures and relationships of the modern industrial world that the right-wing madness will lose its attraction. . . ."*
> *—Gabriel J. Sackre*

Where appropriate throughout this report, we have cited how workers with this or that set of social and psychological characteristics voted in the 1968 Presidential election—with special focus on the Wallace vote. We should put those separate findings in one place, and introduce additional comparisons between the Wallace and non-Wallace voters in our sample of white male union members.

We have already learned that the pro-Wallace worker is more likely than others to be alienated—at least as measured by agreement with the proposition that, "it is hardly fair to bring children into the world with the way things look for the future." He is also more likely to be discontented, as defined in Chapter 2. Discontent not only refers to the discrepancy between a worker's aspirations and his achievements, but also to: (a) whether he feels there is any chance for advancement in his job, or (b) whether he feels his take-home pay is adequate.

With respect to one of the critical typologies used in this study—dealing with personal and political alienation combined—the Wallace voters are much more characterized by the tendency to be *high* in personal alienation and *low* in feelings of political efficacy, relative to their proportion with the opposite characteristics, when compared with the Humphrey and Nixon voters. These Wallace voters include more workers with the negative than with positive tendencies, while workers with low alienation and high political efficacy outweigh by more than 2 to 1 their opposite numbers, in the case of the Humphrey and Nixon groups.

Exactly half of the Wallace voters were discontented, in contrast to only 31 percent of the Humphrey, and 18 percent of the Nixon voters.

Furthermore, we have pointed out the large proportion of the very young workers (under 30) who voted for George Wallace—in contrast to just a few among the oldest workers (55 and older). Indeed, the median age of the Wallace voters is only 38, in contrast to 46 among the Humphrey and Nixon voters.

Because they are so much younger, it is not surprising that the median schooling of the Wallace voters is the highest. In fact, a much larger proportion of them had at least one year of college. This by itself suggests that young workers with that much education, who nevertheless find themselves in blue-collar jobs, may tend to be disgruntled and discontent with their actual "life chances." Another finding is in keeping with all this: one of the questions used to construct the Discrepancy Index, asking the workers whether—compared with what they had hoped for when they finished school—they are better off, or not as well off, as hoped for, reveals a high proportion of the Wallace voters saying they are *not* as well off. Two-fifths of them, compared to slightly more than one-fourth of the Humphrey and Nixon voters, feel this way. More Wallace voters express disappointment than express satisfaction with their life outcome so far. The opposite was true of the other voters.

On one of the other items used to make up this Discrepancy Index, asking if they were further ahead, or behind, compared with where they were ten years ago, a smaller proportion of the Wallace workers than of the others felt that they were ahead. And nearly one-fourth of the Wallace voters, contrasted to only one-eighth of the Humphrey and hardly any among the Nixon workers (1 percent!), said they were *behind*.

Higher education and youth are associated with higher expectations. If these expectations are not fulfilled, the odds for political "deviance" are multiplied. The dynamics of this deviance do not necessarily involve income *per se*. At least this is my interpretation of the fact that the wages of the Wallace voters are not very different from those of the other workers. Neither is their total family income very different from the non-Wallace voters. And all the voters are uniform in their judgments as to how *adequate* their take-home pay is to meet their usual family bills. On the other hand, the Wallace voters are slightly more likely to feel that they don't get enough income to live as comfortably as they'd like. Once again, the importance of aspirations is confirmed.

It is not enough merely to cite changes in actual income or wages among the white working class, as many economists are prone to do, in examining the current issue of the "blues" among white workers. Data restricted to actual income are incomplete and inadequate when trying to examine this critical issue. Human *expectations* and human *evaluations* of that income must also be taken into consideration. And these dynamics enter into the political orientation and voting choice of workers.

We are suggesting here that the Wallace voters, with their higher education and lower age, are bound to have higher expectations. We know directly through our interviews that they have not had those expectations realized to the same degree as the other voters, as reflected in their replies to questions about hopes and realities since leaving school, whether they are ahead or behind compared to 10 years ago—and whether their income is satisfactory as measured against their *desired* level of living.

Something else in this connection: the Wallace voters are much more cynical about "how to get ahead." Less than two-fifths cite education and/or working at it as the road to success—as opposed to more than three-fifths of the rest of the sample (non-voters included). They see, instead, "luck" or "knowing the right people" as the explanation for how people get ahead.

Political and Union Orientation. Wallace voters view themselves as liberal to a lesser extent than the pro-Humphrey workers (40 vs. 49 percent), and considerably more than do the Nixon voters, of whom less than one-fourth choose the label of liberal. (By almost a three-to-one ratio, the Nixonites are more conservative than liberal, in their own eyes. It is only among the Humphrey voters that more chose liberal than conservative when asked to give a label to their political viewpoints.)

As for the political party choice, half of the pro-Wallace workers believe that the Democratic Party represents their point of view best of all. But almost the same proportion (47 percent) refuse to choose *either* of the two major parties. As might be expected, more than 8 out of 10 Humphrey voters prefer the Democratic Party, but less than half of the Nixon voters point to the Republicans as representing their point of view best of all.

The following table shows the voting choices of the workers according to their political identification:

Percent voting for:	Democrat	Republican	Independent or other
Wallace	11%	2%	23%
Humphrey	76	5	32
Nixon	14	93	45
	101%	100%	100%

Note: Percentages do not add to 100% because of rounding.

The table indicates, first of all, that few Republicans "defected" from their party's candidate in 1968. In contrast, about one-fourth of the Democrats may be considered "defectors."

Second, it suggests that, among workers at least, Wallace running as a third-party candidate hurts the Democratic contender far more seriously than the Republican.

Third, the Wallace vote is highest among those rejecting both major parties. The emergence of an "independent" mood among workers, and the greater tendency of Democratic than of Republican workers to stray from their party fold, are among the causes of concern to the leaders of the so-called "majority" party. The fact that more Americans call themselves Democrats than Republicans is no guarantee of victory in elections for the Democrats.

Furthermore, the Wallace voters are less favorable in their ratings of how helpful their unions are to the members. Less than three-fifths of them, compared to about two-thirds of the other voters, rate their unions as very or fairly helpful.

Finally, on the matter of what campaign issues they believe political candidates should be talking about, the Wallace voters are actually not too different from the rest of the sample. Viet Nam, for example, is at the top of the list, although not quite as high as among the non-"Wallace-ites." But on one issue, as reported in another chapter, they *are* different—pollution and environmental problems. This issue is apparently not a very critical one among the Wallace workers, at least in comparison with the others. Even among the young Wallace-ites, the frequency of mention of pollution and related matters is only half that among all the other young voters.

Race Attitudes. While the race question was not expressed to any discernible extent when the workers were asked to cite important political campaign issues, the Wallace workers nevertheless show up as unique when asked more directly about such things as Negroes wanting to get ahead using the same ways other Americans have used to get ahead, and about the efforts of unions and employers to get good training and good jobs for Negroes and Puerto Ricans. On both questions, the Wallace-ites are far more negative than the other voters, regardless of whether these other workers voted for Humphrey or Nixon. But on neither of these two questions was there a majority of Wallace-ites expressing such negative racist positions.

On the other hand, a large majority of them (two-thirds) did express an opinion that new workers in their workplace are not as good as they themselves were when they first got their jobs. And as we have already pointed out, this opinion is highly correlated with the negative answers to the questions directly asking about race attitudes. Among the non-Wallace voters, slightly less than half felt negatively about workers recently joining them in their places of employment.

Other Social Characteristics. Our sample, consisting entirely of white male blue-collar union members, revealed the same general finding of nationwide surveys concerning the influence of religion on voting behavior. A majority of the Wallace voters are Protestant, unlike the Humphrey and Nixon workers. This finding suggests that the ethnic question may be more critical among the white Protestants than among the other ethnic groups (Poles, Italians, and others of eastern European Catholic origins).

Our analysis also revealed that size of city was related to candidate choice of the workers. Two-thirds of the Wallace voters live in the smaller urban areas covered in our survey; that is, in places other than the Philadelphia and Pittsburgh urban areas. While a minority of Humphrey's voters (43 percent) live in these smaller urban areas, a majority (57 percent) of the Nixon voters do. The main point is that, in the North, candidates like Wallace apparently find their greatest source of support in the smaller urban areas.

Work and Its Discontents. What about the job itself? Does this factor have any relationship to how the workers voted in 1968? We think it does. For example, nearly half of the Wallace voters, but only one-fifth of the Humphrey and Nixon voters, have thought frequently about making a real effort to enter a new and different type of occupation. This question was found to be related to other features of the workers' jobs. These differences are *not* a matter of age (since it may otherwise be argued that the Wallace-ites are younger, and youth is associated with the desire to change occupations). Regardless of age, the Wallace voters have thought much more frequently about such a change. They are made up, much more than other voters, of men who are "candidates for second careers," as defined and discussed in the next chapter. To sum it up, the Wallace voters are less frequently satisfied with their jobs than either the Humphrey or Nixon voters. Furthermore, the Wallace voters are in jobs they consider as having little autonomy to a greater extent than are the other voters.

Finally, they are, compared to other voters, much more likely to be in low-level task jobs with less job security (1 or more weeks of joblessness in the past).

In capsule form, what is the pro-Wallace white male union member like? First, he is young, better educated, but alienated. Second, he is truly the worker with the "blues"—if by that we mean he has not achieved as much as he has aspired for, and if he sees little chance of advancement in his job, or if he judges his take-home pay as not as much as he'd like. He is alienated not only in the social sense (little faith in others, and pessimistic about the lot of the average man), but also in the political sense.

Furthermore, he tends more to be independent of either of the two major political parties, compared to other voters. And, just as he tends to reject one of the pillars of the working class Establishment, the Democratic Party, he also is less favorably inclined toward his union. He is also somewhat more prejudiced.

There are several unique signs of unhappiness with crucial features of his job situation. Even when age is considered, he shows signs of wanting a job really different from the type he is in now, which may be considered a sign of job discontent. This is clearly and directly indicated by his answers to a question that directly asks about how frequently a worker is satisfied with his job. And he judges that job as offering little in the way of autonomy.

We cannot ignore the interplay between the nature of the job a man performs and his moods, outlook, and behavior that spill over into his so-called non-work world. Our political findings are, in our opinion, another argument for the belief that greater attention must be paid to finding remedies to the dissatisfying features of large numbers of workers' jobs—even if those numbers are a proportional minority. In modern mass society, small percentages can mean large numbers, and even small percentages in the political realm can swing elections one way or another.

Neither can we ignore the possibility that such a minority may be growing, either in numbers or as a proportion of all members of the labor force. We may have caught in our net only some of the symptoms of a cutting edge in our society, in which men (and, increasingly, women) enter the labor force with high expectations of their work and their society—expectations that constitute a challenge for that society to fulfill.

Part Four

Opportunity and the Older Worker

Chapter Nine

Mid-Career Blues

> *Perhaps the biggest threat to the human race at the moment is not so much the nuclear weapon as the possibility of eliminating the aging process. . . . If we would rearrange the human genetic structure to program death at the age of 1,000 rather than at 70 . . . the human race would face the highest crisis of its existence, a crisis which I illustrate easily to an academic audience by asking them who wants to be an assistant professor for 500 years?*
> —Kenneth Boulding

The young do not have a monopoly on restlessness and discontent, contrary to what our chapters on the young workers may have seemed to suggest.

The popular press has recently dramatized a number of case studies of older individuals (40 and over), mostly men in professional and business positions, who have made drastic leaps from one type of occupation to another seemingly incongrous one. Here we want to explore the possibility that blue-collar workers, too, are beginning to show signs of a similar tendency.

Call it the middle-age work crisis, male menopause, mid-career depression, or anything else. There do seem to be greater signs of this type of phenomenon. At the very least, counselors and other persons in related behavioral sciences may be conceptualizing old problems in new bottles.

Such a phenomenon does exist—apart from the issue of whether it is any more extensive today than it was in the past. Nevertheless, we would argue that it is more extensive—at least more salient—than it was in the past. But more important, our popular mentality—perhaps even the academic literature—is still dominated by the single career concept; the notion that an individual should have a single lifetime occupational role–identity. Perhaps in a

153

more traditional (in other words, a slowly, if ever, changing society), it made sense from both the individual and societal points of view to stress the acquisition of a single set of skills to be used during one's working life—which, by the way, wasn't very long.

But today, the average age at death is higher, and the social and physical technology of the environment is constantly in flux. Longevity increases the probability that a number of intervening experiences—both environmental and subjective—will affect the individual's occupational self-identity and his continued interest in a given occupation.

Changing technology is naturally accompanied by changes in the skill requirements necessary to use that technology. One of the critical points here is that our sources of socialization—chiefly the family and the school—do little, if anything, to prepare members of society for multi-careers *prior* to their entering the world of work. Such preparation need not be strictly devoted to actual acquisition of specific skills of widely varying character. Perhaps it would be more relevant to prepare young people *psychologically* for the fact that before they die, they may enter a variety of somewhat differing jobs.

With perhaps the exception of the military establishment, our other institutions, which actually or potentially touch the lives of *adults*, are doing little, if anything, to make it possible for middle-aged and older persons to enter really new and different occupations. In fact, one could make a case for the proposition that such institutions do everything in their power to discourage and make it impossible to facilitate occupational change. A more charitable proposition would be that, in our efforts to solve certain problems and to achieve other goals, we have developed solutions and mechanisms that—without malice or deliberate intent—function today as anachronistic obstacles to the encouragement and facilitation of second careers. Typical examples include certain entrance requirements for training and education programs, provisions of pension plans, narrow-range seniority rules, and early retirement as a so-called solution to unemployment or other personal problems.

Dr. Thomas Green, of Syracuse University's Educational Policy Research Center, has argued before the House of Representatives Committee on Science and Astronautics that the post-industrial society will have to be based on the cultivation of knowledge, rather than on craft skills.

The idea of reshaping the education system to encourage multiple careers by individuals, and even to provide for occasional "moratoriums from productive work" was presented by Dr. Green.

> Surely there is nothing more damaging to the human spirit than the knowledge —or belief—that one's capacities are unused, unwanted, or expended in something of no particular value.

Who knows what human misery would be relieved and what human energies released if the possibility of multiple careers were the rule, and if there were, as a consequence, ready means of entry and exit to and from new avenues of work.[1]

Let us cite one more possible factor that may be involved in the emergence of concern about flexible or second careers; namely, the impact among adults of a discrepancy between original aspirations and mid-life achievements, the subject of our chapter on discontented workers. It is interesting, and at first paradoxical to some observers, that the amount of education attained is positively related to the tendency among employed men to define work as an activity that is required, or *not* enjoyed. This is a finding of a 1959 study of Detroit workers by Robert Weiss and Robert Kahn. Weiss and Kahn suggest their own explanations for this finding, but the one we want to add here is derived from a discussion by Orville Brim, in his survey of adult socialization research, cited in the chapter on the discontented workers.[2] In that discussion, Brim points out that the greater the person's educational achievements, the higher his aspirations; *but* that higher aspirations are accompanied by a higher risk of *non*-achievement of those aspirations.

Brim says that a person "handles these discrepancies for a long period of time by successively displacing fulfillment of aspirations into the future, but the day of reckoning does come." For some persons, this displacement of aspirations into the future continues for an indefinite length of time. The point we wish to make is that persons whose occupational achievements do not equal their original aspirations come to look upon their jobs as something which must be performed but which are not necessarily enjoyed. Such persons may constitute the group for whom second-career opportunities may be the most critical. We will turn shortly to our own interviews with white male union members, which may shed more light on the question of identifying such persons as "candidates" for second careers.

This point of view can be strengthened by such arguments as the need for upgrading middle-level workers and professionals to make room for lower-working class men and women who complain about being in dead-end jobs; the needs of society for more people to perform higher-level functions and public service functions now in sad neglect; and the need for workers today to be "loose" when it comes to over-identification with one occupation in times of high unemployment. In a study of unemployed workers by the Upjohn Institute, it was found that workers who looked for jobs really different from what they had been doing regularly had a higher job-finding success rate.[3]

The topic of second careers has been treated as something emerging primarily among professional and technical employees. But is it possible that similar desires—expressed and unexpressed—exist among *working class* men in their mid-career years? And if so, how do workers with such characteristics differ from other workers who apparently are not interested in making any radical occupational change?

In the first place, among the more than 200 men in our sample who were 40 and older, more than one-third (36 percent) indicated that they had thought once in a while, or very often, about seriously making a real effort to enter a new and different type of occupation (or had already made such a shift), and also that they would choose a training or education program making it possible to get a promotion or a better job. In the 40–49 age group alone, the proportion is nearly half.[4]

In what ways do these adult candidates for second careers differ from the non-candidates? The accompanying table presents some of the comparisons.

Comparison of Candidates, and Non-Candidates for Second Careers, 40 or More Years Old (Pennsylvania and Kalamazoo Combined)

Item	Candidates for Second Careers (percent)	Non-candidates for Second Careers (percent)
1. Age:		
40–49	51%	35%
50–54	24	24
55+	25	41
	100%	100%
2. High achievement values	57	46
3. If completely free, would prefer some other job to the kind he now has	38	26
4. Has *actually* tried to get into a line of work really different from any he has been in	37	19
5. Above average chance or excellent chance of mobility opportunities on present job	17	35
6. High aspiration-achievement discrepancy	51	28
7. Low job autonomy	22	8
8. States that job rotation is a very good idea	55	38
9. Satisfied with job "most of the time"	47	57
10. Feels that employers and/or unions doing "too much" in getting good training or good jobs for minority groups like Negroes and Puerto Ricans	29	18
11. High school diploma	45	44
12. Earns $3.50 per hour or less	40	34
13. Says that his take-home pay is good enough to take care of family's usual bills and expenses	68	70
14. Reported family income:		
Under $8000	30	38
$10,000 and over	42	46

First, let us cite the variables on which there is little or no difference between the candidates and non-candidates for second careers. The last four items in the table are especially important: There is little difference between the two types insofar as their hourly wages or reported adequacy of take-home pay is concerned. The same is true regarding family income: They are virtually identical. Economic factors apparently do not provide us with any understanding of the problem. There is also no difference in education, although one might expect to find the higher education level among the candidate group, since they tend to be somewhat younger.

The critical point is that the usually considered variables such as income and/or the adequacy of take-home pay do not appear to contribute to understanding the second-career candidates, or their desire to change to really different occupations.

Rather, it is in the social-psychological sphere and in the nature of their jobs that the differences appear. For example, the candidates for second careers have higher achievement values, and we suspect that if we had administered David McClelland's projective test, they would also register higher in achievement motivation.[5] As further indication of this, on a behavioral level, a much higher proportion of the candidates reported that they actually have tried to get into a really different kind of work—by a ratio of 2 to 1.

Returning to a major focus of this volume, the candidates for second careers express greater dissatisfaction with their jobs, as indicated in several ways:

1. A higher percentage, if completely free to go into any type of job they wanted, would prefer some *other* job to the kind they have now.
2. Candidates for second careers—to a far greater extent than non-candidates—say they would quit their job right now if they had anything else to do, or would take almost any other job in which they could earn as much as they're earning now. (And only 16 percent of them, as contrasted to 45 percent of the non-candidates, say, "I do not want to change jobs even for more money because the one I have now is a good one.")
3. When asked how frequently they are satisfied with their jobs, a smaller proportion of the candidates reply, "Most of the time."
4. Candidates are more likely to report that their current job does *not* measure up to what they wanted when they first took it.

In keeping with this last point, it is abundantly clear that the overall discrepancy between aspirations and achievements is radically greater among the candidates than among the non-candidates. More than half of them score a high discrepancy, compared to slightly more than one-fourth of the workers not experiencing any interest in second careers.

On other job aspects, the candidates report, on the average, a lower degree of autonomy in their jobs: 22 percent of them report little or no freedom on the job. But the corresponding figure for the non-candidates is a mere 8 percent.

Their chances for promotion in their present job situation—as they see them—are far slimmer: only 17 percent of the second career candidates, as compared to twice that proportion among the non-candidates, say there is an above average or excellent chance for getting ahead on their job.

Such men are really more discontented, or more ambitious, or more restless. This is further confirmed by the fact (not reported in the table) that nearly half of them (45 percent) said they would choose a training program that would lead them to a better job *away from their present employer*. But among the group of non-candidates who did say they would take such a program, only one-sixth would choose it for a better job somewhere else. (Non-candidates for second careers included some workers choosing a training program opportunity, but they had rarely or never seriously thought about making a real effort to enter a new and different type of occupation—thus disqualifying them as second-career candidates.) This wide difference once again points up a greater dissatisfaction with the *task* content of their jobs.

All of these and other findings point to a group of men who might benefit from a more structured opportunity program that would allow them to shift to new and different kinds of work life. They would not be the only group to benefit, either. Their job discontent, or their greater aspirations for a different type of occupation, may lead to some questionable positions in the social and political realm—positions or behavior that do other parts of society no good. For example, they seem to be more critical of union and employer efforts to help minority groups. Secondly, the candidates are apparently cynical about hard work and/or education as ways of "getting ahead" (only 49 percent of them, but 60 percent of the non-candidates, believe that most people get ahead in such ways).[6]

Finally, we cannot ignore the fact that in their voting behavior, such a group of men preferred George Wallace to a greater extent than did the non-candidates—slightly more than 9 percent, compared to less than 4 percent (p = .10). As our chapter on the young worker reported, the Wallace support came chiefly from that younger age group. But if we combine second-career candidates of all ages, their vote for Wallace was twice as great among all the non-candidates (14 vs. 7 percent of all those voting).

In summary, one might say that there is a malaise among a significant portion of white male workers in America—the "blue-collar blues," to use a recently coined journalistic expression. Much of this seems to relate to an urgent and growing need for flexible or second careers among such persons. The same may be said even for the technician and professional classes in our society. Neither do we exclude the growing numbers of minority group members of our labor force. (We may be dealing here with a new or growing general symptom of the nature of our industrial or "post-industrial" society.) We have presented here one suggestion for identifying such persons, and have also indicated some of the social-psychological dimensions in which they differ substantially from the so-called non-candidates. This approach might help contribute to a program that conceivably could combine an improved counseling and education effort designed to improve the work lives and social environment of the contemporary generation of men and women in our constantly changing, tense society.

Second career opportunities are not a will-o'-the wisp. Several legislative proposals are now under serious consideration in Congress for "Mid-Career Opportunities." Western European nations have actually begun wide-reaching programs.[7] And the following chapter, by Alan Entine (State University of New York at Stony Brook), is a brief description of a successful project at Columbia University (under his direction), which was designed to enable a group of men—previously in top business positions—to make a major occupational change while between the ages of 40 and 55.[8]

NOTES:

1. "Panel Examines New Technology," *New York Times*, January 30, 1970.
2. John A. Clausen, ed., *Socialization and Society* (Boston: Little, Brown and Co., 1968), pp. 203–205.
3. Harold L. Sheppard and A. Harvey Belitsky, *The Job Hunt* (Baltimore: The Johns Hopkins Press, 1966).
4. In this chapter, we are interested only in 40–plus group of workers, and how the candidates for second careers among them differ from the non-candidates. But we should point out that the desire for second careers (or the candidacy rate) declines with age:

Percent of Workers Who Are Candidates
for Second Careers, by Age

Under 30	30–39	40–49	50–54	55+
76%	60%	45%	35%	25%

5. Without resorting to technical psychological definitions, achievement motivation refers to the individual's willingness and tendency to develop and exploit opportunities, to persist, and to excel in situations leading to success or failure. See David McClelland and David G. Winter, *Motivating Economic Achievement* (New York: The Free Press, 1969).
6. This cynicism applies only to the older candidates, not to those under the age of 40. Could this mean (especially in the light of their high aspiration-achievement discrepancy) that after years of striving, they

have not achieved as much as they had wished, and thus place little faith in such "virtues" as education and hard work?

7. See, for example, *Continuing Training and Education During Working Life*, papers for an International Conference, Copenhagen, July 1970 (Paris: Organization for Economic Cooperation and Development, 1970); also, Herbert E. Steiner, *Continuing Education as a National Capital Investment* (Kalamazoo: Upjohn Institute for Employment Research, 1972).

8. A recent study has been published on the same topic, which contradicts the notion that mid-career changes are rare and that persons seeking such changes "do so out of dissatisfaction with their original occupations." Instead, such persons generally are "actively searching for new interests which they had not previously entertained as career possibilities." The study demonstrates "the changing nature of the middle years and of American society. . . ." Dale L. Hiestand, *Changing Careers After 35* (New York: Columbia University Press, 1971).

Chapter Ten

Second Careers: Experience and Expectations

ALAN ENTINE

> *Middle age is no longer necessarily a period of hopes abandoned and of reconciliation prior to entering upon old age. It has become a period of new options that can provide an increasing number of men and women with new opportunities for developing new sources of satisafaction and meaning.*
> *—Eli Ginzberg*

This volume has focused its attention on a wide range of concerns related to the area of employee satisfaction and performance. My comments are limited to one segment of this topic: the problems of persons who seek vocational and personal satisfaction by changing their careers in middle years.

The observations in this paper are based upon the results of a unique project which existed at Columbia University a few years ago. The project, known as the New Careers Program, did more than uncover some of the basic personal problems which individuals face when they wish to change careers. Although the Program was limited in scope to a selected segment of our work force, its existence attracted and exposed an unbelievably wide spectrum of persons from all vocational backgrounds who desired to make career changes. In addition, the Program pointed up the very important role which institutions of higher education can play in facilitating career changes through imaginative and specially designed programs of study and counseling.

THE NEW CAREERS PROGRAM

The New Careers Program began operating at Columbia University in 1963 with a $100,000 grant from the Ford Foundation. The Program was established originally to enable individuals who held positions of responsibility in business to make career shifts into the not-for-profit service sectors such as education (teaching and administration), social work, library administration, hospital administration, and so on. Participants enrolled on a full-time basis in the regular degree programs at one of the professional schools at Columbia and, in most cases, matriculated toward a master's degree. The Program provided $1000 per year to defray tuition costs. In some cases, these funds were supplemented by fellowship support from the professional schools. While there were no age or educational limitations, preference was given to applicants between 40 and 55 who possessed a bachelor's degree.

The Program began in a small way with no major publicity. By 1965, the Program had enabled some 15 persons to successfully make career changes. In August of that year, a major news story about some of these individuals appeared in *The New York Times* and feature articles appeared subsequently in many magazines. Stories about the New Career Fellows—the interior decorator who became the New York City Job Corps Director, the advertising executive who became a reference librarian, the engineer who became a teacher for the deaf—appeared in *Time, This Week, The Saturday Review,* and a host of other publications.

As a result of these stories—and radio and television appearances—inquiries about the Program mushroomed. More than 4000 letters arrived by the end of 1965, and for the next three years the mail never fell below 75–100 inquiries a month. With the deluge of correspondence and telephone calls came the knowledge that the desire to change careers was not limited to businessmen seeking the non-profit sector: teachers asked to become stock brokers, social workers desired to become accountants, and farmers wanted to be salesmen. A small project at one university could not begin to help all of these people, but we did expand opportunities for study at Columbia to those who did not possess the bachelor's degree, to retiring members of the armed services, and to retiring members of the uniformed service groups in New York City: police, fire, sanitation, etc.

By 1968, more than 50 persons had participated in the program. None dropped out and most had either successfully completed their studies or were embarked upon a second career. We made vigorous attempts to increase the financial support for the program since the limited tuition assistance did not provide adequate aid. Men in their forties and fifties, even coming from good jobs or enjoying retirement benefits, could not easily sustain the costs of attending the University while foregoing other income. Often too, these persons had their own children in college.

During 1967 and 1968, strong efforts were made to secure additional financial support. The Department of Defense, the military Retired Officers Associations, the City of New York, and the city's fire and police service societies all gave vocal support to the program but felt that they could not give financial assistance. The Ford Foundation refused to renew its grant feeling that the program had proved its success and should therefore be able to attract funds elsewhere. Appeals to other foundations were also futile. The needs of businessmen and others desiring to change careers fell low in the priority scale when compared to the needs of the poor and the disadvantaged. As a result, the program came to a quiet close in early 1969. I am told by friends at Columbia that inquiries about New Careers arrive to this day.

OPPORTUNITIES FOR THE FUTURE

Despite its limited scope, the New Careers experience provided several valuable insights into the problems connected with middle-years career changes. Older persons were able to return to a university setting and successfully complete formal programs of study. They were able to matriculate toward a new professional degree which gave them the key to opening the doors to their newly chosen field. Yet, if a significant number of persons are to follow the example of the New Careers participatns, two findings must be emphasized:

1. Adequate financial support must be made available while the individual is studying to embark upon his new career. Generous living allowances and grants may be one solution; another may be release time options from present occupations while the individual pursues his study on a part-time basis. To minimize costs, one might institute a trade-off between release time and additional service in his present job. Thus a policeman might work for twenty-two years before retirement instead of twenty if, during his last four years of service, he obtained one-half release time to pursue studies for a second career.

2. Adequate counseling must be provided at all stages of the career change. Many persons who came to us wanted to make a change but were unsure about opportunities elsewhere. Others asked specific questions about the nature and activities of a new field. Still others were anxious about the specific employment opportunities (where the new jobs will be, what the salaries will be, and so on) and were apprehensive about their ability to successfully complete a program of study which would give them new tools and credentials. From the moment a person seeks a new career to the time he is actually embarked upon it, he needs the support of a trained counselor. At Columbia, we attempted to meet this problem by instituting seminars at monthly intervals for program participants. Studying in various parts of the university, the New Careers Fellows were brought together to share common experiences. Speakers from various professional fields addressed the group to tell them about existing opportunities in each field. These activities were supplemented by counseling on personal problems in the New Careers Office, counseling on academic problems in faculty offices, and counseling on employment problems in the placement offices of the various professional schools.

The Program uncovered a wide variety of persons in all parts of the country who desired to make career changes. This fact was already mentioned; let me simply state that the mail came from persons in all walks of life and from all parts of the country. Often persons would telephone the office after having read about the program in the morning papers. Unless an individual was willing to relocate to New York City, we could not help individuals significantly; we advised many to turn to local colleges and universities for further assistance.

Finally, the Program revealed an important role which higher education can play in facilitating career changes. The New Careers Program participants entered existing degree programs at Columbia's professional schools. For the most part, these were one-year master's level programs, although some, such as social work and hospital administration, took two years to complete. A few of the Fellows needed to complete their bachelor's degree studies and another small number sought doctoral degrees to prepare themselves for college teaching. All were required to attend classes full-time in order to facilitate the career-change process.

In retrospect, the program would have attracted many more persons if part-time study were permitted. Moreover, the numbers served would have been even greater if the professional schools themselves had devised special short-term study programs which would be open primarily to persons in middle years who sought new careers. I believe that the creation of specialized programs to facilitate career changes is a major opportunity for innovation in higher education today. These programs might be pursued on campuses, at one's present job or even in one's home.

It is most likely that mature persons would require shorter educational experiences to obtain the needed skills to enter a new career. The educational process today exists as much to provide young persons with opportunities to mature as it does to obtain specific job oriented skills and tools. Older persons do not need the maturing process; they seek as short an educational experience as possible which will enable them to embark on second careers. For this reason, professional and trade accrediting associations must become more flexible to permit mature individuals to receive professional degrees and licenses after shortened, specialized course work. Naturally, no one is asking that the standards of a profession be sacrificed on the altar of expediency. However, I am making a strong plea for flexibility and a positive approach to this problem. Otherwise, many capable persons with proven abilities in other areas will be unable to enter new careers because of artificially rigid barriers imposed by professional schools and professional accrediting associations.

Where do we go from here? The New Careers Program pointed up a great need in our country—the need to provide a realistic way for persons to change careers in middle years in order to obtain a more meaningful vocational experience. This need is not confined to merely the dissatisfied; it is very real to those close to retirement who wish to contribute to society in their senior years. The program also showed that a small group of individuals were successful in meeting these needs by adapting to the existing institutional framework of one university and several professional fields. If we are to meet the career-change desires of significantly larger groups, more innovative answers must be devised. Some of the possible approaches were touched upon in this paper. I feel certain that community colleges, four year colleges, and universities can play a major role in the process by which most persons seek to change careers. Some agency, however, must take the leadership to mobilize the resources—both financial and academic—to effect change in the existing institutional structures to facilitate career changes. Perhaps some type of National Study Group might be formed initially to suggest positive ways that existing academic programs, accreditation requirements, release time for study plans, and other options might be adapted to meet the needs of older persons. We will need these tools if we are to work successfully with industry, labor, professional associations, and educational institutions so that untold thousands of Americans can find a satisfying second career.

Part Five

Possibilities for Change

Chapter Eleven

Search for Solutions

FRED K. FOULKES

INTRODUCTION

The primary purpose of this chapter is to review briefly some structural changes adopted by companies to meet the work-related problems of contemporary workers. Before dividing the current efforts into two categories (starting from scratch and making changes in the existing organizational arrangements), I want to say that, in my view, the problem is not limited to workers and to emphasize that this paper is concerned only with formal programs.

PROBLEM NOT LIMITED TO BLUE COLLAR WORKERS

Before reviewing the current efforts, it is important to note in passing that the problem—whether it be called worker alienation, the "blue-collar blues," or simply a deteriorating attitude toward work—is not a problem limited to some blue-collar workers.[1] It also affects white-collar workers,[2] engineers,[3] junior managers, students, and even lawyers.

The January 1971 issue of *Dun's Review*, in an article entitled "Executives in Ferment," talks about the mounting wave of unrest that is sweeping the ranks of middle management. Michael Gerson, a management consultant interviewed on the subject, says:

> Like the kinds of the drug culture, most of the middle managers have become alienated from their parent figures. The result is a loss of motivation, a tendency to become bureaucratic and there is a fantastic turnover among male middle managers.[4]

Middle managers seem to be searching for something, and one can make the observation that the way many corporations are structured apparently leaves several middle manager needs unmet. Some have argued that many middle managers fulfill these unmet needs in off-the-job voluntary organizations, such as the Little League, Community Chest, and so on.

Those in education know that from first grade to the graduate school level, teachers are searching for new ways to "turn on" students, whether it be optional study halls, more independent work, student-initiated seminars or student created majors. Students are asking for and getting new rights and responsibilities. In one of my classes, a visiting college president, in office for almost twenty years, said:

> It used to be that when a student asked to see the president you could count on the student appearing somewhat nervous in your office. Today when a student asks to see the president, it is the president who is nervous!

An article in the May 1970 issue of *The Yale Law Journal*, entitled "The Public Interest Lawyers," is very interesting. The article is based on a survey of young lawyers who have left private law firms and have entered public-interest law firms. The article states:

> Many of the lawyers when interviewed complained that the large law firms are dehumanizing. One of the lawyers was particularly disturbed by the impersonality and the cautiousness of his colleages of the corporate firm where he used to practice.[5]

A law firm I am familiar with has for almost two years now permitted, even encouraged, its members to devote up to 15 percent of their time to *pro bono publico* matters of their choice. In addition to permitting the lawyer to engage in some worthwhile work in which he is interested, it also gives a degree of control and autonomy to the lawyer which he did not formerly possess.

Thus, while the problem may be more severe at the blue-collar level, it would be a mistake to assume it is only a factory problem. It is, it seems to me, a societal problem threatening many institutions as they are now structured.

FORMAL PROGRAMS

In terms of an overview about what some companies have done about the problem, it is important to point out that this review will be limited to the formal programs which companies have adopted. This is said because it has to be recognized that much is going on informally, whether it be by an enlightened manager trying to innovate or by an old-line manager doing what comes naturally. In terms of numbers, and in terms of formal programs, my research indicates that in 1971 we are talking about, in total, the work of less than fifty companies, most of which are either non-union or organized by unions which are, relatively speaking, not particularly strong. In examining the formal programs, it is useful to classify them under one of two headings: starting from scratch or making changes in the existing organizational arrangements. Most have to come under the latter category, but a few have the privilege of starting from scratch, and it is here that we shall begin.

STARTING FROM SCRATCH

In terms of starting from scratch—in other words, building a new plant with some of the behavioral science concepts in mind—there are at least seven new plant planning efforts that can be cited: General Foods in Saratoga and Topeka, Proctor and Gamble and Olin Mathison in Augusta, Corning Glass and Polaroid in Massachusetts, and General Electric in Illinois. While there may be others, these are the only efforts known to the author.

In terms of generalizations, one can note that these new plants usually eliminate time clocks, have a minimum of rules, engage the employees in goal setting, and stress communications and team building. The important point, however, is that these companies view these plants as *experiments in management*, with the goal being the creation of a very special organizational climate, one characterized by openness and trust and a strived-for goal congruence between personal and company goals. Generally, those managers who are to be responsible for operating the plant are carefully selected long in advance, and they form a new plant planning team, usually aided by outside organizational development consultants. Needless to say, top management support is very important, and it must include the right to deviate from some traditional company policies and practices, especially in the areas of job design and method of payment.

Although new plants, by definition, lack the traditional climate, rules and practices that are barriers to making changes in a firm's existing organizational arrangements, there are still barriers to be overcome. Traditional thinking, perhaps at headquarters, is one. Another problem can be the transfer of managerial personnel to the operating new plant, for managers operating under old assumptions can make it rough going in the new plant. This is understandable, for they have not had the common development experience that the initial new plant managers had.

MAKING CHANGES IN THE EXISTING ORGANIZATIONAL ARRANGEMENTS[6]

The second of the broad categories is termed "making changes in the existing organizational arrangement." In terms of responsibility for initiating the changes, it seems to lie with personnel, training, industrial engineering or work simplification. But in my experience, it does not succeed unless line management gets actively involved. What is intriguing is the number of different approaches to the same problem that companies have adopted. I'd like to mention three and then give some current examples.

One is job rotation. Polaroid started the Pathfinder Program in this area some while ago; Edwin Land, President, Chairman and Director of Research at Polaroid, talks about a worthwhile work life as a company goal for every employee. Under Polaroid's job rotation program, some factory people were given the option of moving to the job of laboratory technician. Job rotation was to be a way of life; one was to work half his time on his new exciting job and the other half on his old job, the one that was not so exciting. What was soon learned was that once the employees adapted to the new job, they didn't want to go back to the old job. Job rotation as a way of life didn't work out. Polaroid then moved to a career exposure plan where employees have the opportunity to be exposed to new jobs and when a moment of opportunity arises they can bid for the job. Another large consumer products company tried job rotation in a different way. On a particular packing line it was felt that the inspection job was the high status, interesting, fun job. Inspection which used to be done out in the laboratory was now made part of the packing line and employees rotated through the inspection job so that each employee spent two hours a day as an inspector and the rest of his time on other jobs. Management thought that each employee considered himself an inspector, and job satisfaction went up, productivity went up, and turnover and absenteeism went down. There are lots of interesting things that can be done in the job rotation area.

The second approach I would like to mention is what I shall call the "Texas Instruments Approach," and, again, there is much top management support. Pat Haggerty, Chairman, talks about a worthwhile endeavor. He hopes all the employees in the company will become involved in their jobs. He thinks that if you have an alignment of company and personal goals, the company is in much better shape than if the goals get out of line. Texas Instruments defines a meaningful job as one in which the employee has planning and controlling responsibility in addition to the traditional "do" part of the job. Vertical job enlargement is stressed at Texas Instruments, and there are a number of jobs, where, for instance, inspection and testing have become part of the job. These are control functions which the employee now has which, formerly, somebody else had. In addition, Texas Instruments has problem-solving–goal-setting sessions where the supervisor and the employees identify the problems of business, form task forces and make recommendations. Being involved in the process *can*, if it works well, make work a more meaningful experience.

In contrast, the American Telephone and Telegraph approach (Work Itself projects) does not employ, at least initially, employee participation; instead, the managers restructure jobs, trying to build in the Herzberg motivators which give employees the opportunity for challenge, recognition, achievement, and responsibility. Managers implement the changes one by one as the employee demonstrates competence to handle the additional responsibilities. Robert Ford has written an excellent book on the work itself projects, and the reader is referred to his book for the results of almost twenty separate trials.[7]

There are a number of firms that are using AT&T's model of making work more meaningful. One example, at Bankers Trust in New York, took place in the division handling the stock transfer operations.[8] This job involved about 100 employee typists.[9] It used to be their job as typists to type the new stock certificates, after which they went to a production typist to type the transfer sheets. Then there was a person called the "preparation clerk" who punched the denomination of the stock certificates, dated and stamped the certificates, and a checker who proofread the sheets, checked for production debit and credit totals and then reviewed the certificates. There was a correction typist who corrected the errors.

After the change, the functions were combined into one, a newly designed typist job. The typist drew the certificate, typed the transfer sheet, prepared the certificate, checked the work, made her own corrections, and, according to an article in the *Boston Globe*,[10] the bank said they saved $300,000 in this one year trial of job enrichment. Among other things, they eliminated much of the quality review force, increased output, improved production quality, and improved job attitudes.

Some of the banks and insurance companies are now trying to apply some of these concepts to a number of the so-called white-collar jobs. In one large insurance company, the managers came up with a "Green Light" list of twenty-four ways to improve the job of the keypunch operator. Eight of the manager-agreed-to-be-implemented suggestions were:

1. The operator should have total responsibility for a certain segment of work, to provide feedback on performance and establish relationship with their clients.
2. Each keypunch operator should maintain her own production and quality reports.
3. Operators should deal with their clients to research and correct errors that are made.
4. Individual operators will be responsible for weighing their own work, completing their time slips, and punching their time sheets.
5. Individual operators who have demonstrated proficiency should be allowed to have their work go unverified.
6. Individuals should be allowed to correct their own errors.
7. Operators should be allowed periodically to attend classes where other operators are in training in order that they might explain their jobs.

8. Each operator should have full background for the job on which she works.

Particularly encouraging is the "conscious application" of some of the job enrichment techniques to some of the entry jobs which now, for one reason or another, are filled by the so-called "hard-core" minority people. In some cases it isn't only that is it right and there's much pressure to do so, but, in certain cities, they are the only ones available for such work. Permit me to quote briefly from a study of minority employees at one company. This is a study that was done by Settlement Housing Employment in New York. In interviewing, they concentrated on what the minority employees were thinking about, and the study concluded:

> It is encouraging to note that so far as the interviews indicate X company's minority workers were not looking for easy jobs, over-indulgent supervision, a spoon-fed route to higher skills, a better position with the company. Their goals appeared to be quite conventional, such as stepping up from the mail room to the typing pool, a sympathetic and helpful supervisor. It is also clear that the employee had genuine respect for the company's stature and accomplishments. Their doubts (the doubts of the minority employees) centered on themselves in relation to the company; they had deep misgivings about chances of getting promoted, of "making it" at company X because of company and supervisory indifference to them. Moreover, several of the more ambitious and more able workers believed that the absence of opportunity for training and advancement was deliberate and to some degree reflected a racial bias.

My encouraging point is that in a firm in New York which is enriching some of the entry jobs held by blacks, not only has there been a reduction in absenteeism and turnover and an increase in productivity, but the thing that is most impressive is the change in white managerial attitudes as the result of the hard-core blacks performing well in the enriched jobs. The firm's initial experience with the hard-core people was that they came late, or didn't show up, and had bad work records; now, after they were given more meaningful jobs, some of that changed. The other thing that has changed is white attitudes in that the whites initially thought "well I always knew these people were lazy," and "what did you expect?" and now suddenly they're learning that "it isn't necessarily so," because of the structural change, and they are quite pleasantly surprised at what they see happening.

CONCLUSIONS

The most significant conclusion that emerges from the study of the experience of several companies is that for job design work (no matter what you call it, job redesign, job expansion, meaningful work or whatever) to be effective, it has to be associated with a program of organizational development, including changes in management thinking and practices, and lots of training and development. A number of things have to be congruent and consistent with the new job design or else it simply doesn't work. What is being said is that the organizational climate has to be right for it.

One of the interesting points stated earlier was the very different approaches which companies are taking to the same problem, just in terms of how a "meaningful job" is defined. While the definition four companies use are different, the final product is not all that different. At Texas Instruments, it is planning, doing, and control. The AT&T approach is basically defining a module (a certain segment of work that gives the employees new authority), giving new responsibility if the employee demonstrates proficiency, giving feedback, and providing recognition, growth and training opportunities. The job redesign effort at another company listed several criteria which they hoped to have in the redesigned jobs: opportunity for autonomous behavior, useful information flow, reasonably demanding work, full tasks, respect for work, non-restricting boundary conditions, optimal work style, work cycle, absence of high stress, desirable future and learning opportunities. Finally, in one other company a program called a new job design program listed nine characteristics:

1. Change as a regular part of the job
2. Job easily identified with end product
3. Opportunity to act and decide
4. Opportunity to interact with other people
5. Ingenuity and initiative opportunities
6. Freedom of movement
7. Opportunity to learn something new
8. Mental and physical demands balanced
9. Attractive physical environment

Close analysis reveals that the criteria are really quite similar, and while the approaches may be somewhat different, in the final analysis they are really not very far apart.

In implementing these programs, there are certain barriers that one traditionally runs up against. The first one, not very significant, is employee resistance. There is a small segment of employees who are not interested in more challenging jobs. Another is existing policies and practices which conflict with the new job design so that the employee can't carry out the authority and responsibility he has been given. Sometimes there are physical and technological barriers. There are a few jobs which, because of certain technological factors, one cannot do very much for, and the hope is to automate them out of existence at some time. The principal barrier, however, is management attitudes and management resistance. Some supervisors feel it is a threat—if the employee has the responsibility, then what do I do? Some don't understand the approach. Sometimes they understand it, but simply do not agree with it. In the challenging book *Education and Jobs: The Great Training Robbery*, Ivar Berg, during the course of his study, came across one highly placed executive in a very large insurance company who commented that "tender-minded academics" were "downright naive" in their concern about worker turnover and wellbeing. It was the judgment of this highly placed executive that clerical personnel

> ... are easily trained for their jobs, that if they stayed on in larger numbers they would become wage problems—we'd have to keep raising them or end up fighting with them; they would form unions and who knows what the hell else. It's better to hire girls who are too well educated to stay happy with the jobs that we assign them to do. That way they get out before it's too late.[11]

That attitude surely represents a barrier. What job enrichment really is, is manager risk-taking, and unless top management support is behind taking some of these risks, not much happens.

In terms of gateways to this kind of work, there are four worth mentioning. One is top management support, it sure does help. There is also the importance of someone playing the role of catalyst or change agent, both internal and external to the company. External change agents can play a valuable role, and internal change agents that work with the program can become valuable coaches and counselors. Much education and training must accompany job enrichment. In terms of getting started in an organization, there is nothing (like the old story) that succeeds like success in your own organization. If there are a few tries and some small things that are successful, other company managers take note. When there is some hard data that managers can look at, and review the increases in productivity and the reduction in turnover, it is of more than passing interest to line managers. Finally, if companies are to adopt these programs, it must be a way of life. The efforts must be sincere, it must not be viewed as another gimmick. If it is viewed as another gimmick, as a way to get a little more out of the employees, it will just be another program that comes down the pike, and most managers have had enough of those programs coming down the pike.

In terms of challenges for the seventies, one is that we have to try to learn more and get some programs going in the unionized organizations. It may be harder and it will require a cooperative approach, but it can work.[12] The insights of the union participants at the Williamsburg conference are encouraging. In a Ford Foundation financed study done in 1971 for the American Foundation for Automation and involving a survey of 11 industries that upgraded jobs, it was estimated that 34 percent of non-supervisory jobs in these 11 industries, (that's 2.4 million jobs), were what they called dead-end jobs, with dead-end jobs being defined as those which allow minimum opportunity for the exercise of independent judgment and do not provide a reasonable expectation for advancement either through formal or informal job-related training. The study states that when unions have become interested in upgrading, notably in the steel and hotel industries, they saw some real progress. Facing increasingly rebellious factors in the ranks, unions must find upgrading appealing objectives to pursue, the study suggests.

There are a number of reasons for movement in this direction. One is just the kind of ideas that John Gardner articulates so well; his concern with people with dull, monotonous jobs—untapped human potential. We simply have to do something about it, for it is a national problem, and quality of life, quality of working life, are important issues. If, unlike Berg's highly placed insurance executive, we view high turnover as a problem (it is costly), there are ways to reduce turnover, and, consequently, reduce costs. In addition, many now realize there is something that the behavioral sciences have to offer, and the challenge is to translate research into action. Another reason is, of course, increased domestic and foreign competition, with job enrichment becoming a way to increase productivity and become more competitive. Non-union companies see it as a way to stay unorganized. In terms of the labor movement, one cannot ignore the unrest and the contract ratification problem. The high turnover of elected union officials, particularly at the local level, may also indicate it is time to turn new attention to the work setting. Finally, it is consistent with what is going on in society. As Rensis Likert has pointed out, there is a trend in America, in our schools and our homes and communities to start giving individual freedom and initiative; there are few direct and unexplained orders in schools and homes, and youngsters are participating increasingly in decisions which affect them. These fundamental changes in American society result in new employee expectations as to how they should be treated. More autonomy and greater responsibilities in schools means fewer and fewer distribution requirements in freshman and sophomore years, and fewer required courses.

All this indicates to me that what each of us is losing, whether we like it or not, is our right to be arbitrary. And that includes the arbitrary, or at least too often the not well thought-out, assignment of work. None of us want people to be arbitrary with us, and there is no reason why we should be arbitrary with others. This means that we must try to allow for a greater measure of self-determination at work. Utilizing people well may be one of the most important issues of the seventies, one which is worth the attention of each of us. While it will not be easy, there is evidence from the experience of several companies that, in many circumstances, it can be done.

NOTES:

1. Harold L. Sheppard's research findings in this book provides new insights about the way in which "the worker" of the seventies sees himself.
2. See Judson Gooding's "The Fraying White Collar Worker," *Fortune*, December 1971.
3. See Judson Gooding's "The Engineers Are Redesigning Their Own Profession," *Fortune*, June 1971.
4. "Executives in Ferment," *Dun's Review*, January 1971, p. 24.
5. "The New Public Interest Lawyers," *Yale Law Journal*, May 1970.
6. See F. K. Foulkes, *Creating More Meaningful Work*, for a fuller discussion and analysis of several change programs.
7. Robert N. Ford, *Motivation Through the Work Itself* (New York: American Management Association, Inc., 1969). For Herzberg's views, see Frederick Herzberg, and others, *The Motivation to Work* (New York: Wiley, 1960).
8. One of the things that I'm always amazed at is that some of the most routine, simple jobs that one would think are hopeless and that nothing can be done about them, when you get a lot of people thinking about them, the number of changes (and good results) that you can get on these so-called routine, boring dull jobs is surprising indeed.
9. I am in debt to Roy Walters for this example.
10. Donald White, "Turning Off Job Boredom," *Boston Globe*, January 6, 1971.
11. Berg, Ivar, *Education and Jobs: The Great Training Robbery* (New York: Praeger Publishers, 1970), p. 105.
12. M. Scott Myers, "Overcoming Union Opposition to Job Enrichment," *Harvard Business Review*, May–June, 1971.

Chapter Twelve

Organizational Obstacles

*I suggest that the concept of human
organization motivated by material
need has been sufficiently successful
to destroy itself; and that if
we do not enlarge our concepts of
innate human need—our portrait
of a human being himself—that our
societies will eventually collapse
into apathy or explode into anarchy.*
—*Robert Ardrey*

*. . . I feel the main problem lies in
management's assumption that they
are dealing with illiterate, uneducated
morons.*
—*Shop Steward*[1]

Society's increasing concern with the sterility of the workplace is shown by
the kinds of people who are now talking, thinking and writing about human
fulfillment through work. Until fairly recently, the notion that man—by nature—wishes to learn, grow and achieve through his work, and the corollary
notion that work should be structured to allow this inclination full expression,
were pretty much the private property of philosophers and academicians. In
recent years, however, government officials, employers and union leaders have
become involved in a new and growing debate. Private consulting firms offering advice on the restructuring of work to meet human needs are proliferating.

Such new interest suggests a critical need to take a systematic look at how
unions, employers and workers now view the problem. Do they think that it
is important, or do they still regard it as frivolous? Do they think it is feasible
and profitable to enrich work?[2] Are they defensive or open to change? When

the problem is phrased in concrete rather than abstract terms, what are their attitudes? Do they feel their employees or members are—on the whole— satisfied with opportunities for interesting and meaningful work? Do they think that things are getting better or worse? Are unions and employers in touch with the feelings of their members and employees?

My conversations with individual labor leaders and employers led me to believe that the climate for taking institutional action to improve the quality of work has become more favorable. In order to check the validity of these impressions, I conducted a "shoestring survey" of top and middle management in the trade unions and in private industry. I also surveyed small groups of white-collar workers in Washington, D.C. and steel and automotive workers in Kalamazoo, Michigan.[3] All groups were asked essentially the same questions. Since no previous comparable data exist, comments on trends are pure speculation. Nonetheless, I am inclined to think that—as recently as 5 years ago—very few respondents to such a survey would have thought it a matter of serious concern that jobs be changed to allow more opportunity for the worker to achieve and grow. Yet over half of each group in the present survey considered such changes to be "very important."

Certainly, the feelings and opinions of those who make up our institutions are of vital concern to us in considering means by which society as a whole can meet its responsibility to restructure work so that it meets human needs. It is clear that little can be done until workers are somehow given a chance to communicate their views to management. This should be a function of the trade union movement. And the attitudes of union presidents and stewards are pivotal. What's more, the accuracy with which their judgments reflect the attitudes of rank and file should be of interest to union leaders. The future strength and usefulness of unions may indeed depend on a new awareness of changing worker sentiments vis-a-vis the workplace.

A word or two of caution: time and money constraints did not permit the use of samples large enough to produce results which meet the tests of statistical validity. However, the data on union officials is fairly strong since all union presidents listed in the *Directory of National and International Unions in the U.S.* were queried and 34 percent responded. In addition, the data on worker attitudes is generally consistent with the results obtained by the University of Michigan's Survey Research Center (SRC) using a national probability sample.

SURVEY RESULTS

Seventeen corporation presidents and twenty industrial relations directors (more than 50 percent of those surveyed) answered "yes" to the question: "Would you be willing to consider an experimental or demonstration project (in other words, job enrichment) in your establishment?" This illustrates the

message which comes across from employers, middle management, workers—
and even the trade unions: The question of work satisfaction demands urgent
attention. Workers are insisting on more than "just a job" and their behavior
when frustrated is forcing management to sit up and take notice. This is clear
both from the extent to which the various interest groups responded to the
present survey[4] and from the nature of their answers.

The number of top people who chose to give personal attention to the
questionnaire rather than leaving it to subordinates is also significant. Of the
73 employer questionnaires which were returned, 35 were completed by corporation presidents, and of the 81 union responses, 49 were made personally
by international presidents.

The answers given to questions on work fulfillment demonstrated even
more dramatically the changing focus of concern from the economic to the
non-economic benefits of work. More than 2 out of every 3 persons completing the questionnaire felt the need for improving workers' opportunities
to achieve and grow on the job to be "very important." Of the other aspects
of work listed (income, safety practices, fair employment practices, contingency protections), only "improving income" received a larger number of
"very important" votes—and these votes came largely from employers and
union leaders. Substantially higher percentages of both blue-collar and white-
collar workers felt it was "very important" to improve their opportunity to
do interesting and enjoyable work than had that feeling about their pay.

The remainder of this chapter will describe in some detail the specific results of the survey. All groups surveyed were asked to rate the importance
which the respondent attached to the need for improving various aspects of
the work situation at this point in time. Employers were asked about the workers in their establishments; union presidents and stewards were asked about
their members; and workers were asked about the need for improving their
own jobs.

NEED TO IMPROVE THE NONECONOMIC ELEMENTS OF WORK

Management thinks that workers' opportunities to grow and achieve on the
job need improvement as much or more than their pay. Union leaders place
challenging work low on their list of priorities (compared to pay, safety,
etc.).[5] How else could they respond? After all, both groups must keep in mind
their common meeting ground: the bargaining table. However, since workers
rank interesting and satisfying work over pay—indeed, blue-collar workers
rank pay a poor last on their list of needed improvements—perhaps unions
might give some thought to whether or not they are taking the right issues to
the bargaining table.

Rankings were assigned the various elements of work according to the
percentages of respondents who answered "very important"—rather than

"somewhat important," "not too important," or "not at all important"—to the question, "Listed below are some of the elements of the work situation. Please check the box opposite each item showing the importance which you attach to its need for attention at this point in time (in your establishment, among your members, in your job)."

It is important to remember that respondents were not asked how important "adequate income," "good health and safety practices," and so on were to them as a general thing. They were asked how important it was that these elements be given attention in the jobs of their employees, members, and so on (or—in the case of workers—in their own jobs). Accordingly, the results reflect how much the jobs lacked a given quality as well as how important the respondent believed it to be that they had that quality. To illustrate, many respondents commented in narrative form that they considered attention to certain elements (in other words, fair employment practices) to be "not at all important" only because there was no employment discrimination among their employees, members, and so on.

Keeping these qualifications in mind, let's discuss in more detail the conclusions which may be drawn from this part of the survey. First, there appears to be a great deal of consistency within the management and union groups, but very little within the worker category. Both levels of management were quite impressed with the need to improve job content while both levels of the union hierarchy were singularly unimpressed, at least when they stacked it up against the need to improve the economic aspects of the work situation. Even between the two categories of workers (blue- and white-collar), there was not a great deal of *absolute* difference. In fact, only 3 percent fewer blue-collar workers considered it "very important" to give attention to this aspect of work than did white-collar workers. In relative terms, however, there was a difference. White-collar workers ranked the improvement of "work itself" as the single greatest need in the work situation. Blue-collar workers ranked it high, but rated two other work elements even higher.

Since the need for restructuring work is most often argued in the context of the greater need for increased pay, relative rankings of these two items by the various groups are of particular interest. Both management groups ranked them among the top two items needing attention. The union leaders rated pay first and job content either last or next to last. Our sample of blue-collar workers put pay last instead of first and job content in the middle rather than last. White-collar workers considered job content to be the item most in need of attention but also expressed a considerable desire for more pay. It should be noted at this point that, in a nation-wide survey of workers by the University of Michigan's Survey Research Center, the importance of pay and other economic benefits placed a very poor second to the importance of job content. My suspicion is that the reversal of worker priorities by the union hierarchy is largely due to the fact that they are quite comfortable with the techniques for bargaining increases in pay and other tangibles but much less comfortable with the task of translating job content items into specific bargaining issues. They are certainly aware of the problem. Far fewer union officials and union stewards considered workers satisfied with their opportunity to do interesting and enjoyable work than did employers and members of the National Management Association. One last comment on the job content results: although the samples were small and, in the case of the white-collar workers not randomly selected, it is interesting that the higher ranking given job content by white-, as opposed to blue-, collar workers is consistent with the Maslow theory that, once lower order needs are satisfied, higher order needs are intensified.

Apart from the matter of work-fulfillment—but germane to a general concern with working conditions—there are several other points which should be made with regard to the ranking of work elements. First, there were serious differences between management and blue-collar workers with regard to the importance they attach to "occupational safety" and "contingency protections" (workmen's compensation). Second, there were even more serious misinterpretations of worker priorities with regard to these two matters on the part of union officialdom. While stewards were more in touch with the feelings of their constituents on this point than international presidents, even they ranked pay above both safety and contingency protections. Union officials ranked contingency protection as the element least in need of attention while blue-collar workers placed it second only to good health and safety practices. The policy implications of these observations are, with regard to safety and health, only confirmatory. A major and well constructed piece of Federal legislation was passed in 1970 addressing this problem. However, contingency protections, such as workmen's compensation, are in a very sad state indeed and part of this unfortunate situation may be due to a misreading of priorities by union leaders.

JOB FEATURES NEEDING IMPROVEMENT

Considering the close relationship between workplace democracy and the humanization of work, it is important that even management—or at any rate about one of five management representatives—wanted workers to participate more in decision making. The numbers of union representatives who saw this as a very much needed change is even greater. This is contrary to the folk-wisdom which says that both management and the trade-union movement are strongly negative toward the idea of labor participating in management decisions. This survey shows that even in the least positive group (National Management Association members) a full 61 percent thought that at least some improvement in worker participation in management decisions was needed.

Our data allow us to rank ten possible kinds of changes which could be made in jobs according to the percentages of respondents who answered "very much" to the following question: "Please check the box opposite each item indicating how much improvement you feel it needs in (your establishment, the jobs of your members, your job)."[6]

The results on this question were remarkably consistent. Five of the six groups surveyed agreed on the two items most needing improvement. Further, each of these five groups ranked the items in the same order: (1) Full recognition of (their, your) achievements, and (2) Full utilization of skills and education.

Blue-collar workers were the only exceptions to this pattern. They considered the "full utilization of their skills and education" to be the item most needing improvement rather than the "full recognition of their achievements" (which they placed in fourth place). They ranked availability of "free skills training" in second place and the "availability of further classroom education on a no-cost basis" in third place.

All groups except union stewards and blue-collar workers ranked "as much responsibility as (workers, you) can handle" third. More stewards selected "availability of free skills training," an item which was felt by top and middle management to be adequate as things stand. Blue-collar workers seemed relatively indifferent to the notion of increased responsibility.

White-collar workers, corporation management and NMA members also agreed on the item in fourth place: "A chance to participate in management decisions." Union officials placed this item eighth out of ten. Stewards and blue-collar workers placed it sixth but were still generally positive toward the idea.

It is important to examine more closely the fact that the availability of free classroom and skills training, which was considered to need a great deal of improvement by unions and workers, was felt by almost all managers to be an area which did not need improvement "very much." Were managers antagonistic to these ideas or did they simply believe that ample opportunities of these kinds were already available? Their answers to a question to be discussed later on in this chapter (whether they were for or against specific program ideas) would suggest the latter. Well over two-thirds of both top and middle management favored employer subsidy of mid-career skills training and formal education. The seeming inconsistency is further resolved by a closer look at our raw data, which shows that substantial numbers of managers did think that these aspects needed "some"—but not "very much"—improvement.

Several other wide disparities are noted:

Management and white-collar workers had a high regard for increasing worker responsibility, while union leaders and blue-collar workers were relatively unenthusiastic. I would speculate that these latter groups regarded the question as proposing possible exploitation by management.

Management's view of employer-sponsored classroom education and free skills training contrasts sharply with expressions by blue-collar workers of the need for these activities. Union leadership, while positive toward these items, was far more positive toward other items lower down on the blue-collar workers' priority list.

Union leadership seems to have somewhat over-estimated the concern of workers with the right to refuse overtime.

There appears to be a consensus among all six groups that job rotation and increased variety of duties are very low on the list of areas needing improvement. This should not be interpreted as describing negative attitudes toward these pos sibilities. On the contrary, substantial percentages of respondents in all groups felt it was very important that attention be given these elements. What is apparent, however, is that there are many other elements which all groups agreed need attention more.

BARGAINING NONECONOMIC ITEMS

Unions appear less concerned than management or workers about increasing human fulfillment through work: however, this appearance should be taken with a gain of salt since they are doing something about the problem. Sixty-seven of the 81 responding union officials and 77 out of 105 union stewards reported bargaining one or more items which can be regarded as having a relationship to human fulfillment through work. The percentages of respondents who reported bargaining each item were:

Percentages of Union Respondents Reporting Instances of Its Being Bargained

Item	Union Officials	Union Stewards
Freedom to refuse overtime	52%	49%
Right to a different job assignment at the same pay (job rotation)	37	32
Availability of free skills training	37	30
Full utilization of (their) skills and education	22	16
A chance to participate in management decisions	23	10
High degree of freedom to make decisions about (their) work	23	9
Wide variety of duties	19	12
Full recognition of achievements	21	6
As much responsibility as the worker can handle	9	5

In comparing the percentages of union presidents who considered an area to need improvement "very much" with the percentages who reported bargaining the item, we must keep in mind the exact nature of the questions.

That is, a respondent who did not feel that an item needed attention "very much" among his members might well have given that answer because his union has already been successful in bargaining the issue. Thus, it is not necessarily inconsistent that "full recognition of achievements" is a benefit which union officials and stewards thought needed attention "very much" and yet rarely reported having bargained in the past.

However, other explanations are also possible. First, non-economic benefits might simply be too hard to translate into concrete demands. For example, what specific demands do unions make when bargaining "full utilization of skills and education" and "full recognition of achievements?"

Another explanation suggested to me by Bill Dodds, Director of Community Relations for the UAW, is that bargaining demands must have a "common denominator"; that is, they must be desired by all members, not just by segments of the membership. Since there is a high degree of confidence at the bargaining table that all members want more pay, more pay is the most common bargaining issue.

ATTITUDES TOWARD SUGGESTED PROGRAMS

Employers appear quite reticent about surveying workers. Whether they are happier not knowing what's on the workers' minds or whether they don't think surveys would inform then on that question is a moot point. They also seem skeptical about all manner of government training subsidies. The two levels of management saw eye-to-eye on most program ideas, except that nearly twice as many middle as top management people favored the introduction of a Federal work-fulfillment bill. The same difference exists between shop-floor and top union management—which also agreed on the other program ideas. Among union stewards, a whopping 60 percent favored a Federal bill as compared to a still impressive 36 percent of top union management.

With the exception of workers, all respondents were asked to express their opinions on possible work-fulfillment programs. The question asked was: "The following are some possible ideas for work-fulfillment activities. Please indicate your personal feeling about each idea by checking the appropriate box." The available boxes were labeled "for," "against" and "undecided." Appendix A, Table 6, ranks the items according to their overall acceptability and also shows the percentage of each subgroup surveyed which was "for" each idea.

On this question, the differences among the various groups diminished. The item drawing the most approval from all groups but two was "granting workers the right to new job assignments at the same pay wherever possible." Union officials placed this program idea in a tie for second place while union stewards had it third. The other two ideas receiving strong support were employer subsidy of mid-career skills training and employer subsidy of mid-career formal education. These program ideas ranked first, second or third with all groups surveyed except union stewards (who ranked "skills training" first but "formal education" fifth). However, we can infer from management's answers to the previous question on areas most needing attention that—while it is not against the idea of subsidizing mid-career skills training and formal education—it does not regard this as an activity in need of more attention. We can also infer—from the low ranking given "granting workers the right to new job assignments at the same pay" by all groups on the previous question—that this point, while uncontroversial, is also relatively low in priority.

Perhaps the most surprising result from this question was the unexpectedly positive response to the negatively loaded query: "Are you for, against or undecided on the introduction of a work fulfillment bill before the U.S. Congress containing all feasible elements of a comprehensive program?" While this suggestion received less support from most groups than did the other items, the fact that it received any support at all is remarkable. The necessarily vague wording of the question, the adjustment required of the respondent to a new concept and the predisposition most of us have to reject any further intrusion of the Federal government into our private lives, led me to anticipate perhaps a 2 or 3 percent favorable response. Without knowing exactly what the provisions of such a bill would be, there was really no way of reacting—except emotionally—to the notion of Federal involvement. Employers certainly do not wish to have the Federal government inspecting their plants and bringing suit on the basis of poor supervisory training. However, they might favor a Federal bill on work fulfillment which emphasizes the "carrot" instead of the "stick."

Instead of a 2 or 3 percent favorable response, 12 percent of corporation managers were in favor of introducing such a bill and another 17 percent were undecided. Twenty percent of NMA members were for a work-fulfillment bill. A full 36 percent of union officials and a resounding 60 percent of union stewards favored the idea. In these groups, there were also large percentages of respondents who did not reject the idea out of hand but needed more specifics before making up their minds. This suggests to me an extremely high level of concern with the problem of human fulfillment through work among all groups surveyed.

Another finding worthy of emphasis is that top and middle management were overwhelmingly in favor of employer subsidy of both mid-career skills training and mid-career formal education. This is particularly significant since 36 percent of the favorable corporation responses were made personally by corporation presidents. While these groups reacted less favorably to the notion that the government subsidize these activities, their responses might augur well for some kind of a joint program with the brunt of the burden—and authority—on the private sector.

ATTITUDES TOWARD INSTITUTIONAL INVOLVEMENT

Too few employers and members of middle-management are positive toward the union's bargaining work-fulfillment benefits. A strong and clearly defined trade union role is essential to the humanizing of work.

Respondents were asked whether they thought certain institutions should be involved in work-fulfillment activities. The specific questions were:

"Do you think that government should involve itself in promoting more interesting and satisfying work for its people?"
"Do you think that trade unions should bargain job satisfaction items . . .?"
"Do you think that employers and employer associations should concern themselves with making work more interesting and enjoyable?"

Table 7 in Appendix A shows the responses to these questions.

"Do you think employers and employer associations should concern themselves with making work more interesting and enjoyable?" is an indirect way of asking "should anything be done by anybody about improving the quality of work?" The answer from all interested groups was overwhelmingly "yes." While employers and NMA members did not approve of Federal involvement to the same extent as the other groups, the percentages approving were still substantial. The differences in views between management and union-oriented respondents becomes quite marked in the response to the question on trade union involvement. While a not inconsiderable 39 and 35 percent of corporate management and NMA members were in favor of union bargaining of job satisfaction benefits, the figures jumped to 91 and 89 percent for union officials and union stewards, respectively. White-collar workers seemed to line up more closely with management on this issue.

INSTITUTIONAL OPINIONS ON JOB SATISFACTION

The closer one gets to the shop floor, the more negative are the reports of worker satisfaction, particularly satisfaction with job content. Employers saw workers as well-satisfied with their opportunity to do interesting and fulfilling work. Middle management had a somewhat less sanguine view. Top union management was even less optimistic and the working steward on the shop floor reported things to be very bad indeed. The general consensus among most groups was that this aspect of work is about the same now as it was 3 years ago. However, five times as many working union stewards thought it was getting worse than thought it was getting better.

The questions on job satisfaction were:
1. How satisfied would you say (your members, your employees) are *now* with:
    a. Pay, fringe benefits and working conditions

b. Opportunity to do interesting and enjoyable work.
The possible answers were: "very satisfied," "somewhat satisfied," "not too satisfied" and "not at all satisfied."
2. In your opinion, are they more satisfied or less satisfied now than 3 years ago with:
a. Pay, fringe benefits and working conditions
b. Opportunity to do interesting and enjoyable work.
The possible answers were: "more satisfied," "less satisfied" and "about the same."

The following table shows the percentages of respondents reporting that workers were "very" or "somewhat" satisfied and the percentages of respondents expressing the opinion that workers are more satisfied now than 3 years ago.

Institutional Opinions on Job Satisfaction

	Employers	Members, N.M.A.	Union Officials	Union Stewards
Percentage believing that workers are very or somewhat satisfied with pay, fringe benefits and working conditions.	92%	80%	70%	57%
Percentage believing that workers are very or somewhat satisfied with their opportunity to do interesting and enjoyable work.	85	75	58	35
Percentage thinking that workers are:				
more satisfied now than 3 years ago with pay, fringe benefits and working conditions	41	35	47	28
less satisfied now with pay, fringe benefits and working conditions	23	25	21	42
About the same	34	39	32	31
Percentage thinking that workers are:				
more satisfied now than 3 years ago with opportunity to do interesting and enjoyable work	16	18	16	6
less satisfied now with opportunity to do interesting and enjoyable work	15	18	20	32
About the same	66	62	60	62

Management seemed to be more optimistic than union leaders with regard to its view of worker satisfaction with both tangibles and intangibles. All groups thought that workers were more satisfied with tangibles than with intangibles. Except for the union stewards, all groups seem about evenly divided among those who thought things were better at the time of the survey than 3 years previous with regard to the economic aspects of work, those who thought things were worse and those who believed the situation to be about the same. A high percentage of union stewards considered workers to be less satisfied now than 3 years ago with their pay, fringe benefits and working conditions.

This contrasts with opinions about worker satisfaction with "opportunities to do interesting and enjoyable work." On this point, large percentages of all groups tended to think things were about the same with relatively few respondents thinking that workers were either more or less satisfied than they were 3 years ago. However, there were far more union leaders who felt that workers were less satisfied on this score than who believed them to be more satisfied.

Perhaps the most striking feature of these data dealing with institutional opinions on job satisfaction is that, on most points, differences between top and middle management were almost nonexistent and that international union officials sized up the situation much the same way as did management representatives. The shop stewards, however, had different ideas:

> Far fewer stewards believed that workers are very or somewhat satisfied with their opportunity to do interesting work.

> Far more stewards thought that workers are less satisfied now with their pay, fringe benefits and working conditions.

> Only one-third as many stewards as representatives of other groups felt that workers are more satisfied now than 3 years ago with their opportunity to do interesting work.

> A much larger percentage of stewards than of any other group expressed the opposite notion: that workers are less satisfied now with their opportunity to do interesting work.

CONCLUSIONS

The principal conclusions which I draw from the survey results are, first, that all groups involved are remarkably positive towards humanizing work and, second, that both management and labor underestimate the seriousness of the problem and misread worker priorities. The first conclusion is most encouraging in that the solution of job content problems necessarily requires this positive attitude on the parts of management and organized labor and, further, requires them to achieve a meeting of the minds on the specific actions which must be taken to meet human needs through work.

However, while both management and union elements are now willing to concede that the problem should not be the exclusive concern of the "tender-minded" and indeed should reasonably be considered in the same general context as traditional "real" problems, neither management nor organized labor seems to have recognized the shift in worker priorities from economic to non-economic goals. Both groups recognize the fact that there is a problem, but neither considers it to be of the same order of magnitude as do the workers themselves. It is hoped that the findings of research projects such as those described in this book will help close the communication gap between workers and their representatives, and that increasingly negative behavior on the part of workers can be avoided.

NOTES:

1. Comment of a Shop Steward in a questionnaire completed on March 1, 1971.
2. The assumptions on which feasibility views are based can be illustrated by the following quotes.
   Erich Fromm in a letter to the writer of February 24, 1971 said:

   . . . There is a rather large literature mostly of the last few years by psychologists and also neurophysiologists, who have come to the conclusion which I fully share that the whole idea that man is basically passive and lazy and hence works only if he is stimulated by the fear of starvation or the hope for financial reward, is erroneous, and scientifically untenable.

   A National Management Association member in a questionnaire he completed on March 6, 1971, said:

   . . . You overestimate the intellectual and aesthetic goals of hourly employees. You also overestimate the possibilities for "job enrichment" in manufacturing. In general "job enrichment" entails stimulation of some intellectual need and fulfillment of that need. That fulfillment involves a thought process which in turn involves decision making and personal responsibility; both of which will be and are avoided by the average hourly employee.

3. The Kalamazoo survey was part of the project directed by Sheppard.
4. Questionnaires were mailed to *employers* (a sample of 200 selected from Standard and Poor's 1970 Standard Corporation Descriptions); *foremen and supervisory personnel* (a sample of 300 members of the National Management Association); *union officials* (all presidents as listed in the Bureau of Labor Statistics 1970 *Directory of National and International Unions in the U.S.*); *union stewards* (a sample of 300 UAW stewards from around the country; and *workers* (99 white-collar workers in one real estate management firm and one consultant organization, both in Washington; and personal inter-

views with 101 auto and steelworkers in Kalamazoo—all white males). Response rates varied from 34 to 65 percent.

5. Nonetheless, a sizeable majority of union leaders (about 6 out of 10) considered it very important that workers be given more opportunity to grow and achieve on-the-job. But even more sizeable majorities emphasized the importance of improving the economic aspects of work.

6 These improvements were: (1) Full recognition of (their, your) achievements; (2) Full utilization of skills and education; (3) As much responsibility as (workers, you) can handle; (4) Availability of further classroom education on a no-cost basis; (5) High degree of freedom to make decisions about (their, your) work; (6) Availability of free skills training; (7) A chance to participate in management decisions; (8) Freedom to refuse overtime; (9) Right to a different job assignment at the same pay (job rotation); (10) Wide variety of duties.

Appendix A

Statistical Tables

Table 1. Percentages of Workers Expressing Negative Attitudes toward Work and Life by Age, Occupation, etc.

		Negative Attitudes Toward Work	Negative Attitudes Toward Life
AGE			
Under 20	(N=97)	25	20
20–29	(331)	24	14
30–44	(491)	13	15
45–54	(340)	11	10
55 and older	(265)	6	10
OCCUPATION			
Professional, Technical and Managerial	(392)	9	10
Clerical and Sales	(331)	18	14
Service	(184)	23	24
Machine Trades	(120)	15	11
Structure Work	(157)	10	7
PERSONAL INCOME			
Up to $3,399	(212)	20	21
$3,400–$4,999	(223)	21	17
$5,000–$7,499	(380)	13	14
$7,500–$9,999	(264)	14	11
$10,000 and over	(337)	8	6
INDUSTRY			
Contract Construction	(123)	5	7
Manufacturing	(381)	17	12
Wholesale, Retail	(274)	23	18
Services	(397)	12	14
RACE			
Black	(157)	23	21
White	(1,352)	14	12
OCCUPATIONAL GROUP			
Blue-Collar	(709)	17	15
White-Collar	(753)	13	12
EDUCATION			
0–6th Grade	(241)	13	19
7–12th Grade	(822)	14	12
13th Grade and over	(465)	13	12
SELF-EMPLOYED	(205)	5	6
WAGE AND SALARY	(1,324)	16	14
SEX			
Male	(990)	12	12
Female	(448)	19	17
MARITAL STATUS			
Unmarried	(261)	21	26
Married	(1,002)	13	9

Table 2. Summary Scores of Political Efficacy-Alienation, by Age and Job Task Rating (Pennsylvania and Kalamazoo Combined)

Total Sample		Under 40		40–54		55 and older	
Postive Rating	Negative Rating	Positive Rating	Negative Rating	Positive Rating	Negative Rating	Positive Rating	Negative Rating
2.39	1.30	2.15	1.44	3.50	1.86	1.62	0.62

Note: The greater the summary score, the greater the tendency toward high political efficacy and low alienation. Score is derived by dividing percentage with low efficacy-high alienation into percentage with high efficacy-low alienation.

Table 3. Summary Scores of Achievement Values—Political Efficacy, by Age and Job Task Rating

Total Sample		Under 40		40–54		55 and older	
Positive Rating	Negative Rating	Positive Rating	Negative Rating	Positive Rating	Negative Rating	Positive Rating	Negative Rating
2.31	1.29	3.33	2.36	2.79	1.42	1.12	0.43

Note: The greater the summary score, the greater the tendency toward both high achievement values and political efficacy. Score is derived as explained in previous table.

Table 4. Percentage of Respondents Expressing Negative Attitudes toward Work by Race, Education, etc. within Age Groups*

	Under 30	30–44	45 and older	Total sample (number of cases)	
RACE					
Black	37%	21%	7%	*23%*	(155)
White	22	12	9	*14*	(1,349)
EDUCATION					
HS Diploma or less	21	14	9	14	(1,078)
Some Education Beyond HS	29	12	9	17	(364)
SEX					
Male	21	12	8	*12*	(987)
Female	28	17	13	*19*	(534)
MARITAL STATUS					
Married	22	13	9	*13*	(1,167)
Unmarried	26	19	10	*21*	(353)
PERSONAL INCOME					
Up to $7,449	25	18	10	*17*	(810)
More than $7,500	21	10	7	*11*	(600)
COLLAR COLOR					
Blue	24	*18*	11	17	(705)
White	24	*9*	8	13	(751)

*Generally, differences between age groups are statistically significant. This means we are 95 percent confident they are not due to chance. Differences which are statistically significant between other socio-economic groups (such as, black vs. white, male vs. female) are italicized.

Table 5. Demographic Characteristics of Under—30 and 55 and Older
White Male Union Members

MIGRANT STATUS	Under 30	55 and older
Born in city where interviewed	61%	50%
Born in town or village, farm, or immigrant from Europe	6	16
EDUCATION:		
Grade school only	0	49
Some high school	24	22
High school or more	76	29
MARITAL STATUS:		
Married	62	92
Never married	35	4
Other; refused	3	4
NUMBER OF DEPENDENTS:		
None	37	1
One	15	68
Two	20	14
Three or more	28	17
PERCENTAGE WITH ADDITIONAL EARNERS IN FAMILY:	38	25
FAMILY INCOME:		
Under $8,000	32	32
$8,000–$9,999	21	30
$10,000–$12,999	26	16
$13,000 or more	18	16
Refused	4	6
HOME OWNERSHIP:		
Renting	40	12
Paying off Mortgage	33	29
Own free and clear	2	56
Living rent-free	23	—
Refused; other	2	3
RELIGION:		
Protestant	45	51
Catholic	33	35
Jewish; other; none; refused	22	14
ORGANIZATION MEMBERSHIPS (including unions):		
1 only	45	29
2	24	34
3	22	19
4 or more	9	18

Table 6. Percentage of Respondents In Favor of Specific Program Ideas

	Employers	Members, National Mgt. Assn.	Union Officials	Union Stewards
Granting workers the right to new job assignments at the same pay wherever possible	85	80	74	79
Employer subsidy of mid-career skills training	66	80	80	78
Employer subsidy of mid-career formal education	71	68	70	62
Worker surveys by unions and/or management to determine the priority work fulfillment items should have on the bargaining agenda	37	54	69	79
Adoption of work fulfillment goals by national and international unions	27	39	60	72
Government subsidy of mid-career skills training	29	25	49	51
Government subsidy of mid-career formal education	27	17	50	44
Government subsidies to train supervisors and managers in job enrichment techniques	20	21	31	36
Introduction of a work fulfillment bill before the U.S. Congress containing all feasible elements of a comprehensive program*	12	20	36	60

*This question elicited extremely high percentages of "undecided" responses since it is difficult to be either "for" or "against" a bill when its provisions are not described.

Table 7. Percentages of Respondents in Favor of Institutional Involvement

	Employers	Members, National Mgt. Assn.	Union Officials	Union Stewards	Workers Blue-Collar	White-Collar
Employer and Employer Association Involvement	95	96	97	94	98	88
Trade Union Involvement	39	35	91	89	88	49
Federal Government Involvement	39	29	62	68	49	49

Interview Schedule for White
Male Union Workers

WORK AND LIFE ATTITUDE STUDY
W. E. Upjohn Institute for Employment Research
Washington, D.C.

Interview No. _____ Name of Interviewer _____
Interview Date _____ City _____

```
+------------------+
|      Give        |
|  Introduction!   |
+------------------+
```

First of all, let me ask:

1. Were you born in this city (or town)?

Skip to Q 2.

Yes	
No	

   a. How long ago did you move to this city (or town)?

Less than 3 years ago	
3 to 5 years	
6 to 9 years	
10 to 14 years	
15 to 19 years	
20 to 29 years	
30 or more years	

199

b. Was the place you were
    born in:

    Skip to Q 3.

Outside the U.S.? (If YES): Which country? _____	
A large American city or a suburb of a large city (250,000 or more)	
A medium-sized city (50,000-250,000)	
A small city (2,500-50,000)	
A town or village; *or* in the open country but not a farm	
or, on a farm?	

2. (If R. born in U.S.) What is the original nationality of your family on your father's side? _____

    (If answer to Q 2. was "American") What country did his family (your grandparents) come from originally? _____

3. How long have you been living at
    this address?

Less than 1 year	
1 to 3 years	
More than 3, less than 6 years	
6 to 10 years	
More than 10, less than 15 years	
15 or more	

4. Migrant status _____

5. How would you rate the city or town
    you're living in now, as a place to live?
    Is it: (Read choices before circling
    answer.)

The best possible?	
Very good?	
Good?	
Neither the best nor worst?	
or, bad?	
DK, etc.	

6. Are you now employed? (If *"yes"*) Full-time or part-time?

Yes, full-time	
Yes, part-time	
No, not now employed	
Skip to Q 74. Retired, or other (Specify) _____	

7. What kind of work do you do? (Did you do? if unemployed) (Get more than job title!)

_____

_____

_____

8. a. What type of fringe benefits do you now (did you) get on your job? Do (did) you get:

	Yes	No
Vacation with pay?		
Sick leave with pay?		
Health or hospital insurance?		
Life insurance?		
Pension when you retire? (*Not* counting Social Security.)		
A training program to improve your skills?		

Number of fringe benefits _____

b. Are there any fringe benefits that you're not getting now that you'd like to be getting?

Yes (Which?)	
_____	
_____	
Skip to Q 9. No	

c. Which one benefit you're not getting now would you most like to be getting?

_____

d. How much of a problem is it for you not to be getting this particular fringe benefit?

No problem at all?	
A slight problem?	
A sizeable problem?	
A great problem?	

9. What is (was) your hourly wage on your job? (If on salary, get weekly figure.)

Less than $2.00 per hour	
$2.00-$2.50	
$2.51-$3.00	
$3.01-$3.50	
$3.51-$4.00	
$4.01-$4.50	
$4.51-$5.00	
More than $5.00	
If salary: $ _____ (weekly figure)	

10. a. How long have you been doing the kind of work you're in now?

	Less than 1 year	
	1 or more years but less than 5	
Ask Q 10b. and Q 11a.	More than 5 but less than 10	
	More than 10 but less than 15	
	More than 15 but less than 20	
	20 or more years	

b. How long have you been working for
your present employer?

Less than 1 year	
1 or more years but less than 5	
Ask Q 11a. More than 5 but less than 10	
More than 10 but less than 15	
More than 15 but less than 20	
20 or more years	

11. a. You've been with the same company, or doing the same kind of work, for more than five
years now. What about the new people that
have come on the job over the past year or
so—how would you rate them:
Have they been just as good on the job as you
were when you first got it?
Better, or not as good?

Skip to Q 12. Just as good	
Better	
Ask Q b. Not as good	
DK, etc.	
Q not asked	

b. (If better or not as good): In what way?

_____

12. Since the beginning of this year, 1970, how many weeks
have you been laid off—not counting illness or vacation
time? (Not asked in Kalamazoo)

0 weeks	
1-4 weeks	
5-7 weeks	
8-14 weeks	
15-26 weeks	
27 weeks or more	
Don't remember, etc.	

13. Were you ever unemployed last year, in
1969 (1970 for Kalamazoo)? (If "yes," how
many weeks?)

Yes, less than 5 weeks	
Yes, 5-10 weeks	
Yes, 11-14 weeks	
Yes, 15-26 weeks	
Yes, 27 or more weeks	
No, not unemployed in 1969	
Don't remember, etc.	

14. a. The job you have now, is it the best one you've ever had?

Yes	
No	
DK, etc.	

b. Do you think the job you have now is the best one you'll ever
have before you retire?

Yes	
No	
DK, etc.	

15. If you were completely free to go into
any type of job you wanted, what
would your choice be? (Ask first three
questions in box, then circle answer.)

Would you want the same type of job you now hold?	
Would you want to retire, not work at all? *or*	
Would you prefer some other job to the kind you now have?	
DK, etc.	

16. How often have you thought very seriously about making a
real effort to enter a new and different type of occupation?
(Ask all questions in box and then circle answer.)

Very often?	
Once in a while?	
Hardly ever?, *or*	
Never?	
Already did it.	
DK, etc.	

17. Have you ever actually tried to get into a line of work that was really
different from any you've been in?

Yes	
No	

18. Check one of the
following state-
ments which best
tells how you
feel about chang-
ing your job.

I would quit my job right now if I had anything else to do.	
I would take almost any other job in which I could earn as much as I am earning now.	
My job is as good as the average and I would just as soon have it as any other job but would change jobs if I could make more money.	
I am not eager to change jobs but would do so if I could make more money.	
I do not want to change jobs even for more money because the one I have now is a good one.	

19. How well would you say your job measures up to the kind
you wanted when you first took it? Is it very much like the
kind of job you wanted? Somewhat like the job you wanted?
or, not very much like the kind you wanted?

Very much	
Somewhat	
Not very much	
DK, etc.	

20. a. Some jobs provide a great
deal of opportunity to
learn more about the work
and enable a person to increase his knowledge of the
process and his skill; other
jobs provide few such
opportunities to learn more.
How is it on your job?

Skip to
Q 21.

Ask Q b.

There are very great opportunities to learn more.	
There are fairly good opportunities to learn—above average.	
There is little opportunity to learn.	
There is almost no opportunity on my job to learn more about the pro-cess or to increase my skill.	

b. How frequently does it bother you that there is little or no opportunity on your job to learn more about the work? (Read first four choices, then record answer.)

Nearly all the time?	
Very often?	
Sometimes?	
Rarely or never?	
DK, etc.	

21. a. Different jobs and types of work vary in how much opportunity they provide a person to advance himself, to get ahead in that line of work, or to be promoted. How is it on your job?

Ask Q b.

Skip to Q 22.

On my job there is no real chance to get ahead.	
There is *some* chance to get ahead on my job, but very little.	
The chances of getting ahead are above average.	
On my job there are *excellent* chances of getting ahead, in comparison with other lines of work.	

b. How frequently does it bother you that there is very little or no chance to get ahead on your job?

Nearly all the time?	
Very often?	
Sometimes?	
Rarely or never?	
DK, etc.	

22. a. Does management where you work put emphasis on your doing quality work, or do they emphasize other things such as quantity of output?

Skip to Q 23.

Ask Q b.

Management puts *heavy* emphasis on the quality of my work	
Management emphasizes the quality of my work more than they emphasize other things such as quantity.	
Management emphasizes other things such as quantity more than they do the quality of my work.	
Management puts almost *all* the emphasis on things other than the quality of my work.	

b. How frequently does it bother you that management emphasizes other things more than the quality
of your work?

Nearly all the time?	
Very often?	
Sometimes?	
Rarely or never?	
DK, etc.	

23. a. Do you have
variety on your
job (can you
do different
things, change
methods, loca-
tion, speed of
working, and
so forth)?

Ask Q b.

Skip to
Q 24.

I always do the same thing on my job; there is no variety	
I mostly do the same things, but there is a little variety.	
I have to do quite a number of different things on my job.	
There is a fair amount of variety.	
I have to do a lot of different things on my job; there is a great deal of variety.	

b. How frequently does it both you that there is only
a little or no variety on your job?

Nearly all the time?	
Very often?	
Sometimes?	
Rarely or never?	
DK, etc.	

A Score (Q 23a × 2) _____

24. a. Which statement
best describes the
kind of job you
have?

Ask Q b.

Skip to
Q 25.

I have no freedom at all to do my work as I want.	
I have little freedom to do my work as I want.	
I am fairly free to do my work as I want.	
I am completely free to do my work as I want.	

b. How frequently does it both you that there is little
or no freedom to do your work as you want to?

Nearly all the time?	
Very often?	
Sometimes?	
Rarely or never?	
DK, etc.	

25. Which one of the following items best describes how much of their potential ideas and skills are being used on the job by the people working on the same general kind of job as yours?

Almost none of what they can offer.	
About one-fourth of what they can offer.	
About half of what they can offer.	
About three-fourths of what they can offer.	
Almost all of what they can offer.	

B Score (Q 24a + Q 25) _____

26. Is the quality of your work the most important thing to you, or is it less important than quantity, speed of working, or other things?

Quality is by far the most important thing on my job.	
Quality is the most important thing, but quantity or other things are important too.	
I emphasize quality but not as much as quantity or other things.	
I give quality very little importance on my particular job.	

27. Which of the following statements fits your job?

Almost anyone could do my job.	
A good many people could do my job.	
Only a limited number of people could do my job.	
Very few people could do my job.	
Can't answer; hard to say.	

C Score (Q 20a + Q26 + 27/3) _____

Total Task Index (Scores A + B + C) _____

28. Do you agree or disagree with this statement: Most Negroes want to get ahead using the same ways other Americans have used to get ahead.

Agree	
Disagree	
DK, etc.	

29. If you could retire with as much money as you need for a good pension, and not have to work anymore, would you do it right away, or would you wait for a while? (If "wait a while"): About how many years would you wait?

Retire right away.	
Wait less than 1 year.	
Wait more than 1, less than 3 years.	
Wait 3, but less than 5 years.	
Wait 5, but less than 10 years.	
10 or more years.	
DK, etc.	

30. Do most people get ahead more as a result of:

Luck	
Education	
Right people	
Working at it	

31. Do you think that is more true today than it was about 10 years ago? Less true today? Or is it about the same today as it was 10 years ago?

More true today	
Less true today	
Same	
DK, etc.	

32-49. Now I'd like to get your reactions to some things that people have different opinions on. Do you *strongly agree, agree, disagree,* or *strongly disagree* with these statements? (Read each item and the response alternatives for Questions 32 through 49.)

32. In his work, all a person should want is a secure, not-too-difficult job, with enough pay for a nice car and home.
Do you strongly agree, agree, disagree; or strongly disagree?

33. Nowadays a person has to pretty much live for today and let tomorrow take care of itself.

34. When a person is born, the success he will have is in the cards, so he may as well accept it.

35. It is best to have a job as part of an organization all working together, even if you don't get individual credit.

36. Don't expect too much out of life and be content with what comes your way.

37. Planning only makes a person unhappy since your plans hardly ever work out anyway.

38. Score of Q 32-37_____

39. There's little use in writing to public officials because often they aren't really interested in the problems of the average man.

40. The way people vote is the main thing that decides how things are run in this country.

41. People like me don't have any say about what the government does.

42. Score of Q 39-41 _____

43. These days a person doesn't really know who he can count on.

44. In spite of what some people say, the lot of the average man is getting better, not worse.

45. It's hardly fair to bring children into the world with the way things look for the future.

46. Score of Q 43-45_____

47. The most important thing to teach children is absolute obedience to their parents.

48. Any good leader should be strict with people under him in order to gain their respect.

49. A few strong leaders could do more for this country than all the laws and talk.

50. Score of Q 47-49_____

51. When someone says such and such a group is "active in politics," what does that mean to you?
    (Record verbatim answer.)

52. Are there any particular groups or organizations that you think should not be allowed to give money to parties and candidates?
    (Record groups and organizations.)

53. In the Congressional elections coming up in November of this year, what do you think are the three most important issues the candidates should be talking about during their campaign?

54. a. During the presidential campaign, many business groups were for Nixon, and many unions were for Humphrey. Do you think it was all right for business groups to work to get Nixon elected, or that it was not all right?

All right	
Not all right	

b. Do you think it was all right for unions to work to get Humphrey elected or that it was not all right?

All right	
Not all right	

55. Which political party do you think represents your point of view best of all?

Democrats	
Republicans	
None	
All about the same	
Other: Which one?	

56. If you were registered to vote, did you vote in the last presidential election in 1968?

Skip to Q 58.

Yes	
No	
Don't remember	
Refuse	
Not registered	

57. If you did vote, would you mind telling me who you voted for as President?

Humphrey	
Nixon	
Wallace	
Other, DK, etc.	
Refused	
Did not vote	

58. Compared with what you had hoped for when you finished school, are you better off than you hoped for at that time? Not as well off? Or just about as well off as you had hoped for?

Better off	
Not as well off	
As well as hoped for	
DK, etc.	

59. Suppose your employer, the government, your union—or some other organization—offered you a training and education program—with enough money to support yourself and family—to make it possible to get a promotion with the employer you have now, or to get a much better job somewhere else.

Would you choose the program leading to a promotion with your present employer? Or the program leading to a better job somewhere else? Or would you just not take any program like that?

With present employer	
Better job elsewhere	
Would not take any program	
DK, etc.	

60. a. If you could be trained to rotate, where you work, between 2 or 3 really different jobs over a period of a year, do you think that would be a very good idea, or not a very good idea?

   b. (If "very good idea" circled:)
   How important would that idea be to you?
   (Circle appropriate box)

Very important?	
Somewhat important?	
A little important?	
OR, not important at all?	
DK, etc.	

61. Compared with where you were 10 years ago, are you further ahead in the things you've wanted out of life? Behind? OR just about the same as where you were 10 years ago?

Further ahead	
Behind	
About the same	
DK, etc.	

Discrepancy Score (Qs. 19, 58, 61)_____

62. a. Is your own take-home pay good enough to take care of
your family's usual bills and expenses?

Skip to Q 62c.	Yes	
Ask Q b.	No	

b. Suppose you added any other income coming to you and
to other members of your family, is all of that enough to
take care of your family's usual bills and expenses?

	Yes	
Skip to Q 63.	No	
	Q b. not asked	

c. Do you feel that this total income is enough to live as comfortably as you'd like to?

Yes	
No	
DK, etc.	

63. As you look to the years ahead, do you expect
a steady rise in your income until retirement?
Some rise and then a decline before retirement?
Or do you expect many ups and downs in your
income before your retire?

Steady rise	
Some rise, then decline	
Ups and downs	
DK, other	

64. Suppose people like yourself lost their jobs. Out of every 100
people like yourself in that situation, how many do you think
would find a new job in about one month?

0-10	
11-25	
26-40	
41-50	
51-74	
75 or more	
DK, etc.	

65. Are you a member of any
clubs or organizations like a:

Veterans organization	
Fraternal lodge	
PTA or other school organization	
Nationality or ethnic club (Japanese-American, Italian-American, etc.)	
Labor union	
Church group	
Military unit (reserves, national guard)	
Recreation, athletic, or sport group	
Any others (specify): _____	

66. Total number of memberships _____

67. Suppose you had to classify yourself as either a liberal
or a conservative, which would you say you are?

Liberal	
Conservative	
Neither	
DK, etc.	

68. (If R. belongs to union)
I'd like to ask about your union—do you think it is
very helpful to its members?
Fairly helpful?
Sometimes helpful but not as much as it might be?
Mostly not helpful?
or, not at all helpful to its members?

Very helpful	
Fairly helpful	
Sometimes helpful	
Mostly not helpful	
Not at all helpful	
DK, etc.	

69. If you think just about improving skills, or promotion to a better job,
do you think the union could be doing more for its members than it
is now?

Yes	
No	
DK, etc.	

70. a. Some people say that employers have been
helping minority groups like Negroes and
Puerto Ricans too much in getting good training or good jobs for them. Other people say
that employers are not helping them enough.
What do you think—are they helping too much?
Helping in just about the right amount? Or not
enough?

Too much.	
Are helping in just about the right amount.	
Not enough.	
DK, etc.	

  b. How about unions? Are they helping Negroes
and Puerto Ricans too much? Helping in just
about the right amount?
Or not enough?

Too much.	
Helping in just about the right amount.	
Not enough.	
DK, etc.	

71. Do you read any magazines regularly? (If "yes," which ones?)

72. How about weekly or monthly newspapers—especially from organizations you belong to?

73. If you watch TV regularly, could you name three or four of your most favorite programs?
(Record names and total number.)

74. How old are you?

24 or younger			40 to 49	
25 to 29			50 to 54	
30 to 34			55 to 59	
35 to 39			60 to 64	
			65 or older	

75. What is your marital status?
(Read items, then circle answer.)

Married?	
Separated?	
Divorced?	
Widowed?	
Never married?	
Refuse, etc.	

76. What was the highest grade in school you
completed?

8th grade or less	
9 to 11	
12 (high school degree)	
Some college or college degree	

77. How many people do you support—*not* counting yourself? _____

78. If you have a religious preference,
would you mind telling me what is
is?

Catholic	
Jewish	
Protestant (Which denomination?)	
Other	
Refused	

79. (If R. has religious preference:)
How often do you usually attend religious
services?

Once a week or more often	
Once or twice a month	
A few times a year	
Hardly ever, or never	
Refused	

80. How do you think of yourself as far as age goes—do you
think of yourself as:
(Circle only one.)

Young?	
Middle aged?	
Late middle aged?	
or Old?	

81. a. Would you take a look at this list and tell me which
         of these is nearest to your total family income for
         last year, 1969, before any tax or other deductions?

Under $2000	
$2000-$4999	
$5000-$7999	
$8000-$9999	
$10,000-$12,999	
$13,000-$14,999	
$15,000 or more	
Refused	

     b. How many people in your family worked to receive that much, including yourself?

82. Are you renting this (home) (apartment)—paying
     off a mortgage on it—do you own it free and clear—
     or are you living rent-free with parents, relatives,
     or friends?

Rent	
Paying off mortgage	
Own it free and clear	
Living rent-free	
Other	

83. Let me ask just one more question:
     How much of the time are you sat-
     isfied with your job? Are you satis-
     fied:

Most of the time?	
A good deal of the time?	
About half of the time?	
Occasionally?	
Hardly ever or never?	

ASKED OF THE KALAMAZOO SAMPLE ONLY

84. Please tell me how important it is to you that each of the following things be improved in your job.

	Very Important	Somewhat Important	Not Too Important	Not at All Important
a. More Pay				
b. How about better contingency protection (for example, work-men's compensation or unemployment insurance?)				
c. Better health and safety practices				
d. Improved Fair Employment practices (no discrimination on account of sex, race, or age)?				
e. Increased opportunity to do interesting and satisfying work?				

85. I'm going to name a number of things which some people feel are desirable in their jobs. Please tell me how much improvement you feel each thing needs in your job.

	Very Much	Some	Not Too Much	Not Any
a. Freedom to refuse overtime				
b. How about right to a different job assignment at the same pay (job rotation)?				
c. Wide variety of duties?				
d. Full utilization of your skills and education?				
e. High degree of freedom to make decisions about your work?				
f. Availability of free skills training?				
g. Availability of further classroom education on a no-cost basis?				
h. A chance to participate in management decisions?				
i. Full recognition of your achievements?				
j. As much responsibility as you can handle?				

86. Do you think that unions should bargain job satisfaction items like the kinds I've just asked you about?

Yes	
No	

87. Do you think the Federal government should involve itself in any way to promote more interesting and satisfying work for all people?

Yes	
No	

88. Do you think employers and employer associations should concern themselves with making work more interesting and enjoyable?

Yes	
No	

89. How satisfied would you say you are now with:
   a. Your pay, fringe benefits, and working conditions?

Very satisfied	
Somewhat satisfied	
Not too satisfied	
Not at all satisfied	

   b. Your opportunity to do interesting and enjoyable work?

Very satisfied	
Somewhat satisfied	
Not too satisfied	
Not at all satisfied	

90. Are you more satisfied or less satisfied now than you were three years ago with:

	More Satisfied	About the Same	Less Satisfied
a. Your pay, fringe benefits, and working conditions?			
b. Your opportunity to do interesting and enjoyable work?			

Index

Perlman, Selig, 58
Polaroid Corporation, 171, 172
Political efficacy, 32–33, 36
   alienation, 34, 86–88
   achievement values, 88–89
   blue-collar workers, 32–36, 86–89
   young workers, 133–34
Pollution, as campaign issue, 134–35, 147
Potential, use of, 79
Presidential election (1968), 35, 90, 135,
   144–48
Procter and Gamble Distributing Company,
   171
Professionals, second careers and, 161–65
Promotion opportunities, 55, 61–62
Puerto Ricans, 72, 138

Quality of work
   job enrichment programs, 170–77, 181–88
   management interest in, 52–54, 78, 127
   organizational obstacles, 179–92

Race attitudes
   as campaign issue, 147
   in job task ratings, 71–72
   young workers, 137–38
Reich, Charles, 122
Religion, voting behavior and, 147–48
Republican Party, 135, 147
Responsibility, 47–48, 79–80, 124–25
Retired Officers Associations, 162
Retired persons, life dissatisfaction, 6, 13
Retirement policy, 6, 31, 52
Reuss, Henry S., 14
Rosen, Bernard, 88
Rosow, Jerome M., 7, 12

Scharr, John H., 99–93
Second careers, 154–65
Self-employment, 5, 12–13
Settlement Housing Employment, 174
Single career concept, 153–54
Skill level, 83–85
Small businesses, 12–13
Social Darwinism, 97
Socialization and Society (Clausen), 23
Strikes, 105
Survey Research Center (University of
   Michigan), 4, 180, 182

Take-home pay, *see* Income adequacy
Texas Instruments, 172, 175
Turner, Arthur N., 29, 45, 66, 67, 84
Turnover rates, 3, 172, 176, 177

Unemployment, 59–60, 98–99, 105–8, 115
Unions
   blue-collar workers' evaluation of, 105–6
   job enrichment and, 177, 185–86
   on mid-career skills training, 186–87
   minority workers, 72
   on worker participation in management
      decisions, 183–84
   young workers and, 115, 120, 129–30, 140
United Auto Workers of America, 130
United States Congress, 63, 159, 187

United States Department of Defense, 162
United States Department of Labor, 12
United Steelworkers of America, 130
University of Michigan, 10, 122
   Survey Research Center, 4, 180, 182
Upjohn Institute, 155

Variety, 29–30, 45–46, 78–79, 123–25
Viet Nam War, as campaign issue, 134–35,
   147
Volunteerism, 6
Voting behavior
   alienation, 89–90
   pro-Wallace worker, 144–49
   religion, 147–48
   young workers, 135–37

Wages, *see* Income adequacy
Wallace, George, 34–36, 91
   voter characteristics, 70, 86, 90, 99, 108,
      135–37, 144–48, 158
Watson, Sir William, 5
Weiss, Robert, 155
Weston, M. C., Jr., 140
White-collar workers, 13–14, 169–70, 180,
   184
   job enrichment, 181–83
   vs. blue-collar workers, 7–8
Williamsburg Conference, 176
Women
   income, 9
   job dissatisfaction, 8–9
   life dissatisfaction, 13
   working wives, 25, 27–28
   young workers, 114, 117
Work, quality of
   job enrichment programs, 170–77, 181–88
   management interest in, 52–54, 78, 127
   organizational obstacles, 179–92
Work Itself projects, 172–73
Workmen's compensation, 183

Yale Law Journal, The, 170
Young workers, 5–6, 113–43
   achievement values, 133
   alienation, 131–32
   aspiration–achievement discrepancy, 137
   authoritarianism, 130–32
   blacks, 115–16
   education, 114, 116–17
   evaluations of new workers, 137–38
   income, 114, 117, 125–26
   job advancement chances, 127–28
   job rotation, 128, 140
   job satisfaction, 125
   liberal vs. conservative identification, 134
   marital status, 117
   party preferences, 135–36
   political efficacy, 133–34
   race attitudes, 137–38
   task levels, 123–25
   unions and, 115, 120, 129–30, 140
   voting behavior, 135–136
      Wallace voter, 136–37, 144–48
   women, 114, 117
   work values, 118, 119